BECKETT'S *BREATH*

Edinburgh Critical Studies in Modernism, Drama and Performance

Published
The Speech-Gesture Complex: Modernism, Theatre, Cinema
Anthony Paraskeva

Irish Drama and the Other Revolutions: Playwrights, Sexual Politics and the International Left, 1892–1964
Susan Cannon Harris

Modernism and the Theatre of the Baroque
Kate Armond

Beckett's Breath: *Anti-theatricality and the Visual Arts*
Sozita Goudouna

Forthcoming
Russian Futurist Theatre: Theory and Practice
Robert Leach

Greek Tragedy and Modernist Performance
Olga Taxidou

www.edinburghuniversitypress.com/series/ecsmdp

BECKETT'S *BREATH*

Anti-theatricality and the Visual Arts

Sozita Goudouna

EDINBURGH
University Press

Edinburgh University Press is one of the leading university presses in the UK. We publish academic books and journals in our selected subject areas across the humanities and social sciences, combining cutting-edge scholarship with high editorial and production values to produce academic works of lasting importance. For more information visit our website: edinburghuniversitypress.com

Edinburgh University Press Ltd
The Tun – Holyrood Road
12(2f) Jackson's Entry
Edinburgh EH8 8PJ

First published in hardback by Edinburgh University Press 2018

Typeset in Sabon and Gill Sans by
Servis Filmsetting Ltd, Stockport, Cheshire,
and printed and bound by CPI Group (UK) Ltd, Croydon, CR0 4YY

A CIP record for this book is available from the British Library

ISBN 978 1 4744 2164 5 (hardback)
ISBN 978 1 4744 5270 0 (paperback)
ISBN 978 1 4744 2165 2 (webready PDF)
ISBN 978 1 4744 2166 9 (epub)

CONTENTS

ACKNOWLEDGEMENTS

I would like to thank the A. S. Onassis Public Benefit Foundation for the award of a four-year scholarship to pursue this research (2003–7); Professor David Bradby at Royal Holloway University of London for his supervision and for encouraging me to pursue this research, that was initiated in 1999 during the MA Text and Performance Studies at Kings College University of London in conjunction with RADA Royal Academy of Dramatic Art; Professors Dr David Cunningham, Christa-Maria Lerm Hayes, Jen Harvie, Olga Taxidou, Adrian Heathfield, Joe Kelleher, Dr Sophie Nield, Dr Mischa Twitchin, and the anonymous reviewers for their precious feedback; Professor Leonee Ormond for her exceptional kindness and generosity and Professor Katherine Worth, leading authority on Beckett; Professor RoseLee Goldberg for selecting me as the inaugural Andrew W. Mellon Curatorial Fellow at Performa Biennial in New York, and for her trust, long-lasting inspiration, personal vision and insight for the future of interdisciplinary arts; Professors Helen Spackman, Anna Furse and Stella Sandford for the initial stimuli; all my collaborators for their trust; my friends, family and Gerasimos for their solid love and support. And most importantly Beckett and the conspirator(s) for letting me conspire.

PREFACE

FOR A *RESPIRATEUR*: GOUDOUNA'S BECKETT

David Cunningham

> I do not know what it is, having never seen anything like it before. It seems to have nothing to do with art, in any case, if my memories are correct. Samuel Beckett, *Three Dialogues*

Visitors to the remarkable collection of Marcel Duchamp's work at the Philadelphia Museum of Art currently pass through an installation by the American artist Joseph Kosuth with the enigmatic title *Plays of / for a Respirateur*. Occupying an entire room, and juxtaposing facsimiles of various Duchamp works with nine of Kosuth's own pieces, the title is taken from Duchamp's famous reply to the question of how, in the last years of his life, he spent his time: 'I'm not an artist. I'm a breather.' *Je suis un réspirateur.* Strictly speaking, the claim is a typically Duchampian feint: Duchamp's supposed artistic silence actually hid the fact that he was secretly making his final work *Étants Données*, which today holds pride of place in the Philadelphia collection. But as an articulation of a blurring of the lines between art and non-art, the poetry of the work and the prose of the world, which Duchamp's career always seemed to emblematise, one can see its obvious appeal not only to Kosuth but to an entire generation of post-war artists and thinkers. The great contemporary German thinker of *Pneuma*, Peter Sloterdijk, connects, in this vein, the (near) silence of this late Duchamp as *réspirateur* to the concerns of a much earlier work, also included in the Philadelphia collection.[1] A gift to his patrons Walter and Louise Arensberg, *50 cc of Paris Air* was 'constructed' in 1919 when, before boarding a ship to New York, Duchamp purchased an 'empty' vial from a pharmacist in Le Havre who he had persuaded to pour out its contents and reseal. One of Duchamp's first readymades, as well as, characteristically, a joke shared with these patrons – who, he said, already owned

---

[1] Sloterdijk, Peter. *Terror from the Air*, trans. Amy Patton and Steve Corcoran. Los Angeles: Semiotext(e), 2009.

everything else he could have bought them – *50 cc of Paris Air* also posed a typically Duchampian question concerning what might be the most insubstantial artwork possible, a work that was barely there at all.

Sozita Goudouna's book is perhaps, first and foremost, about this question too, although its nodal point is neither Duchamp not the readymade but Samuel Beckett's 1969 *Breath*; a literal 'play of / for a Respirateur' that is a work of theatre in much the same sense that *50 cc of Paris Air* is a work of visual art. The problem of what to make of such work, which is, as two of his most astute readers put it, precisely 'nothing on the order of what we have been trained to think of as significant or interesting in art', is of course a common one in criticism of Beckett – indeed, in some senses, defines it – and would often seem to place the challenge posed by Beckett at the very limits of criticism itself; particularly as regards the later works.[2] But it is a problem into which Goudouna breathes new life – something worth bearing in mind when considering what might otherwise seem the extraordinary gall of a book such as the one which you have in front of you. No doubt monographs devoted to single works always have a job persuading the reader of the necessity of such sustained attention, but when that work is not *The Divine Comedy*, *King Lear* or *Ulysses*, but instead a piece that lasts less than half a minute, without dialogue or characters, supposedly written for an erotic review – a play that literally invites the accusation that it is a load of rubbish – it would seem the author has their work cut out. And in fact this is precisely the point. For while it has, until Goudouna's excellent book, yet to receive anything like the level of academic attention that the likes of Duchamp's *Fountain* and John Cage's *4'33"* have acquired, *Breath* belongs with them in being one of those modernist works that, in operating at the very historical and formal limit of what might be thought of 'as significant or interesting in art', paradoxically generates, from very little, almost nothing, a kind of centrifugal force that is immensely productive of critical discourse, as *Samuel Beckett's Breath* itself makes clear.

As far as its own critical discourse is concerned, the crux of Goudouna's study could perhaps, first and foremost, be identified in an exploration of the transmedial meanings and histories of artistic Minimalism – both in its narrow sense, as a specific moment of post-war art, literary and musical history, and in its wider significance as what is a central dynamic of modernist practice in general. As Jean-François Lyotard has suggested: 'Whether or not they belong to the current that art history calls Minimalism or *arte povera*, the investigations of the avant-gardes question one by one the constituents one might have thought "elementary" or at the "origin" of the art of painting

---

[2] Bersani, Leo and Dutoit, Ulysse. *Arts of Impoverishment: Beckett, Rothko, Resnais*. Cambridge, MA: Harvard University Press, 1993: 53.

[or theatre]. They operate *ex minimis*.'[3] However, there can be little doubt that this more general dynamic of subtraction or elimination is taken to an extreme in *Breath*. One result is that that any presentation of it as a work of art or theatre must assume what would appear itself to be an irreducibly para-doxical but productive form: on the one hand, as something like the purest art – utterly autonomous and utterly abstracted, referring seemingly to nothing outside of itself, a form stripped of any readable social or historical content, artistic form *as* form and nothing else – but, on the other, as art converging on the condition of what would in fact be *non-art* – utterly literal, devoid of all traditional aesthetic semblance, a blank 'this-ness' repelling all those forms of experience that we would conventionally associate with the artwork. The 'one object of fifty years of abstract art', asserts Ad Reinhardt, writing in 1962, 'is to present art-as-art and as nothing else, to make it into the one thing it is only, separating it and defining it more and more'.[4] Yet, if this objective broadly conforms to the dynamic of Lyotard's 'ex minimis', the reduction of art to what Reinhardt calls its solely 'art meaning' also threatens to become perversely 'unartistic' at this point, indistinguishable from 'no meaning' and from 'non-art'. It terminates, as Adorno puts it, 'in a literal facticity' which undoes the very making of it 'into the one thing it is only' that Reinhardt's art-as-art seeks.[5]

Such 'literalism', as Michael Fried terms it in a still influential 1967 essay, entails what is a 'projected and hypostasised' objecthood that, he asserts, makes it fundamentally 'antithetical to art'. In this respect, it also intersects, as Goudouna reminds us, with what Fried notoriously defines as *theatre*: a 'profound hostility to the arts', 'the illusion that the barriers between the arts are in the process of crumbling'. The spectre of the *Gesamtkunstwerk* (as of Duchamp and the early twentieth-century avant-gardes) looms large here, and as a threat to the delimitation of modernist reduction as progressive purifica-tion of a specific medium – a conception that Fried takes over from Clement Greenberg – in which 'quality and value' are only 'meaningful' *within* 'the individual arts', the aetiology of Fried's anxiety is clear.[6] Against this, however, would be a view for which, as Adorno writes around the same time, 'art stirs most energetically' precisely *where* 'it decomposes its subordinating concept'.

[3] Lyotard, Jean-François. *The Inhuman: Reflections on Time*, trans. Geoffrey Bennington and Rachel Bowlby. Cambridge: Polity, 1991: 103. See also David Cunningham, 'Ex Minimis: Greenberg, Modernism and Beckett's Three Dialogues', *Samuel Beckett Today / Aujourd'hui*, 13 (2003): 29–41; 'Asceticism against Colour, or, Modernism, Abstraction and the Lateness of Beckett', *New Formations*, 55 (Spring 2005): 104–19.

[4] Reinhardt, Ad. 'Art-As-Art', in *Art-As-Art: The Selected Writings of Ad Reinhardt*. Berkeley and London: University of California Press, 1991: 53.

[5] Adorno, Theodor. *Aesthetic Theory*, trans. Robert Hullot-Kentor. Minneapolis: University of Minnesota Press, 1997: 220.

[6] Fried, Michael. 'Art and Objecthood', in Battock, Gregory (ed.). *Minimal Art: A Critical Anthology*. Berkeley and London: University of California Press, 1995: 141.

'In this decomposition, art is true to itself: It breaks the mimetic taboo on the impure and the hybrid.'[7]

Among the many and extensive merits of Goudouna's book is the way in which, then, it inserts Beckett's *Breath*, as a historically and aesthetically specific 'interface between the theatre and the visual arts', into the broader context of this 'decomposition' or 'crumbling' across the arts, and the arguments surrounding it, while, at the same time, never effacing the singularity of the work itself. In this way, *Samuel Beckett's Breath* may well be said to echo what another art critic, Rosalind Krauss, has to say of her own juxtaposition of Beckett with Sol Le Witt: 'To speak of what Le Witt shares . . . with his generation is not to diminish his art; rather it is to help locate the real territory of its meaning.'[8] Yet this 'territory' is far from simply historical, or of a merely scholarly interest, in Goudouna's book. For it also provides the ground for what is an extraordinary critical meditation upon our *own* 'post-medium condition', and the inescapable paradoxes and tensions that define it. Here, the reader finds not only Beckett and Fried, Donald Judd and Tony Smith, but also Bill Viola, Valie Export and Marina Abramovic, Gary Hill, William Kentridge and Lygia Clark. If, like Duchamp, Goudouna's Beckett is *un réspirateur*, it is through the works of such contemporary artists, and their perceptive and remarkable reading here, that he continues to breathe new life today.

---

[7] Adorno, Theodor. *Aesthetic Theory*, trans. Robert Hullot-Kentor. Minneapolis: University of Minnesota Press, 1997: 182.
[8] Krauss, Rosalind. *The Originality of the Avant-Garde and Other Modernist Myths*. Cambridge, MA: MIT Press, 1987: 256.

Edinburgh Critical Studies in Modernism, Drama and Performance
Series Editor: Olga Taxidou

Editorial Board:

Edinburgh Critical Studies in Modernism, Drama and Performance addresses
the somewhat neglected areas of drama and performance within Modernist
Studies, and is in many ways conceived of in response to a number of intellectual and institutional shifts that have taken place over the past 10 to 15
years. On the one hand, Modernist Studies has moved considerably from the
strictly literary approaches, to encompass engagements with the everyday,
the body, the political, while also extending its geopolitical reach. On the
other hand, Performance Studies itself could be seen as acquiring a distinct
epistemology and methodology within Modernism. Indeed, the autonomy of
Performance as a distinct aesthetic trope is sometimes located at the exciting
intersections between genres and media; intersections that this series sets out
to explore within the more general modernist concerns about the relationships
between textuality, visuality and embodiment. This series locates the theoretical, methodological and pedagogical contours of Performance Studies within
the formal, aesthetic and political concerns of Modernism. It claims that the
'linguistic turn' within Modernism is always shadowed and accompanied by
an equally formative 'performance / performative turn'. It aims to highlight the
significance of performance for the general study of modernism by bringing
together two fields of scholarly research which have traditionally remained
quite distinct – performance / theatre studies and Modernism. In turn this
emphasis will inflect and help to re-conceptualise our understanding of both
performance studies and modernist studies. And in doing so, the series will
initiate new conversations between scholars, theatre and performance artists
and students.

Joseph Kosuth, Plays of / for a Respirateur An Installation by Joseph Kosuth [2015] exhibition installation view, Philadelphia Museum of Art. Photograph Joseph Hu

Joseph Kosuth, Plays of / for a Respirateur An Installation by Joseph Kosuth [2015] exhibition installation view, Philadelphia Museum of Art. Photograph Joseph Hu

Feminist Art Workers (Nancy Angelo, Cheri Gaulke, and Laurel Klick), interactive performance, This Ain't No Heavy Breathing 1978, Photograph by Sheila Ruth.

INTRODUCTION: IN THE SAME BREATH – FROM THE BLACK BOX TO THE WHITE CUBE AND BEYOND

Expecting every breath to be its next[1]

I don't know whether the theatre is the right place for me anymore[2]

Nothing could be more over-determined, unpredictable, nonlinear, and even mysterious than the notion of a writer's 'legacy'[3]

The front curtain is drawn open from both sides of the proscenium to reveal a stage set littered with miscellaneous, 'scattered and lying rubbish' and closes at the end of the play, which has no intermissions. The classic raising and lowering of the curtain establishes the temporal boundaries of drama, the viewers here are watching the spectacle thinking that the curtain might be part of an installation and that the piece is an interlude (inter 'between' ludo 'I play') or an intermède (a play in-between plays), given that *Breath* (1966–9)[4] lasts for thirty-five seconds and has no plot, protagonists, character portrayal, dialogue or acting, but consists only of stage directions that designate a visual and sound installation:

CURTAIN
1. Faint light on stage littered with miscellaneous rubbish. Hold about five seconds.

2. Faint brief cry and immediately inspiration and slow increase of light together reaching maximum together in about ten seconds. Silence and hold about five seconds.

3. Expiration and slow decrease of light together reaching minimum together (light as in 1) in about ten seconds and immediately cry as before. Silence and hold about five seconds.

CURTAIN

RUBBISH

No verticals, all scattered and lying.

CRY

Instant of recorded vagitus. Important that the two cries be identical, switching on and off strictly synchronized light and breath.

BREATH

Amplified recording.

MAXIMUM LIGHT

Not bright. If 0 = dark and 10 = light, light should move from about 3 to 6 and back.[5]

The stage directions enfold the entire playlet that consists of a still image of found objects staged like a temporally situated event as a consequence of the addition of the sounds of breathing, and of two identical cries (recorded vagitus). This time-based event does not include action and any performative element or aspect associated with the constitution of meaning such as words, speech, movement and voice.

'Beckett's *Breath*: Anti-Theatricality and the Visual Arts'[6] explores the dynamic interface between the theatrical and the visual in Samuel Beckett's *Breath* and appraises the writer's exceptional impact on conceptual and minimalist artists, by tracing Beckett's attachment and contribution to the visual arts and to visual modernism (and its critical reception). The book introduces a critical framework that aims to analyse the interplay and interconnectedness of media and the tension between theatricality, high-modernism, materiality and the visual arts in the context of *Breath*. Within its historical milieu, the playlet appropriates techniques of the visual arts, and stages a sustained investigation of abstraction within but also outside the theatre. *Breath* is examined as the culmination of Beckett's late 'style'[7] in the theatre and as a minimalist[8] art work, with conceptual overtones, in order to elucidate how it might contribute to debates led by modernist critic Michael Fried around (anti)theatricality and minimalism, and Fried as the theorist who shaped the contours of late modernism in the visual arts, by arguing that minimalism blurs the boundaries between artistic media and thus cannot be situated in the visual modernist narrative.[9]

The survey also focuses on the impact of visual modernism on contemporary art and on the development and historicisation of modernism and employs an interdisciplinary model so as to elucidate this historical flux and the relationship between past art practice, theoretical discourse and contemporary practice by charting a chronological parallel between *Breath*, as a representative piece of minimalism in the theatre (one of the shortest stage pieces ever written and staged), and Fried's programmatic claims in his essay 'Art and Objecthood'.[10]

This chart attempts to formulate a framework for thinking about the intersection of critical discourses on theatricality in the visual arts and the theatre, specifically about the notion of anti-theatricalism in the theatre and the modernist anti-theatrical impulse in the visual arts.[11] The chronological chart is drawn despite the different geographical (different versions of modernism in the United States and Continental Europe) and cultural contexts, however the book does not attempt to resolve the opposition between formalist and anti-formalist theories or to appraise the differences between American and European formalism, but rather to rethink the relations and the common ground between the different aesthetic, geographical and cultural milieus and the ways these theories are revised and critiqued by practices that engage alternative modernities and a wider global history. It is worth noting that the histories and debates that surround high modernist discourses (specific to the late 1960s) share a number of implications and consequences that exceed the parameters of this book. Moreover, this research focuses on visual modernism and does not consider classical criticism of literary modernism nor the criticism of modernism from a literary arts perspective.

A wide range of possibilities of understanding and redefining the context in which the corporeal function of breathing is represented in art, during the performative turn, and in relation to debates concerning modernism and presence are examined in relation to the special significance that respiration acquires by means of an artistic system. The book argues for the distinctiveness of the core focus on breathing, art making and aesthetic theorisation in reference to the historical, formal and contextual intricacies of Beckett's playlet (the writer's broader *oeuvre* is beyond the scope of this survey), as well as on the interface between the ways a high-modernist art theorist and art historian (Fried) approaches the term 'theatricality' and the ways a playwright (Beckett) approaches the expanded field of art practice, the visual arts and anti-theatricality, both as a productive and as a receptive phenomenon.

Contextualised and historicised readings of Beckett's writings and conceptual strategies are provided so as to situate his playlet in the late modernist context by drawing connections and points of convergence between late-modernist art theory and the writer's own aesthetic 'theory'. Analysis builds upon the investigation of Fried's polemical essay against the new tendencies of minimalism and conceptual art that first appeared in the issue of *Artforum* devoted to American sculpture in the summer of 1967, and Beckett's aesthetic approaches in the

'Three Dialogues with Georges Duthuit'(1949);[12] while both discourses are considered in relation to disciplinary or medial entanglements so as to provide ways of thinking within inter-media synergies that open up 'new' domains of research and artistic inquiry.

At the crux of Fried's essay is the equation of medium-specificity with the possibility of good art as well as his objection to that which he terms the 'theatricality' of the minimalist work and its staging of 'presence'. Aspects of such staging include the addition of installation elements and oversized objects so as to relate to the beholder. According to Fried minimalist works set up an invidious relationship with their spectators.

As a formal movement, minimalism is restricted to those artists (primarily in post-war USA)[13] who share a philosophical commitment to the abstract, anti-compositional, material object and is understood in relation to the critical discourse that emerged between 1963 and 1968.[14] The term refers primarily to sculpture or three-dimensional work, in which geometry is emphasised and expressive technique avoided. Minimalist works are often indistinguishable from raw materials or found (non-art) objects. Nevertheless, the development of minimalist practices also defines the shift from object to place, and as Dennis Oppenheim argued in 1969:

> the more successful work from the minimal syndrome rejected itself, allowing the viewer a one-to-one confrontation with pure limits or bounds. This displacement or sensory pressure from object to place will prove to be the major contribution of minimalist art.[15]

The ways that actual space becomes an element in a three-dimensional composition is the focus of the survey, as well as the ways that minimalist practice opens the pictorial and sculptural to actual space and everyday life thus leading to the development of installation art and to the growth of mediated formats (that Fried decried); yet the book argues for the distinctiveness of Beckett's mediated formats and techniques that express a critical resistance to aestheticism by producing immediacy. The different media do not conflate or become indistinct in Beckett's *oeuvre* and rather than instigating detachment these mediations produce advanced forms of immediacy; an intrusive actuality and immediacy – through mediation,[16] that owing to its anti-theatrical effects resists mainstream appropriation and sublimation.

In the explorations below, we follow the ways these two theoretical texts (by Fried and Beckett) come into existence and critical validity, and how, through the process of negotiation between theatricality and the visual arts, they may be useful for analysing *Breath* as a text for and related to contemporary intermedial production and to 'new' understandings, for example of the body's intermedial relationship to the world. Consequently, the study mobilises an analysis grounded in complexities and attempts to contextualise *Breath* within minimalism and the intermedial cultural discourse of visual practices that was first formulated in 1965 by Dick Higgins,[17] and to make a contribution to intermedial Beckett criticism, a discourse that has not developed yet.[18]

The analysis of the anti-theatrical associations between the theoretical systems of Beckett and Fried illustrates that both the theatre and the visual arts appropriate similar conceptual systems and share a common theoretical ground concerning issues of representation. In this context, Fried is perceived as a modernist art critic who intended to intervene polemically in the discourse of the period with what is now considered as a historical debate in the theory of art, and who criticised minimalism and theatricality by arguing that theatre and theatricality were at war with art as such, and Beckett as a playwright who attempted to formulate a unique aesthetic theory and who had a distinctive impact on minimalist aesthetics and on the American minimalist movement of the 1960s, despite the fact that he only visited the United States once, in 1964, on the occasion of the shooting of *Film*.[19]

Notwithstanding the diverse and often conflicting interpretations of minimalism by theorists such as Hal Foster, Rosalind Krauss and Brian O'Doherty, and the impossibility of framing Beckett's work in any specific art movement and within a single aesthetic trajectory, it is significant to stress the fact that Beckett contributed an audio version of *Text for Nothing #8*,[20] in the 'Minimalism' issue of *Aspen* magazine entitled *Aspen: The Magazine in a Box*, 1.5 and 1.6 (1967),[21] during the same period that *Breath* was published. This multimedia magazine was packaged in a cardboard box and included pamphlets, posters, film, flexi-disc records and other art objects designed by artists.

Beckett's work had an exceptional impact on minimalist and conceptual artists such as Sol LeWitt, Robert Morris, Bruce Nauman,[22] and it was LeWitt and Morris who reacted against the dominance of formalist criticism that Fried and Greenberg had espoused throughout the post-war period both in the US and as representatives of the US abroad.

Specific to the mid-60s moment, Beckett's ultimate anti-theatrical and minimalist challenge to the theatre is the writing of this intermedial playlet that resists character representation, textual production, dialogue, drama and theatricality as this is conveyed by acting, while Fried, in his influential analysis imagines a visual art context that is liberated from the notion of theatricality. Fried's polemic is directed not against the theatre per se, but against certain categories of sculpture, 'the new art of minimalism', that he labels 'theatrical', with regard to the terms of its appeal to the viewer, yet Fried's definition of the theatrical and performative is not transparent. The writer attempts to define theatricality in relation to temporality, anthropomorphic attributes and spectatorship (the relationship between space, work and beholder), since he principally criticises the notion of the bodily experience of the minimalist work, the body's orientation, and the points of view that make it so theatrical and against the temporal dimension of the work that differentiates it from the medium of painting.

The literalist preoccupation with the duration of the experience as the artwork isolates the viewer, marking the passing of time, is for Fried a paradigmatically theatrical process since the work provides an 'inexhaustible' and repetitive serial experience. As he argues, the minimalist preoccupation with time is theatrical:

> as though theatre confronts the beholder, and thereby isolates him, with the endlessness not just of objecthood but of time; or as though the sense which at bottom, theatre addresses is a sense of temporality, of both time passing and to come, simultaneously approaching and receding as if apprehended in an infinite perspective [. . .][23]

A number of affinities and differences can be traced between Beckett and Fried concerning their approach to theatricality, spectatorship, temporality, space and anthropomorphism, as well as to medium purity and biomorphism. It was in fact Fried who mentioned that the need to defeat theatricality is nowhere more evident than in the theatre. Nonetheless, he was critical of intermediality and installation aesthetics and of the 'biomorphic' attributes that respiration shares such as in the 'pneumatic sculptures and readymades' *Paris Air* (1919) by Marcel Duchamp, *Artist's Breath* (1959) by Piero Manzoni, *Difficult Breaths* (2004) by Nikos Navridis and *Souffles* (1968 and 2005) by Gérard Fromanger. The prejudice against biomorphic attributes considers these features as hollow and identifies them with nature; Fried points out Donald Judd's (and Smith's) notion of order and simplicity are principles associated with biomorphism:

> Smith's interest in pneumatic structures may seem surprising, but it is consistent both with his own work and with literalist sensibility generally. Pneumatic structures can be described as hollow with a vengeance – the fact that they are not 'obdurate, solid masses' (Morris) being insisted on instead of taken for granted. And it reveals something, I think, about what hollowness means in literalist art that the forms that result are 'biomorphic'.[24]

Fried's theoretical arguments gained a far wider attention than he was able to imagine when he wrote his polemical essay and they are still prevalent in art theory, since they involve categorical claims about the nature of art and cognition. According to the theorist, the experience of literalist (minimalist) art is one of indefinite duration or endlessness, since it produces 'theatricality-objecthood', namely, an over-awareness of the situation in which the object stands, owing to the conscious use of objects sized to relate to the 'beholder' and a heightened sense of the object as an obdurate entity.

Fried's long-term art-historical project is principally completed in three books: *Absorption and Theatricality: Painting and Beholder in the Age of Diderot* (1980), *Courbet's Realism* (1990), *Manet's Modernism, or, the Face of Painting in the 1860s* (1966).[25] The critic applied his ideas on theatricality through the attendant term, 'objecthood', and for him 'art' and 'objecthood' represent two conflicting terms, as he argues:

> it is as though objecthood alone can, in the present circumstances, secure something's identity, if not as non-art, at least as neither painting nor sculpture; or as though a work of art – more accurately, a work of painting or sculpture – were in some essential respect not an object. There is in any case a sharp contrast between the literarist espousal of objecthood – almost, it seems as an art in its own right – and modernist painting's self-imposed imperative that it defeat or suspend its own objecthood through the medium of shape. In fact, from the perspective of recent modernist painting, the literalist position evinces a sensibility not simply alien but antithetical to its own: as though, from that perspective, the demands of art and the conditions of objecthood are in direct conflict.[26]

Fried argues that the minimalist works 'stage' presence and engender a strong physical immediacy, yet because of their human scale and hollowness they simulate the presence of another person, thus they control both the situation and the beholder's body and they reduce the role of the spectator to a state of unquestioning awareness, since s/he stands in an open-ended, indeterminate and wholly passive relation to the object as a detached subject. According to Fried:

> something is said to have presence when it demands that the beholder takes into account, that he takes seriously – and when the fulfilment of that demand consists simply in being aware of it and, so to speak, in acting accordingly.[27]

In view of the proliferation of contemporary art practices that challenge the objecthood, permanence, temporality and the material status of the artwork, Fried's theory has received criticism. On the other hand, Beckett's anti-theatrical playlet continues to shed light on a contemporary reading and understanding of the interdisciplinary and dialectical nature of theatricality.

Beckett's pervasiveness in contemporary art and the impact of his *oeuvre* on visual artists is diverse, far-reaching and continuous but this legacy is also marked by the writing of this playlet in the borders of the visual arts and the theatre. *Breath* not only combines two art forms (theatre and plastic arts) into a single visual experience but has also spawned experiments in the nature of theatre opening up to extra-theatrical forms, including installation, environmental art, readymade and assemblage.

Cutting across diverse thematic interests and modes of investigation, the book expands beyond the primary contexts in which these texts were written and explores the impact of both writers on aesthetic theory and practice by offering an insight into the emerging and rapidly changing set of concepts and practices proposed by contemporary artists, and by acknowledging that Beckett's experimentations still influence visual artists who employ performative elements in their work and present live performance pieces in a visual art context.

The on-going importance concerning 'liveness' in contemporary artists' work and the engagement with more recent investigations of the temporal within curatorial practice, that focuses on notions of respiration, are significant parameters in the context of the book. Live art offers different potentials for contemporary performance and currently theatricality is being integrated in every artistic domain such as installation art, video, photography, sculpture and visual art performance.

However, the prevalent use of staging and performative strategies in the visual arts is often not recognised, while at the same time contemporary performance employs anti-theatrical strategies similar to the plastic arts. According to Shannon Jackson, the intermedial puzzles of contemporary art create new performative realities (and new performative problems) for receivers trying to make sense of them. As she argues, in the face of critical confusion, the term 'performative' 'comes in to save the day. It seems to provide an umbrella to cluster recent cross-disciplinary work in time, in space, with bodies, in relational encounters – even if the term does this work without saying anything particularly precise'.[28] The theorist calls this phenomenon the intermedial use of the performative vocabulary. Jackson considers that in the navigating of this intermedial interplay, audience-receivers play a central role depending on what art form they understand the work to be challenging, and they will both receive and judge the piece differently from each other. As she argues, the audience's responses,

> gauge a work's closeness and distance to sculpture, to dance, to theater, to film, to painting, or to other mediums. Indeed, such calibrations will in turn affect whether the receiver calls herself a beholder, an audience member, a spectator, a viewer, a visitor, or a participant. The imprecision of 'performative work' in terms of medium thus gets tested most urgently in the encounter with someone who is deciding what kind of receiver she wants to be.[29]

ANTI-THEATRICALITY AND THE VISUAL ARTS

The aim of this survey is to demonstrate that theatricality and performativity cannot be isolated and conceptualised strictly within the field of theatre, by arguing that *Breath* points to an understanding of 'theatre' precisely through an 'anti-theatricality' that is not simply removed from the theatre and displaced into a visual or live art context, and that Beckett's anti-theatrical strategies can play a productive role in the theatre. The book also argues that the dialectics of theatricality and anti-theatricality constitutes an ideological and creative force both for practitioners of contemporary performance and for visual artists, taking into consideration that a large number of contemporary art practices focus on the role of live art in their work, while they aim to integrate the spectator in the creative practice whether in object or time-based works. The inclusion of the viewer, the increasing significance of 'experience', the focus on physical participation and on the extended situation are seen as theatrical 'attributes' that are integrated in contemporary visual art practice.

Critical problems that pertain to the term (theatricality) are examined in the context of the interface between the theatre and the visual arts, the interconnections between theatricality and intermediality, the eradication of the theatrical text, dialogue and character and the objectification of art, by analysing aspects of the formal achievement of this playlet that was written on the paper tablecloth of a café and that attempted to reshape the contours and possibilities of theatre practice in the 1960s by opening up areas of aesthetics that contemporary artists are only beginning to fully explore.[30]

The modernist concern focuses on the literality, durationality, the 'in-between-ness' as an intermedial form and also on the intermedial nature of so-called performative work. Intermedia theorists Freda Chapple and Chiel Kattenbelt locate intermediality at a juncture in-between the performers, the observers and the confluence of the media involved in a performance at a particular moment in time. The intermedial, as they argue:

> inhabits a space in-between the different realities that the performance creates and thus it becomes, at the minimum, a tripartite phenomenon. Intermediality is a powerful and potentially radical force, which operates in-between performer and audience; in-between theatre, performance and other media; and in-between realities – with theatre providing a staging space for the performance of intermediality.[31]

The basic assumptions of this methodological approach is that the interaction with performativity is missing in *Breath* as a result of the anti-theatrical strategies that lead to the eradication of the subject and the performer, thus the formative relationship between mediality and (anti)theatricality becomes critical in understanding the application of the term in *Breath*. It is significant to consider Patrice Pavis' insightful statement that intermediality does not only mean the addition of different media concepts, 'nor the act of placing discrete works in relation to particular forms of media, but rather the integration of aesthetic concepts from different media into a new concept'.[32]

Intermediality draws from the creation of new concepts that focus on inter-generic interfaces and on the mobility of aesthetic media and shared theoretical concepts, namely, on a common practical ground between different disciplines. The interdisciplinary mobility of aesthetic concepts and especially the interdisciplinary mobility of theatricality (between the visual and performing arts) draw from the appropriation of similar conceptual systems with regards to issues of representation. Accordingly, anti-theatricalism is appropriated by both disciplines as a formative process that affects the ways theatre and art practitioners work in, and work between, artistic media respectively. Concepts, as Mieke Bal argues, can travel from one discourse or context to another and they are able to 'carry across their particular histories but at the same time they are in a state of disentanglement or deterritorialisation, thus providing new ways of thinking within their newly found territory'.[33]

Recurrently, anti-theatricalism restricts the use of theatrical metaphor and retains a suggestion of negativity about the formal codes of theatre. However, the anti-theatrical discourse can be decidedly imprecise, particularly in the contexts where it is used and depending on the discipline that examines it. Theatricality was applied as a term to installation strategies after the late 1960s, however both the theatre and the visual arts introduce similar resourceful practices that attempt to abolish the separation between audience and stage, spectator and exhibition space. Modernist aesthetic theory is critical of theatricality, of the hybrid nature of installation art and intermedial practice, and theatre has usually played two different and incompatible roles for high-modernist aesthetics: that of its paradigm and that of its opponent.[34]

According to the theorist Shannon Jackson, it might be imprecision and self-contradiction that make theatricality so resilient and often anti-theatrical discourse links theatre with the degradations of artifice, as 'they appeared variously in Plato's condemnation of its tertiary status, Austin's repudiation of its "etiolated" form or even in naturalistic theatre's attempts to avoid its own artificiality'.[35] It is noteworthy that despite the spatial and participatory engagement of the audience in works of art from minimalism to relational works, the theatrical has diverse manifestations and is not interpreted with consistency by art theorists. It is quite disorienting for the theatre historian, as Jackson argues, 'to learn that the traditional terms of one's own workaday world are the very same terms used to mark the disruption of visual art traditions, whether that disruption is celebrated as a liberation from the object or castigated as the end of art as we know it'.[36]

Depending on the discipline (performance, visual arts, philosophy, anthropology) they represent, these anti-theatrical aesthetics and discourses that emerged in the 1960s have different understandings of the referent in words like 'theatre' and 'theatricality'. Thus, theatricality is considered to be a relational concept, connected to the functioning of metaphor and the term, as

Ragnhild Tronstad argues, 'relates to real life in the same way as the metaphor relates to literal language. Theatricality's way of being is structurally identical to that of metaphor: their creation is contingent upon a gap, a deviation, a difference and the degree of deviation creates different degrees of theatricality'.[37]

The term derives its meanings from the world of theatre but various theorists have abstracted theatricality from the theatre and have applied it to many aspects of human, social life and the visual arts. Yet there is a danger in the flexibility of the uses of the term, as Davis and Postlewait argue, '[M]aking it everything from an act to an attitude, a style to a semiotic system, a medium to a message, can mean too many things, and thus nothing. If it serves too many agendas, it is in danger of losing its hold on both the world of theatre and the world as theatre.'[38]

Notwithstanding the flexibility of the applications of the term it becomes evident that theatricality does not merely indicate a clash between the visual image presented on stage and the verbal image created by the spoken word, as several theorists argue. On the contrary, the intergeneric treatment of theatricality and the visual arts, as well as the interface of the visual and the theatrical produces an ongoing formative process that transforms both disciplines, while it challenges the relationship between theatricality and textuality, actuality and theatrical representation, as well as the concept of mimesis and theatrical practice, speech, voice, language and non-linguistic processes of signification. Vanden Heuvel draws from media theorist Marshall McLuhan who argues that 'two cultures or technologies can, like astronomical galaxies, pass through one another without collision; but not without a change in configuration. In modern physics there is similarly the concept of "interface" or the meeting and metamorphosis of two structures'.[39]

The dynamic interface between the theatrical and the visual in the later work, and in particular in *Breath*, questions conventional and realistic representational strategies and leads to a medial confrontation, as McMullan suggests:

> between the attempt to assume a position of control and judgment in relation to the visual and verbal representations of the self and the laws of representation in general, and the opening up of spaces, which challenge and disrupt the construction of the roles posited by representation, including those of self and other, spectacle and spectator. Beckett's drama frames the operations of authority, but also stages the drama of a subjectivity, which resists or exceeds the dominant codes of representation, questioning in the process the languages and limits of theatre itself.[40]

Beckett challenges the limits of theatre so as to explore and define what theatre is and what can be included in the theatrical frame as well as what can be named and defined as a theatrical event. More specifically, in the late plays, as Brater suggests, the writer reaches for something far more concrete 'what remains in the theatre, live and palpable and real, after so much has been taken away, how much doesn't have to happen onstage for a lyrical dramatic moment to expand and to unfold'.[41]

The consideration of *Breath* in more depth within its historical and formal context elucidates the ways in which certain features of anti-theatricality play out in theatre practice and theory and the differences between visual anti-theatrical discourse and anti-theatricality as it is traced in theatre production and discourse. Moreover, modernist discourse often associates what it considers as the negative elements of theatricality with intermedia practice that is identified with lack both of taste and artistic autonomy. Intermedia practice according to this reading is a symptom of the decline of 'taste', and as Greenberg wrote 'what's ominous is that the decline of taste now, for the first time, threatens to overtake art itself. I see "intermedia" and the permissiveness that goes with it as symptoms of this'.[42]

Making the Audible Visible

High-modernist discourse, that is specific to the late 1960s, has been critical of intermedial practices based on the understanding that their methodologies reinforce the interconnectedness of all kinds of media; old and new, artistic and non-artistic. Even though there are media types that ostensibly demonstrate the presence of several media, Michael Fried's and Clement Greenberg's criticism is founded on media formations that are intermedial in the sense that they share basic properties.

The term 'intermediality' refers both to combinations and integrations of media types and to transformations between these types. This includes media aspects having to do with different material forms, different sensory modes, various spatiotemporal configurations of media and different semiotic characteristics. The term also refers to media types that are created and remodelled in changing historical, cultural, social, aesthetic and communicative contexts.

Moreover, intermediality is not only reliant on technology, but on the interaction between performance and perception, and this survey draws from Yvonne Spielmann's reading that treats the term as a combinatory structure of syntactical elements that come from more than one medium but are combined into one and are thereby transformed into a new entity. Contemporary discourses on the conceptual structure of intermedia are often describing the phenomenon of crossing the borders between traditional media (such as painting and photography), contemporary media (such as cinema, television, video, computer and other hypermedia), live and animated stage production, and attempt to understand the methodological challenges of converging different media, live performance, animation, film, music and design.

Intermedia theorists Chapple and Kattenbelt define the term as 'a powerful and potentially radical force that operates in-between theatre, performance and other media; in-between performer and audience; and in-between realities – with theatre providing a stage space for the performance of intermediality'[43] while both of the constituent parts of the term 'intermediality', 'inter' and 'media', designate 'between-ness'.

The attempt to contextualise *Breath* within this potentially radical force and within intermedial discourse is substantiated in several respects in the analysis below: firstly, *Breath* opens the pictorial and sculptural (readymade) to the spatial and oscillates between the pictorial and three dimensional; secondly, it oscillates between different realities (see below); thirdly, the playlet experiments with media technology and as a 'technicule',[44] it operates in-between a live and a mediated reality; it is an amplified, mediated respiration (a recorded breath and an instant of recorded vagitus) that is presented live on stage; and fourthly, it is the culmination of Beckett's late style in the theatre that is characterised by an aesthetic of media cross-fertilisation. *Breath*'s intermedial 'between-ness' is analysed both in the context of this cross-fertilisation, namely, the multifaceted nature of Beckett's choice of media in an *oeuvre* that includes text, stage, film, radio, television, mime, and performance and in relation to Beckett's reductionist representational strategies.

Breath is intrinsically intermedial given that it operates in-between realities (art and body/biology/life/non-art), in-between the boundaries of artistic media (theatre and visual arts/installation art), the verbal and the visual, the audible and the scenic (sound as stage presence), in-between visibility and invisibility (light and darkness), in-between presence and absence/emptiness, embodiment and ambiguity of corporeal experience, in-between life and death (movement and stasis) and in-between an inhalation and an exhalation (silence and sound). These different aspects of intermediality are unravelled throughout this survey, and the term (intermediality) is analysed in the context of the quasi-generic and inter-generic features of Beckett's late style in the theatre, in conjunction with the de-centred field of subjectivity and its polysemous modes of absence and presence.

The above issues are addressed by focusing on the question of the relation between the work (of art) and what is outside of it (surroundings, author, painter, reader, beholder), through an examination of the artistic use of, and critical commentary on, media and of the artistic treatment of the process of the physical act of respiration, as it is traced in *Breath* but also in the artworks of selected artists that have marked the history of the visual arts and performance.

The topic of respiration, that the book identifies and aims to historicise, can provide an insight into such discussion of aesthetic media. This is not least in terms of the on-going revaluation of the legacy of the 'immaterial' and of the methodologically richly-faceted tension between materiality and immateriality

BECKETT'S BREATH

in debates in, for example, the curatorial projects by theorists such as Lucy R. Lippard, Jacques Derrida, Bruno Latour, Jean-François Lyotard and Georges Didi-Huberman.[45] It is, as well, on the focus on the temporal dimension of exhibiting and on the processual and performative shifts that curatorial practice has undergone over the past twenty years, in reference to breath related curatorial projects that employ intermediality such as Koan Jeff Baysa's *OXYGEN*, (2002) and Autogena Projects *The Breathing Project* (Lise Autogena and Joshua Portway Goldsmiths Curating Project, 1996).

The question of the interface between these disciplines and fields of practice (and their institutional supports) remains very 'current', while the book's particular lens, concerning an aesthetics of respiration, attempts to reflect on the history of these debates, addressing questions of the body (as 'a site of signification'), aesthetic specificity (which is precisely what the intermedial challenges), the interface between the museum and the theatre, and presence and/or 'presentness' (in relation to the 'live and mediated').

The enduring binary between live and mediated performance, as well as the binary between the theatre and the visual arts is primarily founded on different representational attitudes towards the live body, the human figure, corporeal presence, subjectivity/subjecthood and agency. The human body is either physically present or technically represented/mediated in video, film, television and the digital, and intermedial exchanges (in the theatre and the visual arts) manage to reconcile this binary by integrating a variety of technical media into a large medial framework. The blurring of the boundaries between theatricality and the visual arts, just like the question of intermediality in the context of installation art, and the problem of theatricality, continue to problematise aesthetic theorists.

FROM THE SPECIFIC TO THE GENERIC

The history of art has experienced several significant paradigm shifts that reframed modes of spectatorship and long-established notions of the visitor, the audience, the listener and the spectator. The sixties' artworld transformation is seen in conjunction with these scientific paradigm shifts. Theorists like Caroline Jones trace significant affinities with the persuasive account of the enterprise of science put forward by Thomas S. Kuhn in *The Structure of Scientific Revolutions*, and of the complexities between the artworld and Kuhn. Adding to this, the contemporary critic and theorist Hal Foster refers to the paradigm as embedded in the context of a historical shift specific to this mid-1960s moment; the paradigm's identification as modernism (or its scion) is left intact.

At present, medium specificity is set against a critical backdrop and diverse artistic strategies introduce unfamiliar situations, forms, media and materials and engage audiences to embrace new and hybrid forms of immersion, viewing, responsivity and modes of participation. The terms 'participatory'[46] and 'relational'[47] become increasingly important for the visual and performing arts in describing both an aesthetic of making and an ethics of spectatorship. Art practitioners are constantly on the search for innovative ways to engage participants in their work, by shifting the meaning of the art object completely to the experience that is made with and through this work. The focus on individual artistic practice, the experience of this process and the attitudes towards the creative act are some of the guiding principles that inform the expanded and unbounded relationship between space, subjecthood, objecthood, materiality and artwork.

Modernist art critics (Fried and Greenberg), however, claim that these practices and the performative and theatrical elements damage the essence and autonomy of the individual arts. The modernist discourse against the theatricality and performativity of the visual artwork is also related to a general attitude against 'conventional' realistic representation and artistic illusion. The critics consider that the tendency of categorising art as an event means that the viewers do not appreciate the artwork itself but rather its broader cultural context (i.e. Abstract Expressionism, colour field painting, as opposed to a specific painting by Pollock or Rothko).[48] The identification of art to a cultural event leads to a form of reception that is conditioned by surrounding socio-historic circumstance and this means that the artwork is not appreciated as an independent entity.

According to this perspective, the artists do not define what the final work exactly is and the work's aesthetic values are contingent upon the many variables that shape the viewer's experience. These additive components mean that the viewer can relate with the whole, having a more encompassing experience determined not only by the work, but by the different elements of the artistic experience including the event, the architectural space, the social environment etc. Modernist criticism, however, argues for the eradication of these additive components and the exclusion of the viewer, as the work should be closed to the outside and should have an inherent structure.

Clement Greenberg, the writer of 'Modernist Painting'[49] and 'After Abstract Expressionism'[50] (in 1960 and 1962 respectively), identifies this inherent structure and source of value with the intrinsic properties of each art's medium, and argues that modernism works by gradually abolishing all norms and conventions that prove inessential to a work's instantiation of a given art form, and that every art medium has to eradicate everything it shares with any other media. Despite the theoretical differences between Fried and Greenberg, the former endorses Greenberg's view that the arts have distinct essences and acknowledges his debt to Greenberg, who claims that modernism is each art's attempt to locate the essence of its medium through a process of immanent self-criticism and that the structural concerns should be contained within the work of art.

Mid-century aesthetics is therefore partly dominated by the rhetoric of isolated and purified opticality[51] and modernist sensibility is in favour of the difference between formal and conceptual frameworks; and while the distinction between these different frameworks is formulated in relation to 'non-artness', the conceptual framework is reduced to 'non-artness' and to three-dimensional art that focuses on the primacy of the literal over depicted shape.

Greenberg acknowledges that the 'cutting edge' works have the look of 'non-art' at their 'arrival', and for the theorist this means that most paintings that look like 'non-art' are considered as art, though not necessarily a successful work of art. The look of 'non-art' had to be sought in the three-dimensional and Greenberg argues that minimalist work has gone so far in the extreme of being 'non-art' that it is as 'non-art' as a 'door, a table or a blank sheet of paper'.[52] Consequently, minimalist art remains too much a feat of ideation and not enough anything else; as he states, 'its idea remains an idea, something deduced instead of felt and discovered [. . .] There is hardly any aesthetic surprise in Minimal Art [. . .] Aesthetic surprise hangs on forever – it is there in Raphael as it is in Pollock – and ideas alone cannot achieve it'.[53]

The minimalists' failure to formulate anything but interest in their work marks a deviation from modernism, because if a work is merely 'interesting', it is not aesthetically comparable to modernist works preceding it. This is problematic (for modernists), not only because of the 'non-artness' of the minimalist work, but also because these artworks are not concerned with the pictorial or structural elements contained within the work of art. The minimalists' failure to formulate anything but interest in their work marks a deviation from modernism, because if a work is merely 'interesting', it is not aesthetically comparable to modernist works preceding it. This is problematic (for modernists), not only because of the 'non-artness' of the minimalist work, but because these artworks overlook the significance of the pictorial or structural elements contained within the work of art. For modernist critics, conceptual artworks share the same problem.

Contemporary art theorists question modernist notions of the viewing experience as either a pure optical experience or as a strong gestalt, as well as the limits and subjective conditions of modernist discourse as to what can count as art, and hence as an object of aesthetic judgement based on specific practices of painting and sculpture. The question of aesthetic knowledge has been opened and reopened by contemporary critical discourses that resynthesise, reschematise critical methodology based on diverse methodologies and that invent new contexts for their discipline, instead of turning to theoretical schematism and closure.

High-modernist aesthetic positions have been rearticulated by twenty-first-century discourses in performance and art history with a view to developing an aesthetic that can respond to contemporary issues. Thus, contemporary discourse interrogates the platitudes and the tone of certainty that is predominant in formalist criticism. A 'specific knowledge of art', as the art theorist Didi-Huberman notes, 'ended up imposing its own specific form of discourse on its object, at the risk of inventing artificial boundaries for its object – an object dispossessed of its own specific deployment or unfolding'.[54]

Reflective rather than prescriptive, intermedial discourses that are critical of high-modernist formalism emphasise instead of making obscure the limits of interpretation in art and argue in favour of the ambiguity of meaning and the plurality of interpretations of the art work by introducing openness, disorder, chance, mobility and indeterminacy within its structure. Marcel Duchamp's constant questioning of the nature of the work of art and his emphasis on the work of art's 'completion' by the spectator highlights this 'openness', that is primarily based on the ideological[55] and contextual issues surrounding the artwork.

Scholars have been debating the interrelations between the arts of time (theatre, music, literature, film) and the arts of space (the visual arts) since the first formations and writings on art theory and this debate shifts to a more self-reflexive critical dialogue between media as it is expressed in the progressive intermedial networking of the arts. As a consequence, rigid discourses are inadequate to provide a comprehensive analysis of the far-reaching ramifications of works that stimulate an embodied and open sensorial engagement similar to the selected breath related artworks.

EMBODIED VISION

These artworks focus on embodied vision and on respiration as a physical act, an interactivity that produces, invents and 'demands' the viewer/spectator/listener's participation. The visualisation of the complex, minimal and abstract processes of the respiratory system draws from the language of physicality and from the human body as a primary force of signification and discloses the 'sensuous' nature of form. The selected artists look into breath's actuality and immediacy and prioritise the immediate response to the artwork since the act of immediate perception is primarily located in the body. At the same time, artists experiment with processes and materials to transpose this natural process into the artwork.

The cross-disciplinary interest in the artistic, cultural and scientific ramifications and the focus on the complexities of respiration raise questions about the relationship between aesthetics and medical humanities. The 'sensuous' approach that characterises the selected artworks draws from the viewer's corporeal experience and from the interpretive competence of the human body as well as from the ways respiration affects the nervous and visceral systems. This process can offer a glimpse into a possible new reading of breathing, one that intertwines the aesthetic with the biomedical.

Biological metaphors often appear in discourses about the relations of human nature to art and various biologically based theories of aesthetics see biological phenomena and aesthetic practices in a shifting and reciprocal relationship to each other. There is an on-going parallel between the 'visualisation of energy' in the scientific and in the artistic domains and both disciplines are preoccupied with the visual paradigm; nevertheless, the primacy of visual perception (the interplay of the visible and the 'invisible') maintains an ontological status in the artistic domain.

The intermedial intersects with the sensorial; while the sensory, perceptual and sensate approaches are focusing on the aural, visual, tactile and haptic resonance of 'corporeal language' that go beyond the significations and the interpretation of the written text. The selected breath-related artworks employ diverse languages such as the verbal, the corporeal, the visual, the aural and the technological. The potential of the body as the site of signification and as the modality for, and site of, experiential interpretation is highlighted in these works, such as the focus on the somatic rather than the semantic.

Breath, as a medium, is commonly understood as the physical basis of the organism and of the body's manifold sensory apparatus. This bio-process mediates and is mediated and a 'fundamental' reading of the respiratory system emphasises its formative value as a communicative agent between the individual, the outside world and time. The act of mediation is a process and in this sense the medium of breath always internalises a singular engagement with temporality, and thus defines the way in which we, collectively and individually, perceive and understand our environment.

EXHALING THE FIELD

The philosophical and aesthetic questions dealt with throughout the book are wide-ranging but gain their specificity from the focus on *Breath*'s intermedial contours. In turn the ramifications of this analysis are worked out in the specificity of respiration but are far-reaching in relation to an interdisciplinary sensibility. The conceptual and art historical framework is developed in three sections. The first is entitled 'Respiration, Presence, Modernist Discourse and the Question of Medium Specificity'; the second, '(Re)presenting Breath'; and the third, 'The Exhaled Field'. As mentioned, the first section charts a chronological parallel between Beckett's *Breath* as a representative piece of minimalism[56] in the theatre and Fried's 'Art and Objecthood', in an attempt to go beyond a linear and chronological reading and illustrate that some of the larger issues at stake in the critique of theatricality have ramifications that go beyond the confines of the post-war American world. The inflected meanings of terms like 'minimalism' and 'theatricality' across the disciplinary boundaries of the theatre and the visual arts is the focal point of the inquiry on *Breath*'s minimalist aspects as they are unveiled by the lack of the human subject, performer, actor, lack of text, drama, dialogue and plot.

DEEPTIME

The first chapter focuses on the ways that Beckettian aesthetics translates into practice and on how the *Three Dialogues* can be applied to a work like *Breath*, so as to illuminate specific aspects of the playlet, principally Beckett's decision to eradicate the text and the human figure and the ways this decision is affected by Beckett's 'aesthetics of failure'. *Breath* is considered in the context of the expanded field of art practice, whose origins are specific to the mid-1960s moment, the period of the evolution of the minimalist and modernist paradigm.

The chapter consists of a detailed exposition of the concept of objecthood that is central to the critique of minimalism,[57] and draws from the potential of the concept for the analysis, creation and for understanding particular aspects of art and theatre practice with respect to interdisciplinary mobilities. The fact that Beckett's plays approximate the representational conditions of visual art works is, as Hauck observed, 'a purely accidental by-product of the generally "reductive" (by reducing) process of composing plays'. As a consequence, the intermedial aspects of *Breath* are examined in the context of Beckett's progressive diminution of his artistic resources.[58] Hauck argues, 'in the relentless adherence to this process, Beckett has not only created a number of theatrical paintings and sculptures that are as memorable as those of the greatest visual artists, but he has also come as close as it may be possible for a practicing dramatist to get to defining the boundaries between a theatrical performance and a purely visual representation'.[59]

Breath's temporal unfolding is critical for understanding the borders between a theatrical performance and a purely visual representation and an equally important component for the playlet's composition as its materiality (lighting and stage design). *Breath* does not represent time; the playlet takes place at present time (here and now), while Beckett composes an 'aesthetics of presence' (respiration) but also an 'aesthetics of absence' (missing figure). Fried's linkage of theatricality/objecthood to time and his binarism between mere presence and pure presentness are considered through a close analysis of temporalities[60] and temporal unfolding in the production and reception of *Breath*. The playlet's temporal unfolding and its compositional methodology are expressed as a dialectics between duration and 'instantaneousness', a temporal format and modality that characterises installation aesthetics.

The piece is reduced in time and space to the point where it becomes static and 'frozen' both temporally and spatially, in the same manner as a visual artwork. *Breath* operates (or oscillates) between a sound 'tableau'[61] (installation art) and the pictorial, two-dimensional (static image), and the tableau, as Stephen W. Melville argues, is the 'seam along which modern theatre and painting have been historically bound to one another'.[62] Despite *Breath*'s theatrical terms of spectatorship, the playlet reveals aspects and attributes that are characteristic of the visual arts such as flatness, presentness or 'instantaneousness', the presence of the readymade (miscellaneous rubbish); and it is received as a fully realised image (tableau) that has the potential to 'absorb' the beholder.

According to Fried, theatricality and absorption[63] affect how an artwork manifests temporalities and the ways it is received; the effect of absorption is a 'perfect trance of involvement' that draws the beholder into a prolonged concentration on the artwork.[64] This impression is achieved by artists who intentionally ignore the viewer, instead focusing intently on an object in the painting (such as painters Jean-Baptiste Greuze, Jean-Baptiste-Simeon Chardin and Carle Van Loo). Fried draws from Denis Diderot, who wrote during the period that these artists were active, stating that Diderot's ideal for painting rested 'ultimately upon the supreme fiction that the beholder did not exist, that he was not really there, standing before the canvas; and that the dramatic representation of action and passion, and the causal and instantaneous mode of unity that came with it, provided the best available medium for establishing that fiction in the painting itself'.[65]

Fried carries through an art historical project that argues the centrality of a dialectic or quasi-dialectic of absorption and theatricality to French painting from the eighteenth century on, by relating absorption to the effect of the tableau. The term 'tableau' shares a lot of common characteristics with installation art since it ties painting and theatre to each other.

In this framework, the chapter juxtaposes *Breath*'s anti-theatrical use of temporality (minimal duration) and its composition of a 'timeless' moment with two-dimensional works and installations, while it examines the shifts that have taken place from the two-dimensional representation to the intermedial expansion of painting. The selected paintings, such as Bridget Riley's *Breathe* and Gerhard Richter's *Breath*, are representative of the optical art and abstract expressionism movements. Richter's and Riley's paintings, as well as William Kentridge's piece *Breathe* (that is composed of small pieces of torn paper that gather and fall to the rhythm of a singer's breathing), the installation *Sighs Trapped by Liars* by Art & Language and Michael Craig Martin's *Inhale/Exhale* retain a critical inter-mediality that is characterised by a self-reflexive dialogue between the media and resist homogeneous hybrid formations, while other works including James Turrell's *Breathing Light* and Bill Viola's *Fire, Water, Breath* advance forms of aesthetic illusion rather than immediacy.

The chapter focuses on Beckett's critical writings on art, and on the function of art in his own practice, in relation to the dialectics of abstraction and expression and the 'aesthetics of failure'. Beckett is a theatrical writer with a distinctive relationship to theory and art discourse since attempting to express an aesthetic theory. The analysis of the *Three Dialogues* tracks the trajectory of the writer's experimentation with form and narrative and investigates the progressive simplifications and reductions in the writer's *oeuvre* that manifest a self-reflexive concern with medium, genre and the creative act.

The *Three Dialogues*, Beckett's final piece of discursive writing, is considered within the context of its subject matter, the tension between abstraction and expression, the dilemma of artistic expression and the impossibility of expression in painting.[66] As Hugh Kenner's comments in the book *A Reader's Guide to Samuel Beckett*, the 'ostensible subject of these dialogues is painting, a manageable metaphor for any art'.[67] The writer's admiration of the 'old masters' is well-known,[68] along with his dialogue with artists such as Bram van Velde. Yet the writer criticises the work of Tal Coat and André Masson, considering that these artists don't manage to challenge conventional painting, but rather reproduce the aesthetic norms.

In the *Three Dialogues*, the writer speaks of an art that turns from 'the plane of the feasible in disgust, weary of its puny exploits, weary of pretending to be able, of being able, of doing a little better the same old thing, of going a little further along a dreary road',[69] and dreams of an art 'un-resentful of its insuperable indigence and too proud for the farce of giving and receiving'[70] as it is expressed in the work of Bram van Velde that Beckett supports. According to the dialogue:

> Duthuit – One moment. Are you suggesting that the painting of van Velde is inexpressive? Beckett (a fortnight later) – Yes. D – You realise the absurdity of what you advance? B – hope I do.[71]

The notion of the 'inexpressive' is based on the philosophical quest of the expression that 'there is nothing to express, nothing with which to express, nothing from which to express, no power to express, no desire to express, together with the obligation to express'.[72] The writer's aspiration to write an art theory reveals certain of his aesthetic approaches and this unorthodox theory can be applied for understanding his aesthetic quests like his direct or indirect collaborations with painters[73] and his continuing relevance and enduring impact for the visual arts in the twenty-first century. Beckett's aesthetics and the 'fidelity to failure' have influenced contemporary visual artists, composers, musicians, dancers, choreographers, architects and other artists[74] and his work has dominated contemporary discourse, art practices and theorists, curators, art historians, curatorial practices and art movements in the last half century.[75] Most importantly, with his preoccupation with the visual as a paradigm of creativity and with the metaphor of painting in his works, Beckett's 'painterly writing'[76] determines the ways his aesthetics translates into practice.

THE DURATIONAL TURN

The second chapter focuses on the structure of Fried's aesthetic judgement and critique in order to expose a number of concealed assumptions that underlie the criticism of minimalist art and the presuppositions and narrow ideology that Fried covers over with the veil of authority by means of questioning narratives about the viewing experience of visual art, as either a pure optical experience or as a strong gestalt. Fifty years after the writing of 'Art and Objecthood', Fried's fundamental schematism, the binary structuring of his themes, the evaluative hierarchy he sets up between theatrical and anti-theatrical art, the normative dimension of his criticism, the rhetorical style, the oppositional logic, the lack of self-reflexivity and his conception of artistic value have been considered as anachronistic, conservative, unrepentantly formalist and idealist, as since the 1960s the art world has taken a performative and durational turn. This 'turn' has determined the way art is received and has altered the interaction between spectators and works of art. The 'performative turn' draws on a shift from the paradigm of 'representation' to techniques of art/performance and focuses on the exercise of a bodily expounded, 'performative approach'.

Nonetheless, the chapter acknowledges that Fried's reconsideration and revision of his theories in 1998, and from a 1998 perspective, with the book *An Introduction to my Art Criticism*,[77] chart the theorist's own critical and intellectual development and accepts that a series of misconceptions have also marked the reception of his criticism. Most recently, and following Fried's introduction to his criticism,[78] his writings receive varied responses and more elaborate discussions rather than an outright rejection, while critics also contend that it is very challenging to go beyond his theoretical schema and aesthetics imperatives. Critics who appreciate artworks that challenge medium specificity and autonomy are not always able to go beyond the underlying structure of Fried's aesthetic judgement, or to question his theory, given that it is challenging to criticise what can count as an object of aesthetic judgement and not remain internal to the very framework that these discourses criticise.[79]

The chapter questions the ways visual modernist discourse invents artificial boundaries and the imperative that the essence of a given art endures independently of its ongoing practice, by demonstrating the broad challenges of contemporary art practice to many of the dominant assumptions of high-modernist theoretical inquiry that promote received disciplinary categories and forms of practice. The intention is to examine the framework underwriting Fried's evaluation rather than the evaluation itself, by aligning with critics such as Diarmuid Costello who argues that Fried's response to minimalism exemplifies a refusal to judge aesthetically, an approach that determines the criticism of modern art, rather than a negative judgement. The statements in 'Art and Objecthood', according to Costello, 'have not derived from a theoretical position about what can and cannot count as an object of aesthetic judgment but as a description of the experience of minimalist works that is itself the elaboration of a judgment to the effect that this is not an experience of art'.[80]

In the same context, the chapter is critical of Fried's binarism between modernist 'presentness' and minimalist real time by arguing against his claim that the worst aspect of minimalism is the manifestation of unlimited durationality, and concludes by recognising the paradox that the theorist established a discourse that made it possible to theorise postmodern performance, a phenomenon that is virtually the antithesis of the hermetic modernist abstraction he sought to protect.[81]

Fried's theory has been applied by prominent theatre theorists to assess the differences between performance and theatre, despite the fact that his treatise was not originally intended to examine the aesthetic assumptions of performance. Consequently, the chapter integrates the analysis of breath related works by visual artists who work with performance in an attempt to examine the durational and 'experiential' turn in contemporary art and the disparities between the theatre and the medium of performance, in conjunction with the ways that performance merges with politics and feminism in the works of Marina Abramović and Ulay *Breathing In Breathing Out*, Janez Janša's *Something's in the Air* and The Feminist Art Workers' (FAW) *This Ain't No Heavy Breathing*.

Shortness of *Breath*

The third chapter focuses on *Breath*; on the historical and aesthetic context of its production and reception, as well as on Beckett's aspiration to find a means to transform language into a kind of erasure and to find a means to 'literature's end', since, as he argues, language must be shattered in order to reveal what was previously 'unseen'. The chapter elaborates further on visual art and theatre discourses that are specific to the mid-1960s moment and investigates key moments in the history and theory of the theatre and the visual arts so as to identify the piece's original context, explore the aesthetic implications with more depth and open up the possibility of a new framework – one that relates to both the original and the current context, since the critic should not impose, as Pattie suggests, 'a periodization on Beckett's work; rather, he or she should examine the writer's work in relation to its time – without expecting that a simple correlation between the writing and the time might emerge'.[82]

Hermeneutic perspectives of the formal principles that underlie the playlet's structure and pattern are reviewed, as well as the ways in which the writer experiments with the notion of the 'well-made' play by inverting the conventional well-made play with a remarkable precision to the pyramidical structure.[83] As Ruby Cohn argues, these acts form a symmetrical whole, since Act I is repeated in Act V (the cry) and Act II is repeated in Act IV. Symmetry, repetition and inversion establish a cyclic structure, namely an archetypal use of the cyclic form.[84]

The piece shares all the elements of the 'well made' play, including the 'rising action' of the second 'act', the pause, the climax and the third 'act', the culmination, the apex, the exhalation (advancing) and death (declining) (i.e. complete exhalation)' that represents the 'falling action', the fourth 'act' that is followed by the reiterated cry, the 'resolution', and the final silence before the curtain descends. Its formal structure shares the classic Aristotelian narrative technique of tumescence and detumescence (namely a dialectics of inflation and deflation).[85] Yet Beckett employs this classic Aristotelian form (inhalation-deflation) in its complete reduction, with no overtones, since he calls the play 'a farce in five acts' and refutes any formal and contextual interpretations of the playlet.

Breath challenges the 'well made' structure through a highly articulate process of erasure and constant disruption of the processes and the kind of terms that surround representational theatre, while it reorients the viewer's and critic's reception concerning the formation of genre, character, place, action, situation and language, turning towards processes and contexts, through which the limits of the work are yet to be defined.[86]

The exposition of the components of a medium in skeletal form and the decision to eradicate the subject are pivotal for understanding aspects of *Breath*'s intermedial structure, 'visual dramaturgy'[87] and anti-theatrical strategies. The absence of the figure prevails and is not subordinated to the text but rather is illuminated through an audio-visual (intermedial) interplay of sound (respiration), similar to an environmental installation with dispersed readymade objects (waste).[88] This chapter focuses on Beckett's art practice and critical intermediality, as well as on the different stagings of Breath, so as to show that despite Beckett's control of the stage directions, artists overlook the fundamental emptiness and the ideological allusions of the playlet's anti-theatricality.

The chapter juxtaposes theatrical and 'visual stagings' of the playlet by artists such as Damien Hirst, Keneth Tynan, Nikos Navridis, Adriano and Fernando Guimarães and by theatre directors such as Stanley E. Gontarski, Amanda Coogan and Daniela Thomas. The selected productions oscillate between staging performance and displaying art, as they research on the formation of new 'genres' that experiment both with contemporary performance and visual art practices.

The selected pieces by the Guimarães brothers and Amanda Coogan are presented both in a visual and a theatrical context, yet they do not capture the self-reflexive dialogue between the different media and *Breath*'s anti-theatrical aspects, as they fail to reinvent the playlet's minimal context (by adding dispensable elements), as well as Beckett's constant aspiration to expose the components of the medium he is using in skeletal form. The decision to present the human body[89] is in contrast to Beckett's pivotal decision to eradicate the body/ subject from the stage. Consequently, the existential and ontological importance of Beckett's decision to remove the figure of the performer by presenting the 'absence' of the human subject is disregarded.

EMPTIED FIGURE

The fourth chapter considers the ramifications of the subject/actor/figure eradication as an anti-theatrical strategy that highlights *Breath*'s intermedial structure and the playlet's experimentation with installation practices. The theatrical implications of emptiness and its effect on the spectator are seen in conjunction with Beckett's decision to eradicate the figure of the stage by removing the performer/actor/figure/theatrical subject. The intermedial relationship between non-textual frames of representation (in performance) and text oriented drama results in a redefinition of the concept of the character in contemporary performance. Character has dissolved into the flux of performance elements and playwrights abandon many elements long thought essential to drama, including plot, action and character.[90]

The gradual revision of character's representation is based on complex models of representation beyond narrative and language and Beckett's anti-theatrical project integrates strategies in order to eradicate the presence of the character. His theatre is a theatre of corporeality, however, in *Breath* the space is emptied of the presence of the body, and presence is generated despite the fact that the referent is materially absent. The human icon and body are emptied and the figure is placed beyond the visual spectrum even though respiration is a bodily product that entails presence. The presence of the miscellaneous rubbish as the primary stage prop on stage cannot fill the fundamental emptiness that is caused by the lack of the figure (subject and character). Therefore, Beckett's work unveils an (anti)theatricality through the emptying of theatre that is accomplished when theatre is recurringly emptied of theatre.[91]

The writer opens the pictorial (found objects) to actual space in the same way that the minimalists have been experimenting with these transpositions, and by removing the protagonist subject he is 'emptying' the representational qualities of theatre. The pile of miscellaneous scattered and lying rubbish becomes the protagonist in *Breath*'s setting similar to works by contemporary visual artists including Thomas Hirschhorn, Mark Dion, Abraham Cruzvillegas, Andreas Gursky, Surasi Kurolwong, Vik Muniz, Santiago Sierra and Mierle Laderman Ukeles.

THE POLITICS OF FORM

The concluding chapters intersect in their discussion of form, intermediality and anti-theatricality by providing a far-reaching overview of the topic of breath that is associated to current aesthetic approaches and concerns. This thematic approach brings together art from different historical periods within the same conceptual framework by examining potentialities of knowledge that emerge from the intersections of art and im/materiality and that orientate our notions concerning the artistic work in new intermedial directions. The selected contemporary art practices are characterised by the transformation of completed or finalised objects into open works,[92] in spatially expanded and intermedial situations and thus raise methodological questions from diverse philosophical and aesthetic perspectives.

The 'invisible' aspects of this organic function can be represented with auditory, olfactory, kinetic and tactile media, while its 'formless' qualities provide the possibility of artistic experimentation. Georges Bataille describes the 'formless' as subversive of the traditional duality of form and content, and as Krauss asserts, 'the formless has its own legacy to fulfil, its own destiny – which is partly that of liberating our thinking'.[93] The aesthetic challenge of finding a form for formlessness and of showing a form that has no form or even the negation of form has aesthetic and ideological ramifications.

The depiction of formless visual shapes (respiration) that become a metaphor for conceptual forms is always a mediated act like any form of representation, even in art practices that involve the immediacy of the body. As Amelia Jones argues, 'there is no possibility of an unmediated relationship to any kind of cultural product, including body art'.[94] Detached from established aesthetic norms the selected corporeal and intermedial art pieces by female artists such as Lygia Clark *Respire Comigo* (*Breathe With Me*, 1966), VALIE EXPORT *Breath Text: Love Poem* (1970–3), Ana Mendieta *Untitled Grass Breathing* (c. 1974), Marina Abramović with Ulay *Breathing In Breathing Out* (1978), The Feminist Art Workers (FAW) *This Ain't No Heavy Breathing* (1978), Nancy Spero *Woman Breathing* (1978), Ann Hamilton *Flour Breath Body Object Series* (1984–93) and Sophie Dupont *Marking Breath* (2011–15) investigate the materiality of respiration; hence the pieces in certain ways echo Beckett's practices and aesthetics by offering an alternative to a particular history of modernism identified with the idealisation of forms and with the tendency by revered figures within the modernist tradition to evaluate artists based on media specificity and autonomy. The intermedial methodological challenge of converging different media and of working in-between the boundaries of artistic media is manifested in these works, as well as the critical attempt to engage the perceptual and political imaginary of the beholders, (their breath, like their voice, ought to be heard).

Intermediality encapsulates the methodological challenges of converging. As a combinatory structure of syntactical elements that derive from more than one medium the term shares a common ground with theories that have been conceived to theorise the interface and in-betweeness of media like Rosalind Krauss' 'differential specificity' and Foucault's 'disguised difference'. Diverse methods and theoretical perspectives are applied in these pieces, however, overall they are characterised by an openness that challenges the ideological effects of the separation and hierarchisation of artistic media. By revising, in wide-ranging ways, the condition of the modernist art object and its historical trajectory into their art practice the artists shake up the notion of a unified and 'disembodied' visual field and attempt to 'open' the work, to juxtapose multiple media – the spatial and the temporal, the textual and the imagistic – into pieces that are intentionally disjunctive and lacking medial autonomy.

Despite the increased sense of heterogeneity in contemporary practice that disallows conceptions of medium purity and specificity the philosophical ramifications of intermediation are still useful for understanding aspects of the operations of a medium, and for the reflection of the ways formal experimentation relates to politics and entails a politics of spectating. Late twentieth and early twenty-first century developments in installation art transform the role of the audience into the key site of installation practices[95] and the development of intermedia art over the past decades culminates in a focus on the spectator's body, as a sentient and active 'agent', in a reciprocal relation with the work of art; similarly, spectatorship, in Beckett's late works, becomes a self-reflective act.

In the same ways that Beckett eradicates those elements most associated with conventional (realist) drama, and negates the material referent (body) through the continual transposition between 'negative' (eradication of subject) and 'positive' (respiration) form, the selected practices (1919–2015) by representative artists of movements like conceptual and corporeal art question dominant forms of representation by stressing the limitations of the body and by showing the obligation to emancipate the individual and the body (breath) through radical notions of embodiment. As Hélène Cixous argues, 'censor the body and you censor breath and speech at the same time. Write yourself. Your body must be heard'[96]

The 'performance of breath' in a visual art context demands the active perceptual and biological engagement of the viewer that also generates an explicit awareness of this activity. Maaike Bleeker introduces the term 'seer'[97] for 'spectator' in order to denote the activity of the former and the passivity of the latter. Thus, the 'seers' are not reduced to a state of unquestioning awareness or a wholly passive relation to the object as a detached subject. Interaction, engagement and response are required for the aesthetic experience of intermedial art.

This emancipatory process for both the artist and the spectator is revealing since it provokes an open sensorial engagement with the work of art and a different approach towards the live and the mediated body. The human body is either physically present in these works, such as in Vito Acconci *Breath In (To) / Out (Of)* (1971), Chris Burden *Velvet Water* (1974), Giuseppe Penone

To Breathe The Shadow, John Latham *The Big Breather Project*, or technically represented/mediated in video, film, television and the digital such as in
Steve McQueen's *Cold Breath* (1999). Accordingly, the selected artists employ
diverse representational attitudes towards the live body, the human figure,
corporeal presence, subjectivity/subjecthood and agency, in the process of
'writing of the body itself',[98] and as in Beckett's late plays, the naturalistic body
is replaced by the intermedial body that oscillates in-between realities, between
the live and the mediated, and in-between liveness and technology.

The intermedial exchanges manage to reconcile these different binaries
by integrating a variety of technical media into a large medial framework.
Intermedial research embraces a contemplative act between the beholder and
the art object as an extension of the physical senses, counter to a modernist
focus on visual form and to a notion of the eye as a purely abstract organ, cut
off from the bodily senses to which it is connected. By challenging the viewer's
expectations of the experience of coherent, bounded and unified form that can
be organised as distinct media or in terms of a stylistic scheme, the artworks
explore the act of the viewer on the art object.

INTEGRATED LIVENESS

The sixth chapter focuses on the use of technology and analyses versions of
intermediality for a broader understanding of the term and its implications for
formal experimentation. The aim is to contextualise the notion of intermediality and address the enduring impact of Beckett's technological innovations
on contemporary art practice, as well as his experimentation with media and
technology in relation to the complex contemporary media culture.

The writer explores cardinal aspects of technology so as to challenge the limitations of the artistic medium, and Ruby Cohn is precise when she characterises Beckett's aesthetics as theatre electronics. The scenic directions, according
to Cohn, 'stipulate that the two recorded cries be identical and that the light
and amplified breath be strictly synchronized. The elemental symmetries of life
on earth rely upon sophisticated theatre electronics'.[99] *Breath*'s innovative use
of medium, technology and its apparently simple staging is one of the reasons
that artists continue to produce this piece in new media[100] and formats.[101]

The revival of interest in respiration in the new millennium is suggestive and
is partly the outcome of the re-emergence of the rhetoric of the human body
and of presence upon the field of theory. The actor's corporeal presence fades
and vanishes on the electronic platform in a way that foregrounds the illusion of substance and presence.[102] Notions of presence hinge on the relationship between the live and the mediated, while notions of immediacy and the
relationship between live, mediated and simulated performance may deepen
an understanding of the performance of presence and of the performance of
breath both in a visual and theatrical context. The advent of new media and

the increasing integration of contemporary performance and media generate ground-breaking engagements, practices and understandings of presence in performance.[103]

Live performance depends on the presence of live bodies, yet contemporary performance stages two kinds of bodies, the 'physical/material' and the mediatised. In live performance, the human body is physically present or is represented by technical means including video, film, television and the digital. Peggy Phelan advances a basic definition of performance as 'representation without reproduction', arguing that performance 'becomes itself through disappearance'. As she argues, in a culture 'obsessed by materiality and its own preservation through recorded images of itself, performance fails to fully coincide with itself, it is less to do with preservation and materiality than emptiness and disappearance'.[104]

Contemporary performance theorists debate[105] the ways the mediatised replaces the live and analyse the interrelations between the live and the mediatised. The integrity of the live is reinforced in contrast to the 'co-opted' nature of the mediatised, yet theorists also see the live as something that can incorporate the mediatised, both technologically and epistemologically.

Beckett's *Breath* is mediatised (recorded respiration, lack of the live performer) and at the same time integrates liveness through the sound of breath; the body is absent, yet the respiratory system is ubiquitous. The essence of existence and experience lies in the respiratory system, nonetheless, in Beckett's late theatre the absence of the human body discloses a subjectivity that is beyond embodiment by staging a disembodied presence.

The absence of the performer generates the intensity of a 'disappearing presence', and as Herbert Blau argues, 'its very corporeality being the basis of its most powerful illusion, that something is substantially there, the thing itself, even as it vanishes'.[106] Beckett is constantly interrogating the dialectics of presence (liveness) and absence; and in the case of *Breath* the presence of miscellaneous rubbish is set against the absence of the human figure. The life giving force of respiration co-exists with the perplexing 'terror' caused by the decay of humankind as it is 'signified' by the presence of waste.

The notion of terror is in 'all cases whatsoever, either more openly or latently the ruling principle of the sublime',[107] as Edward Burke puts it, and both notions (terror and the sublime) are connected with the magnitude of nature to overwhelm humans. For Gene Ray, "terror" and the sublime go together and are even inseparable, and for Burke, there can be no sublime without terror, and wherever there is terror, there is also, at least potentially, the feeling of the sublime.

ASSERTING NEGATION, NEGATING ASSERTION

The first respiration symbolises birth and the beginning of life. As a result the aesthetic response to respiration approaches notions of 'sublimity', given that it is the ultimate organic phenomenon; a life giving quality that strikes with its perplexity. In *Breath*, the sublime expression of life (respiration) is shadowed by an exhalation on a stage filled with rubbish. 'Positive' and 'negative' representation[108] are unfolding in the dialectic of birth (inhalation) and death (exhalation), since detritus alludes to 'negative representation'.[109]

Beckett's representational approach and the 'aesthetics of failure', as analysed in the *Three Dialogues*, connote the failure to represent: 'to fail means to fail to represent'.[110] Yet the author attempts to negotiate this paradoxical state of artistic impotence and 'non-representationality', since he argues 'to be an artist is to fail, as no other dares fail, failure is his world'.[111] For Beckett it is the fissures, the gaps and breaks in the circuit that constitute the 'object' of the theatre and this idiosyncratic approach to 'failure' fosters the notion that performance is premised on the failure to achieve the fullness of presence. Beckett's art, as Terry Eagleton argues, maintains a compact with failure, 'in the teeth of Nazi triumphalism, undoing its lethal absolutism with the weapons of ambiguity and indeterminacy. His favourite word, he commented, was "perhaps"'.[112]

Beckett's interest in indeterminacy and in ignorance rather than knowledge is manifested in the assembled elements of *Breath*'s set design. The scattered rubbish is not sculpted but is selected and assembled as traces of a story, and of the history that the viewer is encouraged to incorporate when interpreting the playlet.

Through the 'negative representation' and criticism of any philosophical certainty, the writer points beyond the scope of representation to a view of history and humanity that is yet to be uncovered, while he 'stages' an environment of a scattered reality that draws attention to the failings and omissions of modern notions of the political, the social and the personal itself. What we see in Beckett's work is not some timeless condition humaine, as Eagleton argues, but 'war-torn twentieth-century Europe. It is, as Adorno recognized, an art after Auschwitz; one which keeps faith in its austere minimalism and unremitting bleakness with silence, terror and non-being. His writing is as thin as it is compatible with being barely perceptible'.[113] *Breath* presents a stagnant landscape[114] filled with uncertainty, disorientation, exile and with the residues of an environmental catastrophe.

The choice to fill the stage with the pile of miscellaneous, scattered and lying rubbish is not just an allegorical statement about the human condition as it is often stated, it is also an ideological[115] and anti-theatrical manifesto that encapsulates a post-war reality. Nevertheless, Beckett manages to provoke a critical historical reflexivity by creating a minimal structure for the playlet, a dialectics of presence and absence (inhalation-exhalation) that attempts to depict the singularity and incomprehensibility of the past, while it remains fragmented and 'open' to the pluralism of modes of understanding, by adapting the strategies that produce hermeneutic undecidability and reflexivity in a critical and historically specific way. Therefore, Beckett's sensibility between the desire to respond to the ethical problems entailed by the representation of historical facts, as the imperative to remember, and his pluralistic approach to an art that evades representation becomes manifest in *Breath*.

Beckett's concerns are immanently historical and ideological and his anti-theatrical approach is predominantly revealed in the social implications of his formalist quests even though the social content of the later work has been repeatedly overlooked. *Breath* in particular is produced by an abstract and distinctive logic of dynamic minimalism that has strong social dimensions.[116] The writer's artistic strategy critically expresses the historical experience but is also detached from established theatrical and aesthetic norms, manifesting his ideological commitment to the sufferings of the post-war humanity that remain diachronic.

Principally, the writer's desire to 'exhaust' the art object (in *Breath*) points to a desire to expose the exhausted project of modernity[117] and Beckett looks into emptiness and absence so as to problematise the modernist aims and concerns by taking the artwork to new levels of complexity and to new meanings beyond the objectification of the formal constituents of a given medium. The writer employs ontological emptiness (absence of figure) to highlight the tension between abstraction and expression, as well as the dilemma of artistic expression and the impossibility of expression. As he comments about his friend and revered artist, 'Van Velde paints because he is obliged to paint. Cannot paint, since he is obliged to paint. Cannot write, since he is obliged to write. Because there is nothing to paint and nothing to paint with.'[118] Thus, Beckett's foremost political and formal instrument to negotiate this paradoxical state of artistic impotence is humour and openness, while his praise of impotence and failure, as well as his syntax of weakness is, as Simon Critchley argues, a comic syntax 'or the syntax of Beckett's dark humour, his humour noir'.[119]

The choice to call *Breath* 'a farce in five acts' and to refute any formal and contextual interpretations of the playlet stresses this aporetic openness and the idiosyncratic humour, that is, as Critchley argues, at the level of idiom, 'in the fine grain of detail [. . .] and it's that, that philosophy misses'.[120] Humour, complexity and ambiguity are also fundamental for Beckett's open-ended discursive criticism in the *Three Dialogues*, since he expounds an aesthetic discourse that not only focuses on failure but defies any philosophical and art historical sense of rationality. It is this unconventional approach that has defined Beckett's contribution and impact on contemporary art; a ground-breaking aesthetic that few artists and art movements, including minimalism, have managed to challenge.

The paradoxical state of artistic impotence and the inevitability of the artist's 'failure' become an expressive recourse for the writer's quest for representational 'openness'[121] and this is 'already a political manifestation, a statement of the active role and the recipients' freedom, which it theorises'.[122] *Breath*'s 'openness' is consequently paradigmatic of Beckett's ideological stance and work that continues to oppose and resist recuperation pointing to a critique of the conditions of art making, display, marketing and interpretation, in contrast to minimalist art that became dependent on these processes.

NOTES

1. Old Irish joke.
2. Samuel Beckett's comments to actress Billie Whitelaw, during the rehearsals of *Footfalls*, quoted in an interview Whitelaw gave to Jonathan Kalb. Kalb, Jonathan. *Beckett in Performance*. Cambridge: Cambridge University Press, 1989: 235.
3. Cohen, T., J. H. Miller, B. Cohen. 'A Materiality without Matter?'. In *Material Events: Paul de Man and the Afterlife of Theory*. Minneapolis and London: University of Minnesota Press, 2001: xvi. Quoted in Lerm Hayes, Christa-Maria (2007). 'Re-inventing the Literary Exhibition: Exhibiting (Dialogical and Subversive) Art on (James Joyce's) Literature', *Working Papers on Design* 2: 6. inhttp://www.herts.ac.uk/artdes1/research/papers/wpdesign/wpdvol2/vol2.html> [accessed 1-11-2016].
4. The playlet was recited by Beckett in the summer of 1966 according to Ruby Cohn, and staged for the first time in Kenneth Tynan's revue *Oh! Calcutta!* in 1969.
5. In Beckett, Samuel. *Breath and the Complete Dramatic Works*. London: Faber and Faber, 1984: 211. Ruby Cohn remarks that, 'although a fair copy of *Breath* has been widely reproduced, no holograph is extant. In summer 1966 Beckett recited it to me in response to my question about what he had written and had sent to Kenneth Tynan for his revue of *Oh! Calcutta*. The staging became the most notorious deviation of Beckett's text first published as the prologue of *Oh! Calcutta* New York: Grove, 1969. It was printed correctly in the second impression (1970) and then by Calder in Gambit 1970. It is found in CDW and in Beckett's French in Comedie et Actes Divers 1972.' In Cohn, Ruby. *A Beckett Canon*. Ann Arbor: University of Michigan Press, 2001: 298.
6. See Goudouna, Sozita. PhD thesis, 'Mediated Breath: Beckett's Intermedial Breath, Fried's Theatricality and the Visual Arts', submitted to Royal Holloway University of London in partial fulfilment of the requirements for the degree of Doctor of Philosophy supervised by Professor David Bradby and Dr Sophie Nield, examined by internal committee member Professor Jen Harvie and external committee member Christa-Maria Lerm Hayes.
7. David Cunningham discusses the dynamics of Beckett's lateness and asceticism in relation to colour, modernism and abstraction, as well as the political terms related to modernism. As he argues, 'lateness itself. This is how the late Edward Said has described Adorno's distinct 'modernist' sensibility – exemplified by the readings of what is, for Adorno, the very beginnings of a musical modernism: Beethoven's "late style" a sensibility which will have a key role to play in what

follows. But contra Said this is not in fact simply a question of "style", but, more crucially, of the artwork's time; a time that is inextricably linked to the temporality of modernism itself as the critical "practice of modernity [. . .] the means by which modernity and its symbolic modes are tested and retested"'. See David Cunningham. 'Asceticism against Colour, or Modernism, Abstraction and the Lateness of Beckett', *New Formations*, 55 (Spring 2005): 104–19.

8. The book considers *Breath* as a minimalist piece, not only owing to its size that is uncommon for the theatre, but primarily owing to the lack of character, dialogue, drama, action and actors.

9. The provocation was given by Donald Judd and principally Robert Morris who argues that the concerns of sculpture are not only distinct from painting but also hostile.

10. Originally published in *Artforum*, 5 (June 1967): 12–13. Republished on several occasions, most importantly in Battcock, Gregory (ed.). *Minimal Art: A Critical Anthology*. New York, 1968: 116–47.

11. See Auslander, Philip. 'Presence and Theatricality in the Discourse of Performance and the Visual Arts'. *From Acting to Performance: Essays in Modernism and Postmodernism*, London and New York: Routledge, 1997: 49–57.

12. The book refers to this essay as 'Three Dialogues', although the complete title as it appears in the original publication is *'Three Dialogues: Tal Coat, Masson, Bram van Velde'*. 'Three Dialogues with Georges Duthuit', is published in the second *Transition*, edited by the art critic Georges Duthuit (between 1948 and 1950). The original *Transition* was published in Paris between 1927 and 1938 by Eugene Jolas, the poet, critic and newspaper columnist.

13. Frank Stella's *Black Paintings*, which were shown as early as 1959 in the Museum of Modern Art's 'Sixteen Americans', inaugurate the period of minimalist practice, while Robert Morris' process-orientated work and Michael Heizer's earthworks of the late 1960s signal its demise. Other prominent minimalist artists include Carl Andre and Dan Falvin.

14. Minimalist art, according to Strickland, is prone to

> stasis (as expressed in musical drones and silence, immobile or virtually immobile dance, endless freeze-frame in the film, event-free narrative and expressionless lyrics, featureless sculpture, monochromatic canvases) and resistant to development. Gridded or otherwise diagrammatic paintings and sculptures repeated modules and held harmonies in music, simple and reiterated movements in the dance and film, the aborted or circular dialogues of the drama and fiction. It tends towards non-allusiveness and decontextualization from tradition, impersonality in tone and flattening of perspective through emphasis on surfaces, neutralization of depth cues in painting or of the space/substance, image/reflection dichotomies in light environments, the restriction of dynamic and harmonic movement in the music, the human "still lifes" of the films, and the analogously univocal description of persons and objects in the painting and fiction.

> In Strickland, Edward. *Minimalism: Origins*. Bloomington and Indianapolis: Indiana University Press, 1993: 7.

15. Lippard, Lucy R. *Six Years: The Dematerialization of the Art Object from 1966 to 1972*. Berkeley: University of California Press, 1997: 21.

16. This immediacy is different from Walter Benjamin's concept of immediacy through mediation. See Walter Benjamin and Hal Foster's works in general.

17. Higgins, Dick. 'Intermedia' was published by Something Else Press in 1965 and reprinted in *Horizons: The Poetics and Theory of the Intermedia* (Carbondale and

Edwardsville: Southern Illinois University Press, 1983). The term 'intermedium' is adapted from Samuel Taylor Coleridge, 'Lecture No. 3, On Edmund Spencer', reprinted in Coleridge's *Miscellaneous Criticism*, ed. Thomas Middleton Rayson (London: Constable and Co., 1936), Lecture III: 21 and 31 ff.

18. Middeke, Martin. 'Minimal Art: On the Intermedial Aesthetic Context of Samuel Beckett's Late Theatre and Drama', *Anglia*, 123.3 (2005): 359–80.

19. *Film*'s opening external shots took place in Lower Manhattan, close to Brooklyn Bridge, and the rest was filmed in Greenwich Village.

20. The contributors to this issue: Roland Barthes, Samuel Beckett, Mel Bochner, William S. Burroughs, Michel Butor, John Cage, Merce Cunningham, Marcel Duchamp, Morton Feldman, Naum Gabo, Dan Graham, Alain Robbe-Grillet, Richard Huelsenbeck, George Kublar, Sol LeWitt, Douglas MacAgy, Robert Morris, László Moholy-Nagy, Max Neuhaus, Brian O'Doherty, Noton Revsner, Robert Rauschenberg, Hans Richter, Tony Smith, Susan Sontag, Stan VenDerBeek. *Text for Nothing #8* was read by Jack MacGowen. Barthes first published his influential and important essay 'The Death of the Author' in this issue.

21. New York: Roaring Fork Press and Aspen Communications, Inc., 1965–71. Phyllis Johnson originally conceived of *Aspen* as a collection of materials that reflected the rich cultural and recreational experience available in the city of Aspen. Later, it became something resembling an art collection in a box, filled with artistic collaborations and experimentations with contributions from artists and musicians such as Eleanor Antin, Dan Graham, John Cage, Carolee Schneemann, Philip Glass and Andy Warhol. The 'Minimalism' issue was edited and designed by Brian O'Doherty, art direction was by David Dalton and Lynn Letterman. The contents list as described by the editor indicated all the objects included in this issue. In 'Succession: Contemporary Artists' Periodicals', Case 7, Ryerson and Burnham Libraries, 8 May–16 July 2012. See http://www.artic.edu/aic/collections/exhibitions/Ryerson/resource/2454 [accessed 1/11/16].

22. See Rosalind E. Krauss, Christa-Maria Lerm Hayes, Coosje van Bruggen, Rolf Glasmeier, Ingrid Schaffner and Derval Tubridy.

23. Fried, Michael. *Art and Objecthood Essays and Reviews*. Chicago and London: The University of Chicago Press, 1998: 157.

24. Ibid.

25. Fried's texts in chronological order: 'Shape as Form: Frank Stella's Irregular Polygons' (1966), 'Morris Louis' (1966–7), 'Jules Olitski' (1966–7), 'Art and Objecthood' (1967), 'New York by Anthony Caro' (1967), 'Ronald Davis: Surface and Illusion' (1967), 'Two Sculptures by Anthony Caro' (1968), 'Recent Work by Kenneth Noland' (1969), 'Caro's Abstractness' (1970), 'Problems of Polychromy: New Sculptures by Michael Bolus' (1971), 'Larry Poons's New Paintings' (1972), 'Anthony Caro's Table Sculptures 1966–77' (1977).

26. Fried, Michael. 'Art and Objecthood', in *Minimal Art: A Critical Anthology*. New York: E. P. Dutton, 1968: 139–41.

27. Fried, M., 'Art and Objecthood', *Art in Theory* (1967): 826. Also see Kiff Bamford, and Lyotard and the 'figural' in *Performance, Art and Writing*. London: Continuum/Bloomsbury, 2012: 40.

28. Jackson, Shannon. 'Performativity and its Addressee'. In Elizabeth Carpenter (ed.), *On Performativity*, vol. 1 of Living Collections Catalogue. Minneapolis: Walker Art Center, 2014, para 2:2. http://www.walkerart.org/collections/publications/performativity/performativity-and-its-addressee/

29. Ibid.

30. See McMullan, Anna. *Theatre on Trial: Samuel Beckett's Later Drama*. London and New York: Routledge, 1993: 117.

31. Chapple, Frieda and Kattenbelt, Chiel. 'Key Issues in Intermediality in Theatre and Performance'. In Frieda Chapple and Chiel Kattenbelt (eds), *Intermediality in Theatre and Performance*. Amsterdam and New York: Rodopi, 2006: 12.
32. Pavis, Patrice. *Analyzing Performance. Theatre, Dance, and Film*. Ann Arbor: The University of Michigan Press, 2003: 49.
33. Bal, Mieke and Sherry Marx-Macdonald (eds). *Travelling Concepts in the Humanities: A Rough Guide*. Toronto: University of Toronto Press, 2002: 17.
34. See Costello, Diarmuid. 'Greenberg's Kant and the Fate of Aesthetics in Contemporary Art Theory', *The Journal of Aesthetics and Art Criticism* 65.2 (2007): 217–28.
35. Jackson also argues that visual art has had a tougher time reconciling anti-artifice discourse with its own enmeshment in a history of pictoriality, so its anti-theatrical discourse often invokes different – though still varied – terms. Jackson, Shannon. 'Theatre . . . Again', *Art Lies: Contemporary Art Quarterly*, 60, (Winter 2008). http://www.artlies.org/article.php?id=1682&issue=60&s=1 [accessed 1/11/2016].
36. Ibid.
37. See Tronstad, Ragnhild. 'Could the World become a Stage? Theatricality and Metaphorical Structures'. *SubStance*, 31.2/3, special issue 98/99: Theatricality (2002): 216.
38. Davis, Tracy and Postlewait, Thomas (eds). *Theatricality*. Cambridge: Cambridge University Press, 2004: 3.
39. McLuhan, M., Fiore, Q., and Agel, J. *The Medium is the Message*. New York, Bantam Books, 1967: 149. And in Heuvel, Michael Vanden, *Performing Drama/ Dramatizing Performance: Alternative Theater and the Dramatic Text*. Ann Arbor: University of Michigan Press, 1991: 20.
40. McMullan, Anna. *Theatre on Trial: Samuel Beckett's Later Drama*. New York: Routledge, 1993: 9.
41. Brater, Enoch. *Beyond Minimalism: Beckett's Late Style in the Theater*. Oxford: Oxford University Press, 1987: 1.
42. Greenberg, Clement. 'Modern and Postmodern'. In Robert C. Morgan (ed.), *Clement Greenberg: Late Writings*. Minneapolis: University of Minnesota Press, 2003: 25; and Greenberg, Clement. 'Intermedia'. In *Clement Greenberg: Late Writings*. Minneapolis: University of Minnesota Press, 2003: 93–8.
43. Chapple, Frieda and Kattenbelt, Chiel (eds). *Intermediality in Theatre*: 12.
44. See Cohn, Ruby. *A Beckett Canon*: 298.
45. Jean-François Lyotard curated 'Les Immatériaux' at the Centre Pompidou in 1985; Jacques Derrida curated the exhibition 'Memoirs of the Blind' at the Louvre museum in 1990–1; Bruno Latour curated 'Making Things Public: Atmospheres of Democracy' at the ZKM Centre at Karlsruhe in 2005; and Georges Didi-Huberman curated 'Nouvelles Histoires de Fantômes' at the Palais de Tokyo in 2014.
46. The participatory shift and practice in the arts has been often appropriated by post-conceptual, socially and politically engaged art, or by art activism.
47. See Nicholas Bouriaud on 'Relational Aesthetics'. Bouriaud has been an effective advocate for the contemporary tendency to emphasise process, performativity, openness, social contexts, transitivity and the production of dialogue over the closure of traditional modernist objecthood, visuality and hyper-individualism. However, his theories have been questioned in terms of the implicit ideological implications. His positioning of relational art as the heir to the twentieth-century avant-gardes has been criticised. As he argues, 'whatever the fundamentalists clinging to yesterday's good taste may say and think, present-day art is roundly

taking on and taking up the legacy of the twentieth-century avant-gardes, while at the same time challenging their dogmatism and their teleological doctrines'. In Bouriaud, Nicholas. *Relational Aesthetics*. Paris: Les Presses du Réel, 1998: 45. However, the Radical Culture Research Collective mentions in its critique of relational art that 'the main limitation of relational art – and one that negates any claim it makes to the legacy of the avant-gardes is that relational art refuses the radical project of the avant-garde legacy'. As they argue,

> while we would defend relational art from its conservative and reactionary critics, we would also insist that it not come to stand in for the radical project it falls short of – and indeed refuses. Undoubtedly, the avant-garde tradition continues to be transformed by its own process of self-critique. But it does not give up the radical, macro-historical aim of a real world beyond capitalist relations. And it doesn't settle for the experience of gallery simulations.

Radical Culture Research Collective (RCRC). *A Very Short Critique of Relational Aesthetics*, published on transform.eipcp.net. December 2011 [accessed 1/11/2016].

48. See Harrison, Charles and Wood, Paul (eds). *Art in Theory 1900–1990: An Anthology of Changing Ideas*. Oxford and Cambridge: Blackwell, 1992.
49. Greenberg, Clement. 'After Abstract Expressionism'. In John O'Brian (ed.), *Clement Greenberg: The Collected Essays and Criticism*. Chicago: University of Chicago Press, 1986–93, vol. 4: 121–34.
50. Greenberg, Clement. 'Modernist Painting'. In ibid.: 85–93.
51. See Jones, Caroline. *Eyesight Alone: Clement Greenberg's Modernism and the Bureaucratization of the Senses*. Chicago: University of Chicago Press, 2008.
52. Greenberg, Clement. 'Recentness of Sculpture'. Exhibition catalogue, *American Sculpture of the Sixties*. Los Angeles: Los Angeles County Museum of Art Publications, 1967. Reprinted in Battcock, Gregory (ed.). *Minimal Art*: 180.
53. Ibid.: 183 and 184.
54. Didi-Huberman, Georges. *Confronting Images: Questioning the Ends of a Certain History of Art*. University Park: Pennsylvania State University Press, 2005: 3.
55. See Francis, Frascina. *Art, Politics and Dissent: Aspects of the Art Left in Sixties America*. Manchester and New York: Manchester University Press, 1999.
56. The book considers *Breath* as a minimalist piece owing to its size, which is uncommon for the theatre, however, with regards to stage design aesthetics the playlet also shares common elements to conceptual art practices. The conceptual aspect of the piece is emphasized by the presence of the heap of horizontal miscellaneous rubbish and by the fact that absolute form and structure is given to a formless notion like respiration.
57. The seminal theory expressed the anti-theatrical aesthetic prevalent within modernism and marked one of the most vexed points of intersection of critical discourses in the visual arts and the theatre. See Philip Auslander. 'Presence and Theatricality in the Discourse of Performance and the Visual Arts'. In *From Acting to Performance: Essays in Modernism and Postmodernism*. London and New York: Routledge, 1997: 49–57.
58. See Cunningham, David, 'Asceticism against Colour, or, Modernism, Abstraction and the Lateness of Beckett', *New Formations*, 55 (Spring 2005): 104–19; Hauck, Gerhard. *Reductionism in Drama and the Theatre: The Case of Samuel Beckett*. Potomac, MD: Scripta Humanistica, 1992.
59. Hauck, Gerhard. *Reductionism in Drama*: 77.
60. In his Laocoön, Lessing defines separate mediums of art through their differing

temporalities: painting and sculpture are 'spatial and simultaneous' while prose, poetry and music are 'temporal and successive'.

61. The idea of tableau possibly first came to light in Yves-Alain Bois' book *Painting as Model*; also in Clement Greenberg's idea of painterly specificity as centred around qualities of flatness and optical events. For Hubert Damisch's complex sense of thickness addressing the minimalist paradigm and Jean François Chevrier's formulation of tableau in relation to photography see http://tableau-project.blogspot.com [accessed 1/11/2016].

62. For an analysis of the 'tableau' see Gilbert-Rolfe, Jeremy and Melville, Stephen W. *Seams: Art as a Philosophical Context*. London: Taylor and Francis, 1996: 115.

63. See Finch, Mick. *Theatre/Spectacle – Absorption / Lived Time. Painting and Time*. Conference paper, Hull School of Art and Design, 17 and 18 April 1998. See http://www.mickfinch.com/texts/theatre.html [accessed 1/11/2016].

64. Fried, Michael. *Absorption and Theatricality: Painter and Beholder in the Age of Diderot*. Chicago: University of Chicago, 1988: 103.

65. Ibid.

66. See Cope, Richard. *Re-reading Samuel Beckett's Three Dialogues with George Duthuit within Context of the Continuum it Nourished*, PhD thesis. London: South Bank University, 2006.

67. Kenner, Hugh. *A Reader's Guide to Samuel Beckett*. New York: Farrar, 1973.

68. James Knowlson and Anthony Cronin both noted that while living in London Beckett was a regular visitor to the major London art galleries: Knowlson, James. *Damned to Fame: The Life of Samuel Beckett*. New York: Grove Press, 1996. Beckett could spend as much as an hour in front of a single painting, looking at it with intense concentration. Thomas MacGreevy introduced James Joyce to Beckett and other prominent writers and painters of the day. The two men became life-long friends and wrote to each other regularly. Beckett met MacGreevy in Paris in 1928 and MacGreevy later became director of the National Gallery of Ireland (1950–63).

69. Beckett, Samuel. *Proust and Three Dialogues with Georges Duthuit*, Calder and Boyars, 1965: 103.

70. Ibid.: 112.

71. Ibid.

72. Ibid.: 123.

73. According to Ulrika Maude, Knowlson

> a scholar of every letter, notebook and diary that has been recovered, charts Beckett's interest in such paintings as Caravaggio's *The Beheading of St John the Baptist*. Beckett's admiration of 'the old masters' is well known. Beckett saw the canvas in 1971, in the capital of Malta, Valletta, while on holiday there with his wife Suzanne. Shortly afterwards, he began to work on *Not I*. The figure of the auditor, as Beckett wrote to Knowlson, was inspired by Caravaggio's painting. It is, however, unfortunate that the reproductions of artworks in the book are in black and white. Colour appears to have been especially significant in the case of works such as Caspar David Friedrich's *Two Men Observing the Moon* that in part inspired Beckett to write *Waiting for Godot*. Knowlson stresses in particular the shades of browns and greys in the painting, and the reader is left to guess what they may have looked like in a colour plate.

In Maude, Ulrika. 'Beckett and Aesthetics' and 'Images of Beckett' (review), *Modernism/Modernity*, 11.4 (November 2004): 845–8.

74. Beckett has influenced the works of certain of the leading artists in several modernist movements, and many canonical post-war artists such as Jasper Johns, Bruce Nauman, Steve McQueen and Doris Salcedo have indicated their indebtedness to Beckett's work and legacy. Also, composers like Philip Glass, Morton Feldman, Mark-Anthony Turnage, filmmakers like Atom Egoyan, and dancers like Maguy Marin, Martin Arnold, Dorothy Cross, Stan Douglas, Gary Hill, Bruce Nauman, Gregor Schneider, Ann-Sofi Sidén, Zin Taylor, Allison Hrabluik, Avigdor Arikha, Geneviève Asse, Georg Baselitz, Hans Jørgen Brøndum, Claus Carstensen, Jean Deyrolle, Hans Martin Erhardt, Max Ernst, Sorel Etrog, Manfred Garstka, Winfred Gaul, Edward Gorey, Stanley William Hayter, Dellas Henke, Jasper Johns, Charles Klabunde, Leif Lage, Bun-Ching Lam, Louis Le Brocquy, Christian Lemmerz, Joseph Mugnaini, Karlheinz Richard Müller, Roswitha Quadflieg, Robert Ryman, Sergent-Fulbert, Bram Van Velde. Henry Hayden, William Stanley Hayter, Werner Spies, Louis le Brocquy, Sorel Etrog, Charles Klabunde, Dellas Henke and many others. See Lois Mitchell. *Word and Image: Samuel Beckett and the Visual Text/ Mot Et Image: Samuel Beckett Et Le Texte Visuel.* Atlanta: Emory University Press, 1999. Adding to this, visual artists who experiment with interdisciplinary practice have also acknowledged their indebtedness to Beckett. These include Gerard Byrne, Duncan Campbell, Janet Cardiff, Paul Chan, James Coleman, Atom Egoyan, Valie Export, Douglas Gordon, Dan Graham, Rodney Graham, Eva Hesse, Nathaneal Mellors, Juan Munoz, Tony Oursler, Richard Serra and Ugo Rondinone (Stan Douglas and Robert Enright; Dan Graham and Ludger Gerdes; Lucy Lippard and Robert Smithson; Sol LeWitt; Robert Morris; Bruce Nauman. See Carla Taban. *Samuel Beckett and/in Contemporary Art since the 1960s.* See https://carlataban.files. wordpress.com/2013/11/research1.pdf [accessed 1/11/2016].
75. Ibid.
76. See Oppenheim, Lois. *The Painted Word.*
77. Fried writes from a 1998 perspective; the book reprints the art criticism, though by no means all of it, that Fried wrote between the autumn of 1961 and 1977. See Michael Fried. 'An Introduction to my Art Criticism'. In *Art and Objecthood Essays and Reviews.* Chicago and London: University of Chicago Press, 1998: 1–74.
78. Ibid.
79. See Costello, Diarmuid. 'On the Very Idea of a Specific Medium: Michael Fried and Stanley Cavell on Painting and Photography as Arts', *Critical Inquiry*, 34 (Winter 2008): 16.
80. Ibid.
81. See Auslander, Philip. 'Presence and Theatricality'.
82. Pattie, David. *The Complete Critical Guide to Samuel Beckett.* London: Routledge, 2004: 246.
83. According to Hutchings, the formal aspects of *Breath* are based on the dramatic technique postulated by Gustav Freytag in *Die Technik des Dramas* in 1863. Hutchings argues that the initial pause and the first cry, representing birth, constitute the introduction and 'inciting moment' of life in general and of this play in particular; secondly, the inhalation, a symbol of growth and development. See William Hutchings. 'Abated Drama: Samuel Beckett's Unabated Breath', *ARIEL: A Review of International English Literature*, 17.1 (1986): 88.
84. See Ruby Cohn. *Just Play Beckett's Theatre.* Princeton: Princeton University Press, 1980: 4.
85. See Hutchings, William. 'Abated Drama'.
86. See Kalb, Jonathan. *Beckett in Performance.*

87. The concept of 'visual dramaturgy' is analysed in Lehmann, Hans-Thies. *Postdramatic Theatre*. London and New York: Routledge, 2006: 93.

88. Gontarski argues that the rubbish is seen as a metaphor for the human body, which is finite and disposable, a similar approach to Damien Hirst who sees medical detritus as a reflection of the human organism.

89. According to Gontarski, Adriano and Fernando Guimarães' 'staging' of *Breath* foregrounds the regenerative potential of the embryo. Corollary productions/ versions of *Breath*, like *Breathᴐ* feature an actor (or actors), as Gontarski describes:

    > in one version, actors immerse their heads in buckets of water at the bell's command. In another, a single fully clothed actor is submerged in a massive fish tank, the duration of his submersion regulated by the bell. In a third image, submerged actors, again fully clothed, are grotesquely contorted in a bathtub and viewed from above. In each case, the actor's breathing appears subject to or regulated by an arbitrary, external force, in this case a bell or buzzer.

    See Gontarski, Stanley E. 'Redirecting Beckett'. In Daniela Guardamagna and Rosanna M. Sebellin (eds), *The Tragic Comedy of Samuel Beckett, Beckett in Rome*. Rome: Università degli Studi di Roma. 'Tor Vergata' o Editori Laterza, 2009: 327.

90. See Gruber, William. *Missing Persons: Character and Characterization in Modern Drama*. Athens: University of Georgia Press, 1994: 10.

91. See Sarrazac, Jean-Pierre. 'The Invention of Theatricality: Rereading Bernard Dort and Roland Barthes', *SubStance*, 98/99, 31.2 and 31.3 (2002): 57–72.

92. See Eco, Umberto. *The Open Work*. Cambridge, MA: Harvard University Press, 1989.

93. See Bois, Yves-Alain and Krauss, Rosalind E. *Formless. A User's Guide*. Cambridge, MA: MIT Press, 1997.

94. See Jones, Amelia. 'Presence in Absentia: Experiencing Performance as Documentation', *Art Journal*, 56.4, (*Performance Art: (Some) Theory and (Selected) Practice at the End of This Century*) College Art Association (Winter 1997): 11–18.

95. See Oliveira, Nicolas de, Oxley, Nicola and Petry, Michael. *Installation Art*. London: Thames and Hudson, 1994. New edition, *Installation Art in the New Millennium: The Empire of the Senses*. London: Thames and Hudson, 2003.

96. Cixous, Hélène. 'The Laugh of the Medusa', *Signs*, 1.4 (Summer 1976): 880.

97. Bleeker, Maaike. *Visuality in the Theatre: The Locus of Looking*. London: Palgrave Macmillan, 2008.

98. See Derrida, Jacques and Chabert, Pierre. 'The Body in Beckett's Theatre'.

99. Cohn, Ruby. *A Beckett Canon*. Ann Arbor: University of Michigan Press, 2001: 298.

100. Damien Hirst directed *Breath* using the voice of comedian Keith Allen in the *Beckett On Film Project* (2002). The project, which was funded by the Irish Film Institute, the Irish broadcasting network RTE and Britain's Channel 4, focuses on the whole spectrum of Beckett's stage works that were filmed by a wide range of artists such as director Harold Pinter and actors Alan Stanford and Barry McGovern and film directors such as Anthony Minghella and Neil Jordan.

101. Six contemporary curatorial projects present innovative approaches to Beckett and deal with three forms of cultural representation: theatrical writing, visual art and the art exhibition, including *Objet Beckett* at Centre Pompidou in Paris, *The Theatre without the Theatre* at MACBA in Barcelona, *18: Beckett* in Blackwood Gallery, Toronto, *Samuel Beckett: A Passion for Painting* at the National Gallery

of Ireland and *Try Again. Fail Again. Fail Better,* Momentum 2006, 4th Nordic Festival of Contemporary Art in Norway.

102. See Auslander, Philip. *Liveness: Performance in a Mediatized Culture.* London and New York: Routledge, 1999.
103. See 'Performing Presence: From the Live to the Simulated'. International conference, Centre for Intermedia, University of Exeter, UK, 26–9 March, 2009.
104. Phelan, Peggy. *Unmarked: The Politics of Performance.* London: Routledge, 1993: 146.
105. See the conflicting theories of Peggy Phelan (*Unmarked*) and Philip Auslander (*Liveness*).
106. Blau, Herbert. *Blooded Thought: Occasions of Theatre.* New York: Performing Arts Journal Publications, 1982: 132.
107. Burke, Edmund. *A Philosophical Enquiry into the Origin of our Ideas of the Sublime and Beautiful.* London: R. and J. Dodsley, 1761. http://academic.brook lyn.cuny.edu/english/melani/gothic/burke2.html [accessed 1/11/2016].
108. See Adorno, Theodor. *Negative Dialectics.*
109. See the history of negative presentation in the visual arts after 1945. Ray, Gene. 'Mourning and Cosmopolitics: With and Beyond Beuys'. In Christa-Maria Lerm Hayes and Victoria Walters (eds), *Beuysian Legacies in Ireland and Beyond: Art, Culture and Politics.* Berlin and Muenster: LIT Verlag, 2011: 118–46; and Ray, Gene. *Terror and the Sublime in Art and Critical Theory.* New York: Palgrave Macmillan, 2005, and 'History, The Sublime, Terror: Notes on the Politics of Fear', *Static,* 7 (2007): 1–15.
110. See 'Three Dialogues with Georges Duthuit'. In Martin Esslin (ed.), *Samuel Beckett: A Collection of Critical Essays.* New York: Prentice-Hall, 1965: 21.
111. Ibid.
112. And Eagleton adds that 'against fascism's megalomaniac totalities, Beckett pits the fragmentary and unfinished. In his Socratic way, Beckett preferred ignorance to knowledge, presumably because it resulted in fewer corpses'. Eagleton, Terry. 'Political Beckett?', *New Left Review*, 40 (July/August) 2006: 67.
113. Ibid.: 71.
114. If the starved, stagnant landscapes of his work are post-Auschwitz, as Knowlson argues, 'they are also a subliminal memory of famished Ireland, with its threadbare, monotonous colonial culture and its disaffected masses waiting listlessly on a Messianic deliverance which never quite comes'. Ibid. Also see Cunningham, Conor. *Genealogy of Nihilism.* London: Routledge, 2002.
115. Beckett is one of the few modernist artists to become a militant of the left rather than the right. See Eagleton, 'Political Beckett?'.
116. See Cunningham, David. 'Ex Minimis: Greenberg, Modernism and Beckett's Three Dialogues', *Samuel Beckett Today/Aujourd'hui,* 13 (2003): 29–41.
117. See Krauss, Rosalind E. *The Originality of the Avant-Garde and Other Modernist Myths.* Boston: MIT Press, 1986.
118. See 'Three Dialogues with Georges Duthuit'. In *Beckett: A Collection*: 21.
119. See Critchley, Simon. *On Humour.* London: Routledge, 2010. In http://dks.thing.net/Critchley-Beckett.html
120. Critchley, Simon. 'To Be or Not to Be is Not the Question: On Beckett's Film', *Film-Philosophy,* 11.2 (August 2007). The New School for Social Research, See http:/www.film-philosophy.com/2007v11n2/Critchley [accessed 1/11/2016].
121. The term 'openness', as discussed in Eco, Umberto. *The Open Work.* Cambridge, MA: Harvard University Press, 1989. 'Closed' versus 'open' form has been a defining attribute of modern works of art; critics have become used to employing

these terms, with their derivations and extensions in the various contexts of literary studies, visual arts and theatre.

122. As Christa-Maria Lerm Hayes argues about the open work of art in 'Re-inventing the Literary Exhibition: Exhibiting (Dialogical and Subversive) Art on (James Joyce's) Literature'. *Working Papers on Design*, 2 (2007). See <http://www. herts.ac.uk/artdes1/research/papers/wpdesign/wpdvol2/vol2.html>[accessed 1/11/2016].

PART I
RESPIRATION, DISCOURSE AND THE QUESTION OF MEDIUM SPECIFICITY

I

DEEPTIME: *BREATH* AND THE LOOK OF NON-ART

The sixties came from an empty room[1]

It's the shape that matters[2]

Total Object, complete with missing parts, instead of partial object.
Question of degree.[3]

Minimalism has ushered art into real time and real space, to borrow
a pair of phrases from the art talk of the late sixties. All the old
hierarchies had collapsed. In real time, no work of art is timeless. In
real space, the art object is no more privileged than any other physical
thing.[4]

Samuel Beckett is a theatrical writer with a distinctive relationship to art
theory and discourse, who attempted to express an unorthodox aesthetic
theory in his final piece of art criticism, but who has also expressed indirectly
aesthetic theories in his criticism of fellow writers and visual artists in his inter-
views and essays. His final piece of art criticism, the 'Three Dialogues with
Georges Duthuit', was published in issue five of the second Transition (1949)[5]
that was edited by the art critic Georges Duthuit (between 1948 and 1950).
Beckett's conversation with Duthuit and his 'words on painters', as well as his

writings on aesthetics and the visual arts, are in dialogue with his earlier and subsequent critical pieces in an edited volume by Ruby Cohn entitled *Disjecta: Miscellaneous Writings and a Dramatic Fragment*,[6] together with texts on *Geer van Velde*, *La Peinture des van Velde* (in French), *Peintres de l' empêche-ment* (in French), *à Jack Butler Yeats* (in French), *Henri Heyden, Bram van Velde, Pour Avidgor Arikha* (in French).

The publication history of the dialogues as David Hatch[7] remarks is very significant since it has defined the interpretation and influential readings of the text. The dialogues have been read initially in a fragmentary form, as the exhibition catalogues and art books were more readily available than the original journal issues. The bibliographical evidence shows that the complete text was not reprinted until 1965, thus it coincided with *Breath*'s publication. The text has been originally reprinted in fragments, out of context, and in publications intended to support the work of Bram van Velde. As Hatch argues, the nature and consistency of the extracted quotes indicate that for the first decade of its existence the text was apparently thought of primarily as a piece of art criticism, and as a work that was specifically connected with van Velde.[8]

Consequently, the text was largely disregarded for nearly a decade following its original publication, but soon after was considered as an essential guide to understanding the ways the writer's aesthetics translates into practice. However, the original context of the publication cannot be reconstructed and Beckett's intentions in writing criticism are not apparent, while the cryptic form of the text often produces misinterpretations and ambiguous readings.

The dialogues represent for critics a platform from which to investigate the writer's aesthetic approach but the text has also been employed for broad and 'erroneous' assumptions. Theorists assume a theoretical, aesthetic and philosophical position that may not be applicable and often ignore the humorous, ideological context and the intentional inconsistencies as well as the text's performative and subversive aspects.

Scholarly research, critical readings and influential approaches are articulated by theorists including Abbott, Acheson, Albright, Bersani, Butler, Cohn, Cope and Esslin, and a variety of meanings have been extrapolated by Federman, Fletcher, Hatch, Hesla, Katz, Oppenheim and, Robinson based on this final piece of criticism, thus manifesting that the text still has interpretive possibilities that remain unexplored, particularly in relation to Beckett's late writings and plays. The writer's artistic and aesthetic intentions as well as the subject and methodology in these performative dialogues remain rhetorical and enigmatic and Beckett continued to research and develop on these aesthetic and philosophical considerations throughout his life.

His statement to John Calder reveals the enigmatic character and ambiguity of the dialogues, as well as his idiosyncratic approach to the text. When Calder asked him to stage a reading of the dialogues in 1965 he turned down the proposal. As he requested, 'what ever you like, but please not the Duthuit dialogues. We can always find something to replace them'.[9] Moreover, the writer apparently refers to his own works when he comments to Tom Driver about his struggle to 'find a form that accommodates the mess' and David H. Hesla contends that the dialogues cannot function as a key to understand his work since what Beckett pronounced in 1949 does not harmonise with what he has practised since.[10] Driver argues that the impossibility of expression discussed in the dialogues was simply a stage for Beckett, a problem for which he eventually discovered a solution, and that his comments in an interview with him in 1961 reveal the writer's new aesthetic programme:

> Beckett insists that art must admit to itself what he calls 'the mess' or 'the confusion', when he writes: the confusion is not my invention. We cannot listen to a conversation for five minutes without being acutely aware of the confusion. It is all around us and our only chance is to let it in. The only chance of renovation is to open our eyes and see the mess. It is not a mess you can make sense of [. . .] One can only speak of what is in front of him, and that now is simply the mess.[11]

At the same time, the text surpasses the specific discussion of the modernist artists Bram van Velde, Tal-Coat and Masson and despite the cross-disciplinary approximation of the formal art of writing with painting, Beckett does not intend to apply a theoretical perspective to visual artists, but rather to juxtapose theory and practice and highlight the expressive paradox (expressive-inexpressive), namely the creative tension between abstraction and expression (absence of expression), the impossibility of expression and the 'notion of failure'. The writer considers ways of escaping the aporia of expressing the impossibility of expression, when he states that there is 'nothing from which to express', as Hatch expounds:

> because self is not a unity, not a coherent entity, but in itself an interplay of presence and absence, a dialectic of the one and the other. There is 'no power to express' because author, narrator, characters and language itself are impotent.[12]

The dialogues can nevertheless be employed to track the trajectory of Beckett's experimentation with form and narrative as well as his 'aesthetics of impoverishment', the progressive simplifications and the reductions in his *oeuvre*. The dramatist published these 'pseudo-dialogues' between 'B' and 'D' in 1949 and 'B' is, usually, identified as Beckett by critics and 'B's' discussion about modern art in the dialogues is often attributed to him. However, recent scholarship refrains from identifying the character B with Beckett's ideas and the character D with Duthuit's, and argues in favour of the dual authorship of the text that reinforces the fictional aspect of the dialogues. In an oft-cited passage from the dialogues, Beckett writes:

> B. – Yet I speak of an art turning from it in disgust, weary of its puny exploits, weary of pretending to be able, of being able, of doing a little better the same old thing, of going a little further along a dreary road.
> D. – And preferring what?
> B. – The expression that there is nothing to express, nothing with which to express, nothing from which to express, no power to express, no desire to express, together with the obligation to express.[13]

BECKETT'S AESTHETIC THEORY AND MODERNIST DISCOURSE

The critical context around the 'Three Dialogues' and its relationship to art and aesthetics is multifaceted. The dialogue form challenges philosophical conventions that allude to the Platonic dialogues and there is extensive debate among critics about the text and as to whether it expounds a coherent theory of art and artistic expression. Theorists like Lois Oppenheim admit that it is difficult to argue that Beckett 'developed any real aesthetic, in the sense of a theory of artistic expression',[14] while Richard Cope suggests that the 'Three Dialogues' is a text that attempts to articulate a thesis, but 'fails' to do so. The failure of the text to articulate its thesis renders the text a failure itself, a failure that parallels the argument within the text. Thus, the text becomes a paradigm of its own thesis, or non-thesis.[15] Beckett's dialogues and *oeuvre* evade exegesis and challenge hermeneutical systems, but in *Breath,* the evasion of exegesis becomes even more subtle, as Blau inquires:

> what is it there in *Breath*, that mimicry of a play, with its two vagital cries, what is it being remembered, except remembered being, being bygone, if it ever was, always nostalgia for it, or something more than being, with nothing there onstage, except a litter of rubbish, as if some token of the ruins of history, which gives another dimension to the birth astride of a grave.[16]

Beckett's language is aporetic, while in *Breath* the aporia of expressing the impossibility of expression is manifested and language is utterly eradicated. Interrogation is for Beckett, as Carla Locatelli suggests, 'the function of art (and thus the function of art is, in a sense, epistemological), art has always been this – pure interrogation, rhetorical question less the rhetoric'.[17]

The dialogues differ from broadly contemporaneous writings on modernist painting and abstraction from the post-war period and are in critical relation to 'Art and Objecthood', both in terms of form (performative/discursive) and content, as well as with regard to their discourse and concerns, even though they seem to share some common ground. Theorists such as Richard Cope argue that Clement Greenberg's 'Modernist Painting' and the dialogues may seem to share a similar agenda, but that the methodology and outcome are vastly different. That is to say, the former is stressing the possible and the latter remains within the impossible. Cope considers that within the argument of the dialogues and its insistence on impossibility there is ample scope for the continuation of painting, as a valid form of art that questions the nature of art by undermining its possibility.

Greenberg's essay 'Modernist Painting' represents a significant attempt to make painting possible in a time in which it was perceived to be in crisis, and Cope argues that the dialogues, seen as a piece of criticism, deserve to be considered more frequently in the debate surrounding the relevance of painting for contemporary art and is able to extend this questioning to other forms of expression. The thesis of the dialogues can highlight the problems inherent within the painting process. As Cope suggests, it can:

> bring into relief the possibility of remaining within these problems as a solution to the impossibility of overcoming the problems [. This] means that the text can be read as being of paramount interest to both artists and art critics alike, when considering the contradictions of painting, the possibility of its impossibility and the impossibility of its possibility.[18]

The critic and his relation to the artist are of crucial importance for the dialogues in relation to the responsibility of the critic in grasping the expressive deadlock and the 'aesthetics of impoverishment', since Beckett praises the artists who continue to struggle painfully with 'the ferocious dilemma of expression'.[19] As he asks, 'does there exist, can there exist or not, an impoverished painting, useless without camouflage, incapable of any image whatsoever, whose obligation does not seek to justify itself?'[20] The aporia of expressing the impossibility of expression and the research on the means to avoid the concretisation of abstraction become the primal concerns.

THE CONCRETISATION OF ABSTRACTION

Beckett's literary corpus, as Pascale Casanova claims, is unified by a singular aesthetic purpose, namely, 'to emulate in literature the abstraction central to modernism in the plastic arts',[21] while the theorist locates the anatomy of a literary revolution in Beckett's abstract writing. The concept of abstraction in relation to the human body and the abstractness of minimalism, as it is associated with the visual arts, are prominent artistic concerns for the writer. The minimalist object destabilises the media of painting and sculpture and opens the way to the invention of new ones – or to the idea that art advances by further displacement, further alienation from the traditional mediums and even from the idea that media can be given coherent definitions.[22] The abstractness of minimalism, as Krauss argues, makes it less easy to recognize the human body in those works and therefore less easy to project ourselves into the space of that sculpture with all our settled prejudices left intact. Yet our bodies and our experience of our bodies continue to be the subject of this sculpture – even when a work is made of several hundred tons of earth.[23]

Beckett extensively discusses representational abstraction, a couple of years before the writing of *Breath*, in the *Gruen Letter* (1964), and considers that he has perhaps freed himself from certain formal concepts. As he writes, 'perhaps, like the composer Schoenberg or the painter Kandinsky, I have turned toward an abstract language. Unlike them, however, I have tried not to concretize the abstraction not to give it yet another formal context'.[24] Thus, Beckett was influenced by Kandinsky's early lyrical abstract style but not his Bauhaus period.

In contrast to modernist discourse Beckett's unorthodox theory challenges aesthetic purity and autonomy, while his sharply critical usage of the term 'abstraction' reveals a suspicion against self-sufficient aesthetic purity. According to Erik Tonning, the reason of this scepticism is summarised in Shane Weller's review of Beckett's 1948 essay 'Peintres de l' empêchement'. As she wrote,

> rather than freeing the artist to pursue some absolutely non-representational art, recognition of the object's resistance to representation, it inaugurates an art whose theme or matter will be that resistance itself: 'Est peint ce qui empêche de peindre'. Art will therefore be forever in mourning for its object: 'deuil de l'objet'.[25]

The writer's ambiguous statement concerning the 'concretization of abstraction' is perplexing and cannot be easily deciphered, while his discussion about abstract language (in the Gruen and Schneider interview) manifests the tension between expression and abstraction during the creative process and Beckett's tendency beyond formalism that is characterised by the necessity of having both components in a dialectic relationship (abstraction-expression). Abstraction, according to the writer, requires new technical means of expression;[26] this is the reason behind the decision to write about the impossibility of writing as a solution to a technical problem, resolutely formalist in nature, with its closest analogue in abstract art.

Beckett is against false attempts to reach beyond, rather than sustain the confrontation with the 'dilemma of expression' (like some kinds of painterly abstraction). As an alternative, he argues that art should accept failure as its inescapable condition. Hence, he praises the work of Bram Van Velde, who is described as the 'first to admit that to be an artist is to fail, as no other dare fail, that failure is his world and the shrink from its desertion'.[27]

The anti-theatrical strategies and his formal game-playing[28] are a product of his aesthetics of 'failure'. The concern about the new formal language is ultimately related to Beckett's preoccupation with the nature of the medium and contains aesthetic and philosophical concerns, while aspects of the formal achievement of *Breath* are considered as an aesthetic breakthrough that led to an 'abstract' formal language. The evasion of figuration, the abeyance of the mimetic, and principally the reduction of duration in *Breath* are related facets of the technique of abstraction. The writer challenges the 'nature' of the medium he is working with, and he then follows, as Francis Doherty argues, 'a path of reduction and diminution, and treads the path of diminution in order to call into question the dominant idea of what constitutes a dramatic script and a theatrical performance'.[29] Through its highly articulate process of erasure and constant disruption of the processes and the kind of terms that surround representational theatre, Beckett's *oeuvre* and especially *Breath* reorient our reflections concerning the formation of theatricality, medium, genre, character, dialogue, drama, place, action, situation and language, turning towards processes and contexts through which the limits of the work are yet to be defined.

The exhaustion of possibilities is Beckett's fundamental artistic strategy, as Gilles Deleuze argues, and according to this reading his art is an art of exhaustion – exhaustion, that is, 'not of the artist, but of his resources and not with the particular artist, but with art itself, always at the mercy of decomposing and perverse media'.[30] The writer's aim is to endorse failure, disjunction, dis-function within his given medium and his work foregrounds schematisation, de-individualisation, bodily constriction and reduction, fragmentation and rapid extortion of speech, as well as expressionless (and occasionally unintelligible) delivery. This was Beckett's way with every artistic medium that he worked in, as Albright argues, 'to foreground the medium, to thrust it in the spectator's face, by showing its inadequacy, its refusal to be wrenched to any good artistic purpose'.[31]

The writer compares his work and method of composing to that of James Joyce and argues that he (in contrast to Joyce) was merely aiming at the essentials. He considers that he was diametrically opposite to Joyce, because Joyce was a synthesiser. As he puts it, 'he wanted to put everything, the whole of human culture, into one or two books, and I am an analyser. I take away all the accidentals because I want to come down to the bedrock of the essentials, the archetypal'.[32] In another passage, Beckett compares again his aesthetic with that of Joyce, by explaining that his investigation was the area of existence, which was by definition incompatible with art. As he writes:

> the more Joyce knew the more he could. He is tending toward omniscience and omnipotence as an artist. I'm working with impotence, ignorance. There seems to be a kind of aesthetic axiom that expression is

achievement – must be an achievement. My little exploration is that whole zone of being that has always been set aside by artists as something unusable – as something by definition incompatible with art.[33]

Beckett is also the inventor of the persona of Jean du Cas, the founder of the movement of Concentrism, a movement that was constantly challenging interpretative strategies, and as Lois Oppenheim argues, his *oeuvre* is perfectly intelligible and perfectly inexplicable at the same time. Any effort to situate and analyse the writer's work risks the epithet of one who bears a marked resemblance to the writer himself. Jean du Cas, as the theorist states, is 'such a threat [. . . and] no less fictive than the movement's leader, both inventions of Beckett – and the belief that a critical exegesis may be just non-reducible enough to respect an art as at once, perfectly intelligible and perfectly unexplicable'.[34]

The resistance to exegesis, and his deprecating of the role of the author as authority, was singular and Beckett is constantly challenging the role of hermeneutics, while his statements have been fundamentally against any attempt at interpretation. As he says, 'art has nothing to do with clarity, does not dabble in the clear and does not make clear'.[35] He also famously refused to offer his readers any help in interpreting his work, as he states, 'my work is a matter of fundamental sounds (no joke intended), made as fully as possible, and I accept responsibility for nothing else. If people want to have headaches among the overtones let them and provide their own aspirin'.[36]

The texts deal with the problem of interpretation itself, as he phrases it, 'no symbols where none intended'[37] and as Steven Connor argues, criticism mimics the gesture of Beckett's 'shrug' in order 'to assert humbly its own limits'. In the very act of making this gesture it (criticism) 'defies those limits affirming the possibility of speech and commentary even when these are denied'.[38] The literal refusal of *Breath* to convey verbal meaning through language is part of this resistance to exegesis and categorisation, despite the fact that, at the same time, Beckett with his writing and directorial vision, maintained the strict composition of his texts and strict control over even the smallest details of the various productions of his plays. Since his death, in 1989, his estate has shown itself committed to the same policy.[39]

The attempt to contextualise the Beckettian aesthetics within a single theoretical framework is very difficult, since his art reveals, as Abbott suggests, 'the semantic porousness of categories'.[40] His *oeuvre* absorbs the arts of painting, music and mime; however, the work can, by and large, be associated to the artistic movement of minimalism, as Blau argues,

> the parsimonious aesthetic, the 'mere-most minimum', of those claustral plays and prose, where 'Words are few. Dying too' (*Monologue*). But when it comes to thinking the worst, *Ill seen ill said*, who was saying it better, *What where*, and who would have thought that in the 'accusative

[of] inexistence', along with a rush of amnesia, 'no notion who it was saying what you were saying', there is also a 'grand apnoea', taking your breath away – what signal from the brain, what particle physics, apnea with a grandeur? 'Whose skull you were clapped up in' (*That Time*), where else would you find that but Beckett?[41]

Minimalist practice experiments with a range of strategies that redefine the structure, form, material, image and production of the art object in its relationship to time, space and to the spectator.

THE TRANSITIONAL SPACE BETWEEN THE PLASTIC AND THE PERFORMING ARTS

These strategies began to imply a different kind of viewer, hence a different kind of engagement with the artwork, where the boundaries between a timeless visual art object and a temporal theatrical work became indistinct. In the well-known statement about the distinction between the temporal and the spatial arts, Gotthold Ephraim Lessing argues that all bodies exist not only in space but also in time and that they continue, and at any moment of their continuance may assume a different appearance and in different relations. Every one of these momentary appearances and groupings, as he states, 'was the result of a preceding, may become the cause of a following, and is therefore the centre of a present action'.[42]

A shift towards a relational understanding of art occurs in twentieth-century sculpture that moves it from being a fundamentally spatial, into an increasingly temporal, art. Temporal consequences of a particular arrangement of form are very significant for art criticism and for the history of art, since, as Krauss argues, in any spatial organisation 'there will be folded an implicit statement about the nature of temporal experience'.[43] Sculpture is a medium located at the juncture between stillness and motion, time arrested and time passing, and minimalist practice stresses the conditions and the significance of temporal experience during the viewing of the artwork. Attitudes towards time, in the work of art, vary and art theorists have given many insights into a notion of temporality and its relationship to 'presentness'. Central to the notion of 'presence' and to the phenomenological ramifications of minimalist sculpture is the idea of direct experience that is related to the 'here and now' of the temporal and material world.

In the critical writings of the late sixties, the notions of 'presence' and 'lived experience' are differentiated from modernism's transcendentalism, while modernist theorists are critical of the effect of 'presence' and the transient situations of encounter. Performance theory focuses on immediacy and 'presence', given the structure of co-presence of artwork and viewer, predominantly in interactive installations and intermedia practices that involve and require the viewer's immediate engagement with the work and her/his ultimate involvement in the creation of the artwork. The theoretical emphasis on perceptual and phenomenal states and the insistence on direct, lived experience, generated through representation, undermines aesthetic boundaries and questions the logic of medium specificity that is prevalent in modernist theories.

The effects of media on perception are extensively addressed in critical literature, particularly in relation to the notion of 'literal presence' in environmental installations. The implications of the relationship between time and medium are imperative for modernism and minimalist sculpture (that is characterised as a matter of time by Fried). Fried sees temporality as connected with the theatre and the performing arts, thus he is critical of the effect of 'presence' of the 'new sculpture of the sixties'. He considers that his invocation of presentness makes him the last in a long time of aestheticians, who (from Lessing to Greenberg through Wölfflin), sought in the instantaneous spatiality of painting the specific essence of plastic art.[44] Fried's linkage of theatricality/objecthood to time and his binarism between 'mere presence' and 'pure presentness' are examined in relation to a close analysis of temporalities and temporal unfolding in the production and reception of *Breath* related works in this chapter.

In his Laocoön, Lessing defines the separate media of art through their differing temporalities; painting and sculpture are considered as 'spatial and simultaneous' while prose, poetry and music are 'temporal and successive'. *Breath* takes place 'here and now', since the time and space of the theatrical event and the time and space of 'the breath and cry' on stage are identical. 'Theatreality'[45] is the term that describes this process, that is, the time and space of drama is sequentially related to the time and space of the spectators. The playlet's temporal unfolding and its compositional methodology lies in the dialectics between duration and instantaneousness that is associated to installation aesthetics and to a durational modality of production and reception. *Breath*'s temporal unfolding is an equally important component for its composition as its materiality (lighting and stage design). The playlet does not represent time, but it takes place at present time (here and now), thus formulates an 'aesthetics of presence' but also an 'aesthetics of absence' (missing figure). *Breath* is reduced in time and space to the point where it is frozen temporally and spatially, approximating a visual artwork.

Audiences can watch *Breath* onstage, but it can also be presented as an installation (of rubbish) or as a sound piece in a gallery space. It is possible to present the piece in situations in a context where viewers can be walking around it and as an installation that can be circled, departed from or returned to at one's will (provided that this durational encounter lasts for thirty-five seconds). The experimentation with the aesthetic and conceptual aspects of duration and repetition, through the minimal duration of one of the shortest plays ever written, manifests a decisive moment in the history of theatrical experimentation, in part because of the new relationship it developed towards the formal possibilities of the theatrical event. Beckett reduces his medium to its most basic form of objecthood by staging a play with theatre's basic essentials and by exposing the components of theatre in skeletal form, given that the work consists solely of stage directions, no literary text, total absence of plot, action, dialogue, and character, hence visual and acoustic, non-textual processes of signification.

Beckett almost reaches this ultimate anti-theatrical desire 'to create a blank or white page',[46] by writing a text beyond the theatrical (literary) text. This intermedial text, in a scale of a fragment almost reaches 'the point zero of language', given that it consists solely of scenic directions based on a pattern of an interplay of silence and sound, light and dark, time and space, covering timing for sound and lights, level and intensity of lights. The scenic text draws from visual and auditory elements that establish an acoustical presence on stage, a 'soundscape', that includes and notates silence. The enigmatic thinness of the late work, the writing of a non-text (only stage directions), as well as the articulation of a non-thesis in the 'Three Dialogues', are related facets of Beckett's *oeuvre*, and his pieces reflect on and explore modes of theatrical production, beyond textual frames of representation, as well as modes of perceiving and perception, by articulating a visual field[47] that is principally a perceptual field.

In the later plays, as Garner states, the writer explores 'the activity lodged within stillness and the sound of the depths of visual latency. The result [. . .] is to etch the contours of performance even more within the spectator and to replace a theatre of activity, with a theatre of perception, guided by the eye and its efforts to see'.[48] Beckett's fundamental intention, as Essif argues, is not to eliminate either visual image or language, 'but to discover images as well as utterances, that, instead of telling a story, would convey to the spectator a profound and complex sense of emptiness and silence'.[49]

The closest to a minimal definition[50] we do get from Beckett are his statements that a perfect play is one in which there are no actors, only text, and that this text must be built up around a 'picture'. Theorists like Gerhard Hauck, therefore, compare Beckett to a painter, 'whose distaste for the excesses of style make him end up with an empty canvas, or the musician whose quest for the origins of art lead him back to primitive forms of tonal and rhythmic expression, such as the sound of the heartbeat'.[51] As Hauck observes, *Breath*'s visual qualities bear a strong similarity to the 'environmental sculptures' and paintings of artists like Joseph Beuys and Salvador Dali. However, Hauck considers that *Breath* would need to be reduced even further, into a single timeless moment, in order to qualify as a purely visual artwork. The ramifications of the relation between a single timeless moment and a temporal composition or in the representation of different 'temporalities' can be traced in the following analysis of practices and shifts in the representation of respiration in two-dimensional art and installation, such as in Bridget Riley's *Breathe* (optical-art) and Gerhard Richter's *Breath* (abstract expressionism) and in installation pieces such as Art & Language's *There were Sighs Trapped by Liars* and Michael Craig-Martin's *Inhale/Exhale*.

The intermedial expansion of painting and the reality-making performativity of painting have taken many shapes in the history of art. According to Shannon Jackson, the theorist Harold Rosenberg defined 'action painting' in the United States and comprehended that the distinctiveness of 'American' abstract expressionist canvases came from a change in attitude toward painting itself. The conventions, as she states, 'of two-dimensional representation were undone by painters who no longer viewed painting as a domain to 'reproduce, re-design, analyze, or "express", instead regarding it as an "arena in which to act". As Rosenberg describes, "what was to go on the canvas was not a picture but an event"'.[52] According to Fried's assessment of the relationship between abstract expressionism and minimalism, a conflict has gradually emerged between shape as a fundamental property of objects and shape as a medium of painting. Roughly, the success or failure of a given painting, as he writes,

> has come to depend on its ability to hold or stamp itself out or compel conviction as shape-that, or somehow to stave off or elude the question of whether or not it does so [. . .] what is at stake in this conflict is whether the paintings or objects in question are experienced as paintings or as objects.[53]

Moreover, Fried adds that what decides their identity as painting is their confronting of the demand that they hold as shapes. Otherwise they are experienced as nothing more than objects and 'this can be summed up by saying that modernist painting has come to find it imperative that it defeat or suspend its own objecthood'.[54]

Intermediality lies in-between the boundaries of artistic media as a term that encapsulates the methodological challenges of converging different media. As a combinatory structure of syntactical elements that derive from more than one medium the term shares common ground with discourses that have been conceived to theorise the interface and in-betweeness of media, such as Rosalind Krauss' 'differential specificity' and Foucault's 'disguised difference'.

'Differential specificity'[55] is a concept that attempts to capture the complexity and interface between diverse media, that Krauss defines as the artist's attempts to reinvent the use of a singular medium. The theorist, who is critical of the formalism of medium specificity distinguishes intermediality and intermedia practices from 'differential specificity', since, as she argues, the term assumes the impossibility of the merger or complete sublimation of one medium in another. The specificity of mediums, even modernist ones, according to Krauss, should be understood as differential, self-differing, and thus as a layering of conventions never simply collapsed into the physicality of their support [. . .] and the onset of higher orders of technology – robot, computer – which allows us, by rendering older techniques outmoded, to grasp the inner complexity of the mediums those techniques support. And continues [. . .] there are a few contemporary artists who have decided not to engage in the international fashion of installation and intermedia work.[56]

Krauss is sceptical of contemporary installation art; she defines such work as a trend that 'essentially finds itself complicit with a globalization of the image in the service of capital (perceiving art in the regime of postmodernity, characterised by Fredric Jameson as "the total saturation of cultural space by the image, whether at the hands of advertising, communications media, or cyberspace").[57] The theorist considers that in contrast to intermediality, the notion of 'differential specificity' of media still assumes that medium is apparent even if as a relation. Krauss argues for a contemporary art that embraces the idea of differential specificity, namely an art practice that 'reinvents or rearticulates the art medium per se and resists to retreat into etiolated forms of the traditional mediums – such as painting and sculpture'.[58] Meanwhile, Rosemary Hawker compares Krauss' differential specificity to a term that describes an 'identity that is inviolable but which can nevertheless be feigned', namely, Foucault's notion of 'disguised difference'. As Foucault puts it, artists 'disguise the differences that constitute their practice. It is not media that are translated in this process, but the idiomatic aspects that every medium possesses and which are visible only in citation'. Hawker considers that both Krauss and Foucault see intermedial relations as productive in their articulation of disciplinarity and media.[59]

In Beckett's *Breath* the complete sublimation of one medium in another doesn't imply or suggest complicity with a globalisation of the image, as Krauss forewarns. The playlet resists homogeneous hybrid formations, and the writer's intention behind the interface of the theatrical and the visual is to decompose and pervert these media by showing their inadequacy, their 'refusal to be wrenched to any good artistic purpose'.[60] Beckett's aim is to show the artwork's resistance to representation, and his art's core and matter becomes that resistance itself,[61] while *Breath*'s 'resistance' to representation is intrinsically related to the reduction and control of time. The pictorial and sculptural elements form a visual presence that cannot be discerned from the theatrical features of the piece owing to the treatment of temporality.

DURATION VS INSTANTANEOUSNESS: BECKETT, RICHTER, RILEY, KENTRIDGE, ART AND LANGUAGE, CRAIG-MARTIN, TURRELL, VIOLA

The terms 'differential specificity' and 'disguised difference' are applicable for the analysis of works of painting that approach the photographic medium and of pieces that work with photography as an image of a painting or in such a way as to stand outside their own medium. Gerhard Richter's painting *Breath* investigates the ways in which the mapping of a structure, originally composed in one medium (photography) is mapped onto another structure in another medium (painting). *Breath* transcribes the photographic medium to the medium of painting with a persistent emphasis on the relationship of painting and photography and their contrasting visual effects.

Richter's early work was influenced by the expressive abstraction of *Art Informel* ('Informal Art'), the French post-war movement, while the post-war period brought the digitalisation of colour in art.[62] The painter's research focuses on the representational limits of the medium of painting and this piece depicts his notion of respiration and its representation in painting. The artist reproduces the photographic medium in painting through the use of the photographic effect of pixelation and electronic blurring. As he argues, regarding his work, 'I am not trying to imitate a photograph; I am trying to make one. And if I disregard the assumption that a photograph is a piece of paper exposed to light, then I am practicing photography by other means.'[63]

According to Gertrude Koch, Richter's blur is 'a mental state in which the relation to the world of objects blurs and the act of blurring causes that world to appear particularly threatening; to appear as an impenetrable presence'.[64] Painting is a synthesising and constructing medium that makes use of all modes of sensory knowledge besides the visual and the tactile. Like Parrhasius' curtain, all representation takes place as a staged, mediated event where curtain, paper, canvas are the conveyance for the idea. This greater, all encompassing truth is only made evident, as Hawker argues, 'through the rendering of the photographic idiom in painting. It is only possible through the effect of painting's idiom, it is not evident – in fact it is hidden – in photography as medium'.[65]

A cinematic wide-screen canvas of repeated curving diagonals presents the effects and process of inhaling and exhaling in Bridget Riley's painting, *Breathe*. The artist draws from respiration to research on abstract forms and optical impression. The illusion of movement is created by the use of pattern and the contrast between black and white, while the visual experience triggers a bodily response that demonstrates the interconnectedness of eye and body. The embodied, dizzying vision evident through the viewing of optical art questions high-modernist claims about the dominance of the optical, while its version of the 'trompe l'oeil', allows the haptic back into an exclusively optical experience. This embodied vision challenges the disembodied, optical experience that is proper and exclusive to the 'advanced' modernist painting of the late 1950s and 1960s. The verb 'breathe' in the title of the work expresses a bodily function and enduringness, while the painting works at the level of the frame or photogramme and indicates a concern with optical and visual impression. Riley introduces a 'new' visual language by experimenting with the static medium of painting and by challenging the visual ideal of a strong gestalt celebrated by a number of minimalist artists.

The performative and intermedial expansion of painting takes many shapes, while the distinctiveness of 'American' abstract expressionist canvases came from a change in attitude toward painting itself. For Rosenberg the conventions of two-dimensional representation were undone by painters who no longer viewed painting as a domain to 'reproduce, re-design, analyze, or express'; instead they regarded the medium as an 'arena in which to act'. As Rosenberg argues, 'what was to go on the canvas was not a picture but an event'.[66] According to Fried's assessment of the relationship between abstract expressionism and minimalism, a conflict has gradually emerged between shape as a fundamental property of objects and shape as a medium of painting. Roughly, the success or failure of a given painting, as he writes,

> has come to depend on its ability to hold or stamp itself out or compel conviction as shape – that, or somehow to stave off or elude the question of whether or not it does so [. . .] what is at stake in this conflict is whether the paintings or objects in question are experienced as paintings or as objects.[67]

The performative and filmic expansion of painting and the reality-making performativity of painting are manifest in William Kentridge's *Breathe*.[68] Krauss argues that, in contrast to artists who have resisted, as impossible, retreating into etiolated forms of the traditional mediums, such as painting and sculpture, artists like Kentridge embrace 'the idea of differential specificity, which is to say the medium as such, which they understand they will now have to reinvent or rearticulate'.[69]

Breathe is part of an installation that consists of the three films *Breathe*, *Dissolve* and *Return* that are projected on the fire curtain, while the orchestra is tuning before the performance. *Breathe* is composed of small pieces of torn black tissue paper that successively swirl and fall making either random patterns or defined images. The performative aspect of the piece is introduced by a singer's breathing that conducts the movement of the paper; the fragments are dispersed and in turn gather and fall to the rhythm of her breathing. The medium exchange in the interface between painting and performing here shows the artist's attempt to rearticulate and reinvent both mediums. The specificity of mediums is thus challenged, but the complete sublimation of one medium in another is avoided.

The conceptual life-size installation *Sighs Trapped by Liars*[70] reproduces inhabited spaces as a research on the linguistic, the pictorial and the dialectic between looking and reading, pictures and words. Michael Baldwin and Mel Ramsden research on the complexity of 'reading by reproducing the text and

Figure 1.1: WILLIAM KENTRIDGE (partial view). *Breathe, Dissolve, Return*: 2008. Installation of three video projections, DVcam, HDV, video transfer. Six minute loop. Courtesy of the Artist and Marian Goodman Gallery

by treating texts as visual objects. The materiality of texts is illustrated in the uncertainty of meaning that is produced by the disjunction between reading or recovering an image. The tables are constructed of canvasses pinned together and photocopied sheets of texts are printed on the canvasses that have then been painted over and are almost obliterated by brightly coloured paint. The installation consists of everyday materials, whereas the viewers have to change their posture so as to read the actual text.

The group collaboration and artistic practice Art & Language (est. 1968)[71] that consists of artists Michael Baldwin and Mel Ramsden, with the art historian Charles Harrison collaborating on theoretical projects, is primarily concerned with institutional critique. This concern is manifest in the piece *Sighs Trapped by Liars* that invites the viewer to question the correlation between 'reading' and 'looking' and to reconsider the relationship of the artwork and the institution. Art & Language bespeak that form of resolution without which art cannot persist in its trust in the potential of a medium. They claim that art must embody some form of resistance to the dominant regimes of the culture – some form of incompetence. It cannot be good unless it does. This is a basic tenet of modernism. They ask:

> Does it follow that it is an out-dated notion? Does it no longer hold true in the post-modern world? Or is the idea of the post-modern, like the idea of the global, no more than a return to the earlier, discredited version of modernism, in which all differences were overcome in the eyes of the global aesthete-cum-consumer?[72]

The neo-conceptual art collective researched on the identity and meaning of medium-specificity during modernism and the postmodern turn; as Donald Judd argues, half or more of the best new work in the 1950s was neither painting nor sculpture. Painting and sculpture became set forms:

> a fair amount of their meaning isn't credible [. . .] because the nature of three dimensions isn't set, given beforehand, something credible can be made, almost nothing. Of course something can be done within a given form, such as painting, but with some narrowness and less strength and variation. Since sculpture isn't so general a form, it can probably be only what it is now – which means that if it changes a great deal it will be something else; so it is finished.[73]

Questions of medium and the relationship between two mediums are staged in the site-specific installation *Inhale/Exhale*, that consists of everyday materials that Martin Craig-Martin magnifies so as to experiment with the interface between painting, sculpture and installation art. As Krauss remarks about media exchanges, 'it is their disciplinary differences that allow each to say something quite different. It is their resistance to homogeneous hybrid formations that allows their greatest effect'. *Inhale/Exhale* is a single painting around the space, from floor to ceiling, a panorama of objects, painted directly onto all four walls. These magnified mass-produced everyday objects are models for works of art, as Craig-Martin notes: 'I try to get rid of as much meaning as I can. People's need to find meanings, to create associations, renders this impossible. Meaning is both persistent and unstable.'[74] And the artist's aim is 'to construct images and pictures, places to use very simple things to describe very complex ideas [. . .] Because they are so familiar, they are like a universal language, anybody can see them'.[75]

Craig-Martin's conceptual and minimal art is characterised by stylised drawing and the depiction or assemblage of everyday objects that challenge the relationships between perspective, form and purpose. The objects are reduced to coloured-in outlines of varying scales while the artist integrates readymade techniques into his compositions. Craig-Martin's medium exchange between painting and sculpture produces a genre that oscillates between the two, the three-dimensional and the object itself. Similarly to Beckett's *Breath*, *Sighs Trapped by Liars* and *Inhale/Exhale* are works characterised by an aesthetic of media cross-fertilisation that open the pictorial and sculptural to the spatial. Thus the pieces retain a critical inter-mediality that is characterised by a self-reflexive dialogue between the media that resists immersion and homogeneous hybrid formations, while other works such as James Turrell's *Breathing Light* and Bill Viola's *Fire, Water, Breath* advance forms of aesthetic illusion rather than immediacy.

Viola's piece is an image sequence projected onto a screen that begins with a small, central, luminous, abstract form shimmering and undulating against a deep blue-black void. The multiple layers transform the medium of video into painting and gradually the luminous shape begins to get larger and less distorted, and a human form appears illuminated, rising towards us from under the surface of a body of water. As Viola describes:

> after some time, the figure breaks the surface, an act at once startling, relieving and desperate. His pale form emerges into the warm hues of a bright light, the water glistening on his body. His eyes immediately open and he releases a long held breath from the depths, shattering the silence of the image as this forceful primal sound of life resonates momentarily in the space. After a few moments, he inhales deeply, and, with his eyes shut and his mouth closed, he sinks into the depths of the blue-black void to become a shimmering moving point of light once more. The image then returns to its original state and the cycle begins anew.[76]

The artist meditates on the themes of human existence and produces spaces of transition between the medium of painting and the medium of video. Similarly to *Fire, Water, Breath*, James Turrell's *Breathing Light*[77] and his light-based installations expand perception and explore illusion and the ways light shapes space. At the same time the pieces mark a shift from pigment to light, the medium that shapes the artist's *oeuvre* . As Turrell states, 'I make spaces that apprehend light for our perception, and in some ways gather it, or seem to hold it [. . .] my work is more about your seeing than it is about my seeing, although it is a product of my seeing.' He adds, 'I want you to sense yourself sensing – to see yourself seeing.'[78]

Coloured light shifts from blue to crimson to magenta become spatial in Turrell's works, and his pioneering experiments in light projection have the ability to transform space. The resulting intersection of light and architecture generates virtual extension and the illusion of flatness. Spaces are filled with shifting artificial and natural light that the artist is using as a material, even though he considers that his indispensable medium is perception.

Turrell's 'post-medium', site-specific installations escape categorisation and according to Gordon Hughes they are an unstable 'mix of not-quite painting, not-quite sculpture, not-quite cinema, not-quite photography, and not-quite architecture'[79] The merging of art and architecture in these pieces and media technologies are used to reflect on the meaning of light, on the modalities of appearance and the ways perception functions. However, the co-mingling of art and architecture and the complete sublimation of one medium in another, as Hal Foster warns, is 'now a primary site of image-making and space-shaping in our cultural economy'.[80] Minimalism, according to Foster, has turned from an artistic movement to an architectural style to an interior design option: 'Office towers purport to be "sculptural," or else use tricks of perception borrowed from conceptual art.'[81]

Beckett aims to stop theatrical time in the duration of thirty-five seconds in *Breath* and to transform the temporal 'events' into an image (lighting field), in contrast to Bill Viola and James Turrell, who are transforming an image into a temporal event so as to produce an illusionistic effect. *Breath* retains a critical, anti-illusionistic approach, despite its minimalism. Beckett stages a 'tableau' in *Breath*, where the viewer's experience of the object occurs through a precise manipulation and reduction of time with accuracy, whereas the single timeless moment that is produced in painting cannot be generated in time based art. From the moment the curtain rises and falls, the minimal 'action', the 'story' of two brief cries, the synchronous inhalation, exhalation, the stage and the light changes differentiates *Breath* from these visual art and installation pieces. A painting, a sculpture, or an 'environmental' piece is not framed in the same way.

The reduction of duration is Beckett's principal anti-theatrical strategy. Temporality is an intrinsic factor and component of responsivity in *Breath* as it is for Fried's criticism of minimalism. The centrality of time, for the theorist's argument, lies in minimalism's relationship to temporality, while the term is problematized within the context of the modernist sensibility as an experience that essentially has a beginning and an end. The minimalist artwork has an inherent relationship to repetition, an element contingent on time as it pertains to infinity.[82]

Single Moments: The Interdisciplinary Mobility of the Concept of Temporality

Hauck portrays the playlet as a work with no beginning and no end, as he argues, *Breath* consists of a single moment stretched out between the point of its completion and the point of its ruination. And while it may tell a story or represent an action, that action, according to Hauck, 'does not move in time and space in the same way it moves even in a minimal play like *Breath*'. Even if *Breath* was shorter than its prescribed (thirty-five-second) run the same conditions would still apply. In order to qualify as a purely visual artwork, the playlet would need to be reduced further still, as Hauck writes:

it would need to be condensed into a single timeless moment. At that point, however, the cry at the beginning and the cry at the end would be one and the same, just as the inhalation and the exhalation, the increase and the decrease of light would collapse into a single moment. *Breath* would no longer be *Breath*, but an exhibition of rubbish. It would turn from a play into an 'environmental' sculpture.[83]

'Environmental sculpture' and installation practices are based on the arrangement of various objects and materials to create a complex spatial environment. *Breath* consists of an installation (stage design) of miscellaneous rubbish that is similar to a display of readymade pieces or to an installation piece that presents rubbish as a focal scenic element. Hauck's statement is critical given that the visual image initially appears to be 'without time', however, while the visual arts and the theatre share common qualities and lexical terms such as temporality, performativity, presence, these terms have varied associations in these different contexts.

Beckett experiments with the 'aesthetics of time' and with the disposition of perception, as well as with the temporal aspects of the image and the temporal movement in the image that depend on the reception of the viewer. The represented time is identical to the time of theatrical representation, while the piece is about the shaping of time; *Breath* appeals to the temporal sense of the viewer by producing a conceptual imagery and an audio-visual displacement of theatrical perception.

The control of time is nowhere more evident and strict than in new media pieces, while the relationship of temporality with the theatre and its durational stasis has concerned Hans-Thies Lehmann in his analysis of 'post dramatic theatre'. The perception of theatre no longer simply prepares for a 'barrage' of the sensory apparatus with moving images. Yet, as Lehmann argues, 'just as in front of a painting, it activates the dynamic capacity of the gaze to produce processes, combinations and rhythms on the basis of the data provided by the stage'.[84] According to this view, the visual semiotics seems to want to stop theatrical time and to transform the temporal events into images for contemplation. As Lehmann writes, 'the spectators' gaze is invited to "dynamize" the durational stasis offered to them through their own vision. The result is a hovering of perceptual focus between a "temporalizing" viewing and a scenic "going along," between the activity of seeing and the (more passive) empathy'.[85]

Breath freezes theatrical time in the duration of thirty-five seconds and transmutes the temporal 'events' into an image, while Beckett's decision to show the piece in a proscenium stage (with the rise and fall of the curtain) in conjunction with his decision to use the structure of the 'well-made play' so as to challenge it, points to strategies and concerns that characterise post-dramatic theatre.

MODERNIST PRESENTNESS VS MINIMALISM'S REAL TIME (PRESENCE)

Fried's essay 'Art and Objecthood' first appeared in an issue of *Artforum* devoted to American sculpture in the summer of 1967, alongside essays and statements by artists associated with the movement that was later described as minimalism and with representative artists such as Robert Morris, Sol Lewitt and Robert Smithson. The issue intended to portray the contemporary debate and the reaction against the dominance of formalist criticism, which Fried and Greenberg had espoused, and the modernist sculpture and painting they had effectively promoted throughout the post-war period both in the United States and as representative of the US abroad. The essay, according to Merve Unsal, represents a breaking point from Greenberg's version of modernism, further modified by Fried, emphasizing the essential, integral, formal values of the work. Continuity is also an integral part of Greenberg's modernism, as he states 'nothing could be further from the authentic art of our time than the idea of a rupture of continuity'.[86] As Merve Unsal argues, the break thus becomes prophetic in art history as later years would point to the different genealogies of modernism to be created, refuted and reincarnated again,[87] but these different versions of modernism exceed the parameters of this book.

Fried is indebted to the writings of the late Greenberg, whom he regards as the foremost art critic of the twentieth century. He knew Greenberg personally and on more than a few occasions visited studios and warehouses to look at recent painting and sculpture with him. For several years he enjoyed not only his friendship but his qualified approval. Then, for reasons he only partly understood, their relationship became impossible. But he remarks that he 'would not have been the art critic he was, he would not have become the art historian he is, had it not been for the need to come to terms with his [Greenberg's] thought'.[88]

Fried argues that the theatre exists for spectators in a way that other arts do not and he characterises the inclusion of the viewer as 'presence', because the medium of theatre and the effect of theatricality presuppose, as one of their indispensable preconditions, some sort of real, immediate, physical presence. 'Presence' suggests the bodily impact of the artwork, an experience akin to encountering another person that Greenberg defines as the 'look of non-art'. Greenberg and Fried ground their argument against minimalism upon this notion, but they radically alter its meaning, attributing presence to a work that lacks aesthetic quality.

Presence in Fried's sense is not, as for Greenberg, the presence of the ready-made that shocks us or awaits our use.[89] It is the presence of the human-scaled unitary shape, a shape that seemed to suggest the gestalt of another body. As Fried argues, 'the entities or beings encountered in everyday experience in terms that most closely approach the literalist ideals of the [. . .] holistic are other persons'.[90] The problem with the literalist emphasis is the phenomenological effect of its wholeness – the disquieting effect that it has on the spectator. This effect of viewing or embodied reception of visual artworks, which is a process that can be engaged as performative, is at the core of Fried's critique.

This takes as its central theme the proposition that art is a performative rather than merely a representational practice. In contrast to the prevailing understandings of art as a representational or a signifying practice, through creative practice, a dynamic material exchange can occur between objects, bodies and images. Fried opposes what he calls the performative, that is, the way in which the event surrounding the exhibition of the work becomes as important as the work itself. This process is primarily related to a total control of the *mise en scène* and of making that situation the primary thing as distinct from the work itself.

Therefore it becomes apparent that a particular critique of the actor is motivating this anti-theatrical stance and, as Puchner argues, in Fried's often metaphorical formulations, 'theatrical paintings or sculptures are described as if they were actors; these sculptures are "aware" of the audience and thus lose their self-sufficient unity and integrity, in the process of which they start to resemble vain human actors pandering to the audience'.[91] In reality, Fried ascribes to such theatrical works an anthropomorphic quality that leads to a form of personalised naturalism. The prejudice against performance is seen in the distrust of the live actor that speaks through Fried's figurative language and becomes more evident when the writer analyses the contrast between theatre and film. The one art form that is safe from such deplorable anthropomorphic effects, Puchner argues, is 'film, in contrast to the endlessly personalizing theatre, film not only removes the actors from the presence of the audience but also cuts them into pieces through close-ups and montage'.[92]

Fried considers that the experience of these artworks is situational and sensory in the sense that the artist places the beholder in a situation of encounter that pushes the object/viewer relationship into sensual realms. In a similar line of reasoning, literalist works are criticised for being fundamentally naturalistic and Fried considers that a kind of latent or hidden naturalism, indeed anthropomorphism, lies at the core of literalist theory and practice.

He argues that the problem with literalism is not that it is anthropomorphic, but that the meaning and, equally, the hiddenness of its anthropomorphism are incurably theatrical; the reasons being the 'size of much literalist work that compares fairly closely with that of the human body. He adds that another reason is that the 'literalist predilection for symmetry, and in general for a kind of order that is simply order [. . .] is rooted, not, as Judd seems to believe, in new philosophical and scientific principles, whatever he takes these to be, but in nature'.[93]

The apparent hollowness of most literalist work – the quality of having inside – is almost blatantly anthropomorphic, according to Fried, and like actual theatre, literalist work blurs the distinction between a timeless visual art and a temporal experience. He writes that it is neither 'the condition of music nor the condition of photography – definitely not theatre – to which art ought to aspire, but to the condition of painting and sculpture [. . .] the condition that is of existing in, indeed or secreting or constituting a continuous and perpetual present'. And he argues that modernist art's effect is a higher effect than mere presence; a presentness that transcends temporality (the condition that is of existing in a continuous or perceptual present). The viewer's experience of such art is, he suggests, 'one of continuous and spontaneous apperception. It is as though one's experience has no duration [. . .] because at every moment the work itself is wholly manifest'.[94]

Fried favours the modernist notion of presentness as opposed to minimalism's 'real' time' aesthetic, a moment of perpetual immediacy in which one could possibly see the work 'in its entirety [. . .] during this moment of presentness, one's conviction and self-knowledge would keep theatre momentarily – and only momentarily, at bay'.[95] This structure delineated a kind of ethics of duration, and taking sides inevitably entailed privileging one of the terms of that binary, modernist instantaneity or literalist duration that became synonymous with the theatre. Not because one in fact experiences a picture by Noland or Olitski or a sculpture by David Smith or Caro in no time at all, but as Fried argues:

> because at every moment the work itself is wholly manifest [. . .] It is this continuous and entire 'presentness' (a term I adopted in opposition to literalist 'presence'), amounting, as it were, to the perpetual creation of itself, that one experiences as a kind of instantaneousness as though if only one were infinitely more acute, a single infinitely brief instant would be long enough to see everything to experience the work in all its depth and fullness, to be forever convinced by it.[96]

The effect of presence has been associated with literalism, but the modernist perception of presence is debatable. According to Sayre, there are two separate poetics of the present, one largely modernist and the other postmodern. The modernist version sees in the 'present' the immediacy of experience, something like an authentic 'wholeness'; a sense of unity and completion that is the end of art. The postmodern poetics defines the present as perpetually and inevitably in media res, as part of an ongoing process, inevitably fragmentary, incomplete and multiplicitous. This would be a straightforward enough situation, however, as Sayre writes, 'for so many the recognition of the latter, in no way mitigates their nostalgia for the former. It is as if, having lost formalism, we necessarily long for its return, as if, having lost the present – or, rather, the fullness of presence – we are some how embarrassed to admit it'.[97]

The discussion about presence draws from diverse perspectives of temporality, and like Greenberg, Fried introduces the problematic distinction between real and conceptual temporality. However, Greenberg employs this distinction in order to underscore what he describes as an effective immediacy or real timelessness at a first glance. In 'Art and Objecthood' Fried insists on the instantaneousness of perception on an intellectual level. In other words, the real duration of experience can and has to be annihilated in the 'as though timelessness' of an intellectual moment. That moment of instantaneousness he defines in terms of a continuous and entire 'presentness' and this perceptual presentness is experienced as a privileged state of grace.[98] As Vickery argues, Fried apparently meant to convey something more precise than a simple striving after theatrical effect, especially in view of the fact that the term was not one that had any particular currency in art critical circles at the time.[99]

Fried's particular understanding of the term derives from Stanley Cavell's anti-Brechtian discussion of the difference between 'good and bad' theatre, between real theatre, as it were, and the constant threat of theatricality. Theatre works compellingly when we feel ourselves to be in immediate contact with the scene being enacted before us and at the same time when, according to Alex Potts:

> we are situated physically in a sphere apart, and thus undisturbed by the compulsion to respond to the actors as we would were we to feel we existed in the same space as them. Theatricality intervenes in this experience when we have the sense that the actors might recognize our being present, and so the question arises for us as to whether the scene taking place is real or illusory.[100]

Situation, duration, temporality, illusion, that is to say, theatricality, meant for Fried a breakdown of the intimate relationship between art and its viewer. Theatre's preoccupation with time, the duration of the event, is what modernist sensibility finds intolerable in the theatre. These experiences that persist in time, and more broadly the 'presentment' of duration, of time itself, as though it were some sort of literalist object, is central to the new aesthetic, in contrast to the experience of modernist painting and sculpture that had no duration (according to this reading). In conclusion, the 'theatrical' effect of these works represented a crisis in the definition of the art object.

Fried's argument associates the open-endedness or sense of duration of the minimalist object with its violation of the medium as theatrical; thus he describes the artworks of artists like Tony Smith, as presences of a sort and not sculptures[101] and these presences persist in time. He wants to emphasise that:

the experience in question persists in time, and the presentment of endless or indefinite duration [. . .] The literalist preoccupation with time – more precisely, with the duration of the experience – is, I suggest, paradigmatically theatrical, as though theatre confronts the beholder, and thereby isolates him, with the endlessness not just of objecthood but of time; or as though the sense which, at bottom, theatre addresses is a sense of temporality of time both passing and to come, simultaneously approaching and receding, as if apprehended in an infinite perspective.[102]

According to this reading, minimalist practice blurs the categorical distinction between aesthetic experience, the specular experience of ordinary empirical objects, and restricts interpretive practices, as a consequence of the notion of 'objecthood'. This term is primarily interpreted in the criticism of these works, as the subversion of artistic style. This is not an 'art-style', as Mel Bochner declares (in 1966): 'it will not "wither" with the passing season and go away. Its objects were industrially produced in rigid materials without any trace of the artist's hand. Its forms were those of an idealistically conceived geometry, rather than intuitive self-expression'.[103]

Nevertheless, since its dominant period (1963–8), it has come to seem a style, so much so that critics use 'minimalist' to categorise any painting or sculpture that is non-figurative, non-referential and non-narrative, or is remotely geometric. What makes minimal art special, though, Bochner argues, is 'its philosophical underpinnings. It expresses beliefs about the self and the self's perception of the world that are based on material – objecthood – and space as occupied by that material and the artists/viewer body. It is the condition of objecthood that elevates the work of art, theoretically from mere things in the world'.[104]

In-Between Objecthood and Personhood

Minimalist choreographers experiment with a range of strategies that redefine the structure, form, material, image and production of the art object in its relationship to space and to the spectator, while Beckett's work provides a closer analogue to minimalism (in the theatre).[105] The persistent search for irreducible essentials that scholars find in minimalist progressive simplifications and reductions is charged as being anti-art, but Strickland argues that it may be more accurate to call it anti-artifice.[106]

Minimalist works by Beckett and by artists including Yvonne Rainer, Simone Forti, John Cage, Agnes Martin and Frank Stella illustrate a significant shift in compositional methods, towards subtraction of representational registers, emphasis on objecthood (literalness), on the sculptural elements of dance practice and on the object of art. These artworks project visuality or literality. As Frank Stella declares, 'it really is an object [. . .] If the paintings were lean enough, accurate enough, or right enough, you would be able to just look at [them]. All I want anyone to get out of my paintings, and all I want to get out of them, is the fact that you see the whole idea without any confusion [. . .] What you see is what you see'.[107]

The minimalist paradigm points out material objecthood and is often employed for defining the spatial, gestural and durational extensions of artistic innovation. Jon Erickson argues that each art form reduces itself to a form of objecthood:

> in part, the rationalization of art, its will to self-knowledge and the attempt to eliminate all but its most absolutely essential features, can be seen as the will to autonomy from other, 'exterior' forces that would define it for their own purposes. Each particular form of art within modernism has engaged in this process – literature, painting, sculpture, music, dance, theatre – and in each, the relentless pursuit for understanding the essence of its formal properties has resulted in one or another kind of minimalism.[108]

For Erickson each medium has reduced itself to its most basic form of objecthood – sound, colour, plastic form and so on, but each has drawn attention to what gives that form its shape – silence, emptiness, stillness. This movement has 'even resulted in certain reversals of work that end up encroaching on the territory of other arts or disciplines: conceptual art's reliance on language, minimalism becoming body art then performance art, which slides into theoretical purview of theatre'.[109]

The notion of objecthood that is central to minimalism in the visual arts is differentiated from the notion of the 'personhood' of the live performer. Theatre is mostly defined by the performers' presence and personhood is the term used to define this notion. Artists emphasise the object-qualities of the human body by simultaneously de-emphasising their human qualities, and as part of their anti-theatrical methods, theatre practitioners, writers and choreographers have integrated strategies in order to diminish the 'personhood' of the performer. Yvonne Rainer writes in the 1970s (shortly after the performance of *Continuous Project – Altered Daily at the Whitney*) that she loves the duality of props, or objects, their usefulness and obstructiveness in relation to the human body. Moreover, Rainer focuses on the duality of the body; she writes of

> the body as a moving, thinking, decision-making entity and the body as an inert entity, object-like [. . .] oddly, the body can become object-like; the human being can be treated as an object, dealt with as an entity without feeling or desire. The body itself can be handled and manipulated as though lacking in the capacity for self-propulsion.[110]

Form is explored through the body's stillness or movement, and minimalist choreographers consider that dance pieces can be in some way plastic, sculptural and that the sculptural elements of the moving body are emphasised in their choreographies. Minimalist dance techniques explore a range of strategies that redefine the structure, form, material, image and production of the art object in its relationship to space and the spectator. The body becomes an exceptional medium for the exploration of the interplay between theatricality and 'anti-theatricality' in Beckett's minimalist practice.

The body is present and active, as object and agent, in a very different way from in other forms of theatre that employ actors. As Pierre Chabert notes, in Beckett's theatre the body is considered with minute attention and it is approached as a genuine raw material, like space, objects, light and language, which may be modified, sculpted, shaped and distorted for the stage. The words 'raw material' should be taken literally:

> whereas the actor's body is usually a 'given', which does not vary – aside from that part, which contributes to the 'composition' of the role (costume and make-up) – in Beckett's theatre the body undergoes metamorphoses. It is *worked*, violated even, much like the raw materials of the painter or sculptor, in the service of a systematic exploration of all possible relationships between the body and movement, the body and space, the body and light and the body and words.[111]

Oppenheim claims that art's 'end' resides in its consciousness and in its self-consciousness in the postmodernist explication of modernist self-definition. According to this standpoint, Beckett's minimalism is something more and not something less. The reduction of genre in the conflation of subject and object, the result of the dramatisation of the self-awareness at hand in his work is precisely what defeats the 'end'. As Oppenheim argues, to the extent that

> Beckett's is a totalizing art, namely, a synthesis of sight and sound, poetry and drama, literature and choreography, within its very minimalism, art as manifestation of the concrete universal has been revived. Its itinerary from a historical to a post-historical effort is accomplished, and the afterlife of Beckett's painterly writing may thus be said to lie – 'beyond minimalism' (to borrow from Brater), beyond the historicity of Hegel-cum-Danto's philosophical analysis – in its re-essentializing, which is to say re-humanizing, of art.[112]

Critics like Bert States and Jon Erickson endow theory with a more comprehensive and far-reaching account of the context of anti-art by contrasting art to aesthetics. Art is a vital force whose force depends upon a free practice, as Erickson argues:

that will posit itself against the standard ethos of its age, attempting to either avoid categorization, and so stand outside of judgment, or create a new category that defies the judgment of its age, as a wilful negation. Art as such can only effectively exist in protean form [. . .] the so-called anti-art movements are but a further extension of the desire for an art autonomous from aesthetic, thereby social control. Anti-art movements are not anti-art at all, but anti-aesthetics. We recall that too many scholars still refer to nouveau theatre as anti-theatre.[113]

Modernist art historians tend to concentrate on the historical contexts of painting and often employ general notions of theatricality as a way to explain the frameworks that establish these contexts. Therefore Fried's theory has provoked countless and intense critical responses, in the field of theatre and art theory, as a distinctly restricted and decidedly negative view of theatricality. Fried has been much criticised by theorists who argue that he explicitly conflates ontological questions with aesthetic ones.[114] Nevertheless, his contemporaries endorse the performative and durational turn and see theatricality as an art historical turning point and indeed after the late 1960s art practice shifted towards the creation of the 'open work of art' and against medium-specificity. The following chapter focuses on alternative interpretations that attempt to uncover the assumptions that prevail in Fried's evaluative discourse, as it is exposed in his criticism of theatricality in the visual arts, while the terms 'non-art', 'presentness', 'conviction' and 'medium-specificity' are set into a critical backdrop.

NOTES

An extract of this chapter was presented at 'Beckett and Company, a Centenary Conference on Samuel Beckett and the Arts'. Part of the 2006 global Samuel Beckett centennial celebrations and in collaboration with the London Consortium; Birkbeck, University of London; and Goldsmiths, University of London. A three-day celebration of Samuel Beckett's continuing impact on contemporary arts, jointly hosted by Tate Modern and Goldsmiths, University of London.

1. Will Insley. In Donald, Droll and Jane Nicol (eds), *Abstract Painting: 1960–69*. New York: The Institute of Art and Urban Resources, 1983: n.p.
2. Hobson quotes Beckett as saying, when he was interviewed as the dramatist of the year, after the production of *Endgame*, 'I am interested in the shape of ideas even if I do not believe in them. There is a wonderful sentence in Augustine. Do not despair; one of the thieves was saved. Do not presume; one of the thieves was damned. That sentence has a wonderful shape. It is the shape that matters' (Harold Hobson. 'Samuel Beckett – Dramatist of the Year', *International Theatre Annual*, 1956: 153).
3. Beckett, Samuel. 'Three Dialogues: Samuel Beckett and Georges Duthuit', *Transition*, 49.5 (ed. Georges Duthuit) (1949): 101.
4. Oppenheim quoted in Ratcliff, Carter. *Out of the Box: The Reinvention of Art 1965–1975*. New York: Allworth Press, 2000: 25.
5. The initial extract, entitled 'Dialogue Samuel Beckett–Georges Duthuit', is

Beckett's own translation of the third dialogue into French, and was published in a brochure by Galerie Michel Warren for a Bram van Velde exhibition held in Paris, 7 May–1 June 1957. The same year, an extract entitled 'Samuel Beckett et la peinture' appeared in the 'Notes' section of *Nouvelle Revue Francaise IX* (1 June 1957). This passage, once again in French (although not by Beckett's hand), quotes a short paragraph from the middle of the third dialogue, as well as the long final response by B. The same passage, and another short selection from Beckett's article 'Peintres de l'empechement (1948)', are quoted in a catalogue entitled *Bram van Velde*, with texts by Samuel Beckett, Georges Duthuit, and Jacques Putman (Paris: Georges Fall, 1958), and in the two variant American editions of this text: a Grove Press edition, in which the shorter passage is eliminated (New York: Grove Press, 1960), and an edition produced by Harry N. Abrams, which includes the short quote from 'Peintres', and adds an extract from 'Three Dialogues' on the dust jacket as well (New York: Harry N. Abrams, 1962). The complete text of 'Three Dialogues' was not reprinted until 1965, when Martin Esslin included the essay in *Samuel Beckett: A Collection of Critical Essays*, and John Calder produced a collection entitled *Proust and Three Dialogues with Georges Duthuit*. Later extracts include an 'Excerpt from a Dialogue between Samuel Beckett and Georges Duthuit', that appeared in the exhibition catalogue for 'Bram van Velde: Paintings 1957–1967' held in New York, 2–7 April 1968 (New York: M. Knoedler, 1968), and two extracts that were used in the exhibition catalogue 'Bram van Velde' (Paris: Centre National d'Arte Contemporain, 1970). In Hatch, David A. *Beckett in (t)Transition: Three Dialogues with Georges Duthuit, Aesthetic Evolution, and an Assault on Modernism*. Tallahassee: The Florida State University DigiNole Commons Electronic Theses, Treatises and Dissertations, The Graduate School, 2003: 3.
6. Cohn, Ruby (ed.). *Disjecta: Miscellaneous Writings and a Dramatic Fragment*. London: John Calder, 1983.
7. Hatch, David A. *Beckett in (t)Transition*.
8. Ibid.
9. Statement on 25 June 1965. See Lois Oppenheim (ed.). *Palgrave Advances in Samuel Beckett Studies*. London: Palgrave Macmillan, 2004: 197.
10. See Hesla, David H. *The Shape of Chaos: An Interpretation of the Art of Samuel Beckett*. Minneapolis: University of Minnesota Press, 1971.
11. Driver, T. F. 'Beckett by the Madeleine', *Columbia University Forum*, iv (Summer 1961): 22–3.
12. Hatch, David A. *Beckett in (t)Transition*: 78.
13. Beckett, Samuel. *Proust and the Three Dialogues with Georges Duthuit*. London: Calder, 1965: 103.
14. Oppenheim, Lois. *The Painted Word: Samuel Beckett's Dialogue with Art*. Ann Arbor: University of Michigan Press, 2000: 3.
15. See Cope, Richard. *Re-Reading Samuel Beckett's Three Dialogues with George Duthuit within the Context of the Continuum it Nourished*, PhD thesis. London: South Bank University, 2006.
16. Blau, Herbert. 'Apnea and True Illusion: Breath(less) in Beckett', *Modern Drama*, 49.4 (Winter 2006): 460.
17. Carla Locatelli concludes from the passage quoted that in Beckett's view, a 'pure interrogation' can only be structured as a subtraction (of rhetoric from the rhetorical question). In Locatelli, Carla. *Unwording the World: Samuel's Beckett's Fiction after the Nobel Prize*. Philadelphia: University of Pennsylvania Press, 1990: 172.

18. Cope, Richard. *Re-Reading Samuel Beckett's Three Dialogues*: 10.
19. Tonning, Erik. *Abstraction in Samuel Beckett's Drama for Stage and Screen 1962–1985*. Oxford: Peter Lang, 2007: 8.
20. Fifield, Peter. *Late Modernist Style in Samuel Beckett and Emmanuel Levinas, New Interpretations of Beckett in the 21st Century*. London: Palgrave Macmillan, 2013.
21. Casanova, Pascale. *Samuel Beckett: Anatomy of a Literary Revolution*. New York: Verso, 2006: 21.
22. See Ratcliff, Carter. *Out of the* Box: 21.
23. Krauss, Rosalind. *Passages in Modern Sculpture*. New York: Viking Press, 1977: 129. Quoted in Bleeker, Maaike. 'Passages in Post-Modern Theory: Mapping the Apparatus', *Parallax*, 14.1 (2008): 56.
24. In Tonning, Erik. *Abstraction in Samuel Beckett's Drama for Stage and Screen 1962–1985*. Oxford: Peter Lang, 2007: 8, 17.
25. Ibid.: 17.
26. As Tonning concludes, it becomes evident from Beckett's writings that an 'abstract language', should develop specific technical means of achieving new kinds of expressive force if it is to be artistically effective.
27. Beckett, Samuel. *Bram van Velde*. New York: Grove Press, 1960: 125.
28. Erik Tonning argues that Beckett's technique approaches mere formal game-playing. See Erik Tonning. *Abstraction in Samuel Beckett's Drama*.
29. Doherty, Francis. *Samuel Beckett*. London: Hutchinson, 1971: 75.
30. Deleuze, Gilles. 'The Exhausted', *SubStance*, 24.3 (1995): 24.
31. Albright, Daniel. *Beckett and Aesthetics*. Cambridge: Cambridge University Press, 2003: 1.
32. Knowlson, James and Knowlson, Elizabeth (eds). *Beckett Remembering Beckett: A Centenary Celebration*. New York: Arcade, 2006: 104.
33. Samuel Beckett is quoted in Shenker, Israel. 'Moody Man of Letters', *New York Times*, Section 2 (5 May, 1956): 3.
34. In Oppenheim, Lois. *The Painted Word*: 1.
35. Devlin, Devis. 'Intercessions', *Transition*, 27 (May–April 1938): 94.
36. Harmon, Maurice (ed.). *No Author Better Served: The Correspondence of Samuel Beckett and Alan Schneider*. Cambridge, MA and London: Harvard University Press, 1998: 24.
37. Quoted in Alvarez, A. *Samuel Beckett*. New York: Viking, 1973: 86.
38. Connor, Steven. *Samuel Beckett: Repetition, Theory and Text*. New York: Blackwell, 1988: 208.
39. See analysis about Beckett's 'closure' in the Conclusion.
40. Abbott, Porter. *Beckett Writing Beckett: The Author in the Autograph*. Ithaca, NY: Cornell University Press, 1996: 23.
41. In Blau, Herbert. 'Apnea and True Illusion: Breath(less) in Beckett', *Modern Drama*, 49.4, (Winter 2006): 452–68, 17, 135.
42. Lessing, Gotthold-Ephraim. *Laocoön: An Essay on the Limits of Painting and Poetry*. Indianapolis: Bobbs-Merrill, 1962: 91.
43. See Krauss, Rosalind. *Passages in Modern Sculpture*: 4.
44. See Fried, Michael. 'An Introduction to my Art Criticism'. In *Art and Objecthood Essays and Reviews*, Chicago: University of Chicago Press, 1998: 1–74.
45. See Cohn, Ruby. *A Beckett Canon*. Ann Arbor: University of Michigan Press, 2001: 298.
46. Quoted in Bair, Deirdre. *Samuel Beckett: A Biography*. London, Picador, 1980: 433.
47. Visual articulation is based on lighting design.

48. Garner, Stanton. 'Visual Field in Beckett's Late Plays', *Comparative Drama*, XXI.4 (1987–8): 371.

49. Essif, Les. *Empty Figure on an Empty Stage: The Theatre of Samuel Beckett and his Generation*. Bloomington: Indiana University Press, 2001: 61.

50. According to Hauck, 'Beckett moved his drama as close to silence and inaction as a playwright can decently get and still remained a practicing playwright [. . .] He has not only changed many opinions on what is supposed to happen when we enter the theatre, but has also redefined the minima of valid theatrical performance'. In Hauck, Gerhard. *Reductionism in Drama and the Theatre: The Case of Samuel Beckett*. Potomac, MD: Scripta Humanistica 1992: 77.

51. Beckett has influenced the development of modern theatre and dramatic literature by defining the boundaries of drama and genre closely, by questioning them more radically. As Hauck argues,

> he researched on form and brought the rhythm, tone, colour and melody of a play to centre stage and that was precisely what was responsible for the crossing of boundaries from drama to something else. His works approximate to the presentational conditions of painting, sculpture and music, while they approach the point where their classification qua drama becomes difficult to maintain. Approaches to Beckett's representational reductionism may all be considered as homogenous or intra-disciplinary, i.e. located within the framework of drama and the theatre. Further complications arise out of the fact that both intra-scientific and inter-scientific reductions are feasible, whereby the former would describe reductions from drama and theatre to some other art form. There is also, appears to be, some evidence of heterogeneous, interdisciplinary reductions taking place. Reductions to other art forms concern the pervasive tendency to reduce drama and theatre to other art forms, notably, sculpture, music and painting'. (Ibid.: 75)

52. See http://www.walkerart.org/collections/publications/performativity/performativity-and-its-addressee/

53. Fried, Michael. 'An Introduction to my Art Criticism': 151.

54. Ibid.

55. See Krauss, Rosalind. *A Voyage on the North Sea: Art in the Age of the Post-Medium Condition*. London: Thames and Hudson, 2000: 53–4. Krauss discusses the work of Marcel Broodhaers along the threads of conceptual art, television and poststructuralist theory.

56. Ibid.: 53–4.

57. See https://monoskop.org/Postmedia#cite_note-8

58. Krauss, Rosalind. *A Voyage on the North Sea*: 64.

59. Hawker, Rosemary. 'Idiom Post-medium: Richter Painting Photography', *Oxford Art Journal*, 32.2 (June 2009): 263–80, and 'Painting over Photography: Questions of Medium in Richter's Overpaintings', *Australian and New Zealand Journal of Art*, 8.1, Post-Medium (2007): 42–59.

60. Albright, Daniel. *Beckett and Aesthetics*: 1.

61. See Shane Weller's review of Beckett's 1948 essay 'Peintres de l' empêchement'. Weller, Shane. *A Taste for the Negative: Beckett and Nihilism*. Oxford: Legenda, 2005.

62. See Batchelor, David. *Minimalism*. Cambridge: Cambridge University Press, 1997.

63. Hawker, Rosemary. 'The Idiom in Photography as the Truth in Painting', *The South Atlantic Quarterly*, 101.3 (Summer 2002): 544.

64. Koch, Gertrude. 'The Richter Scale of Blur', *October*, 62 (Fall 1992): 137.
65. In Hawker, Rosemary. 'The Idiom in Photography': 541–54. Also, see Fried, Michael. *Why Photography Matters as Art as Never Before*. New Haven, CT and London: Yale University Press, 2008.
66. See http://www.walkerart.org/collections/publications/performativity/performati vity-and-its-addressee/
67. Ibid.
68. *Breathe* is a component of the larger project REPEAT that debuted at the Teatro La Fenice in Venice in 2008 and at the nearby Fondazione Bevilacqua La Masa in San Barnaba, Italy. Producer: Wesley Miller and Nick Ravich; camera: Bob Elfstrom; sound: Ray Day; editors: Paulo Padilha and Mark Sutton. Artwork Courtesy: William Kentridge.
69. See Krauss, Rosalind. *A Voyage on the North Sea*: 64.
70. The piece was presented at Documenta X in Kassel in 1997.
71. The numbers within the group fluctuated, and were around thirty from 1976.
72. See http://www.worldofart.org/english/99/99charlytxang2.htm [accessed 1/11/ 2016].
73. See the works of Donald Judd.
74. See Hawker, Rosemary. 'Callum Morton's Architecture of Disguised Difference'. In A. L. Macarthur and J. Macarthur (eds), *Architecture, Disciplinarity, and the Arts*. Brussels: A&S Books, 2009: 151–65.
75. Quoted in *Eye of the Storm*, 'Interview'. In *Michael Craig-Martin: Eye of the Storm*. Exhibition CD-ROM. New York: Gagosian Gallery, 2003.
76. Smith, Terry. *Impossible Presence: Surface and Screen in the Photogenic Era*. Chicago and London: University of Chicago Press, 2001: 3.
77. The installation was presented at LACMA Los Angeles, California, USA in 2013.
78. See http://jamesturrell.com
79. Hughes, Gordon. 'Tangled Up in Blue: James Turrell's Virtual Vision'. In http:// nonsite.org/article/tangled-up-in-blue [accessed 27/07/2017].
80. See Foster, Hal. 'After the White Cube', *London Review of Books*, 37.6 (2015): 25–6. In https://www.lrb.co.uk/v37/n06/hal-foster/after-the-white-cube [accessed 7/07/2017].
81. Ibid.
82. Unsal, Merve. 'Minimalist Art vs Modernist Sensibility: A Close Reading of Michael Fried's Art and Objecthood', in http://www.artandeducation.net/paper/ minimalist-art-vs-modernist-sensibility-a-close-reading-of-michael-frieds-art- and-objecthood/
83. Hauck, Gerhard. *Reductionism in Drama and the Theatre*: 77.
84. Lehmann, Hans-Thies. *Postdramatic Theatre*. London and New York: Routledge, 2006: 157.
85. Ibid.
86. See Greenberg, Clement. 'Modernist Painting'. In John O'Brian (ed.), *Clement Greenberg: The Collected Essays and Criticism*. Chicago: University of Chicago Press, 1986–93, vol. 4: 85–93. In Unsal, Merve. 'Minimalist Art vs Modernist Sensibility: A Close Reading of Michael Fried's Art and Objecthood'. See http:// www.artandeducation.net/paper/minimalist-art-vs-modernist-sensibility-a-close- reading-of-michael-frieds-art-and-objecthood/
87. Unsal, Merve. 'Minimalist Art vs Modernist Sensibility: A Close Reading of Michael Fried's Art and Objecthood'. See http://www.artandeducation.net/paper/ minimalist-art-vs-modernist-sensibility-a-close-reading-of-michael-frieds-art- and-objecthood/

88. Fried, Michael. *Art and Objecthood Essays and Reviews*. Chicago and London: University of Chicago Press, 1998: xviii. See also whole 'Preface' and 'Acknowledgements'.
89. Nevertheless, by and large, Fried and Greenberg express different accounts of modernism.
90. Fried, Michael. 'An Introduction to my Art Criticism': 156.
91. Puchner, Martin. *Stage Fright: Modernism, Anti-Theatricality and Drama*. Baltimore and London: Johns Hopkins University Press, 2002: 3.
92. Ibid.
93. Fried, Michael. 'An Introduction to My Art Criticism': 156.
94. Ibid.: 167.
95. Fried, Michael. 'Art and Objecthood'. In *Minimal Art: A Critical Anthology*, New York: E. P. Dutton, 1968: 45.
96. Fried, Michael. 'An Introduction to my Art Criticism': 45.
97. Sayre, Henry. *The Object of Performance: The American Avant-Garde since 1970*. Chicago and London: University of Chicago Press, 1989: 175.
98. Fried, Michael. 'Art and Objecthood': 141
99. Costello, Diarmuid and Vickery, Jonathan. *Art: Key Contemporary Thinkers*. Oxford: Oxford University Press, 2007: 71–3.
100. Potts, Alex. *The Sculptural Imagination: Figurative, Modernist, Minimalist*. New Haven, CT: Yale University Press, 2000: 188.
101. Tony Smith added that Fried didn't think of them as sculptures, but as presences of a sort, which he speaks of in 'Art and Objecthood'.
102. Fried, Michael. 'An Introduction to my Art Criticism': 167.
103. Quoted in Lambert, Carrie. 'More or Less Minimalism: Performance and Visual Art in the 1960s'. In *A Minimal Future? Art as Object 1958–1968*. The Museum of Contemporary Art Los Angeles. Cambridge, MA: The MIT Press, 2004: 133.
104. Ibid.
105. See Strickland, Edward. *Minimalism: Origins*. Bloomington and Indianapolis: Indiana University Press, 1993.
106. Ibid.
107. Battcock, Gregory. *Minimal Art: A Critical Anthology*. Los Angeles: University of California Press, 1996: 158.
108. Erickson, Jon. *The Fate of the Object: From Modern Object to Postmodern Sign in Performance, Art, and Poetry*. Ann Arbor: University of Michigan Press, 1995: 13.
109. Ibid.
110. Yvonne Rainer, quoted in Banes, Sally. *Democracy's Body: Judson Dance Theatre, 1962–1964*. Durham, NC: Duke University Press, 1993: 10.
111. Chabert, Pierre. 'The Body in Beckett's Theatre', *Journal of Beckett Studies*, 8 (Autumn 1982): 23.
112. In Oppenheim, Lois. *The Painted Word: Beckett's Dialogue with Art*: 62. Bert States introduces the opposition of anti-sign (theatrical anti-conventions) to sign (theatrical conventions). He explains that anti-sign becomes sign through an attempt to break into the circuit of convention, to pester the circuit with nuance, to wound it with the resistance of its presence. As he writes, 'the sign began, as an image, in which the known world was, in some sense being recreated or revised out of its primal linguistic matter. But what human awareness preceded the primal linguistic matter?' States, Bert O. *Great Reckonings in Little Rooms: On the Phenomenology of Theatre*. Los Angeles: University of California Press: 1985: 12.

113. Erickson, Jon. *The Fate of the Object*: 34.
114. See Jones, Amelia and Stephenson, Andrew (eds). *Performing the Body/Performing the Text*. London: Routledge, 1999; and Jones, Amelia (ed.). *A Companion to Contemporary Art since 1945*. Malden, MA: Blackwell Publishing, 2006.

2

THE DURATIONAL TURN: ABSORPTION AND THE SPECIFICITY OF TEMPORALITY

Ever tried. Ever failed[1]

The ever-expanding site of practice in the sixties and the forms of art that flourished, in which the common distinctions between media were deliberately transgressed, is at the core of Fried's critique, since it challenges the conventions of spectatorship. The experience of the artwork related to a widespread shift in spatiotemporal conditions of artistic practice, credited with drawing attention to the temporal and contextual realities of the viewer's experience in relationship to art. Nevertheless, the move to installation practices certainly has not resulted in a complete dissolution of the sculptural object, as Alex Potts argues, 'not the distinctive structures of response elicited by a traditional sculpture. Rather it has entailed a progressive abandonment of the assumption prevalent in much nineteenth- and twentieth- century aesthetics that the authentic art object has to be completely self sufficient, its significance unaffected by the circumstances of its display'.[2]

The minimal object's very resistance to the viewer's effort to 'read' its terms served only to force what would be 'the work' back toward the viewers, prompting their own engagement with performance. This shift from a representational to a performative practice meant that the event surrounding the exhibition of the work became as important as the work itself. Fried realised that this shift and the multifaceted discourse that was developing on aesthetic perception, dislocation and experience alluded to a total control of the mise-en-scène, that becomes as significant as the work itself, while the embodied reception of visual artworks is a process that can be engaged as performative. By placing the work outside the gallery, land art and site-specific sculpture generated a phenomenologically informed focus upon the conditions of encounters with artworks; that is to say the embodied perception of physical objects and events in time and space.

Fried's account of the relationship between the visual arts and the theatre is problematic since he considers that installations offer their audience a kind of heightened perpetual experience. He wanted to understand the nature of 'that surefire', and therefore to his mind 'essentially inartistic (I should have said unmodernist), effect'. As he argues, he quickly realised that the basis of that effect was that both:

> work and installation (in a sense the installation was the work, as Thierry de Duve has emphasized) solicited and included the beholder in a way that was fundamentally antithetical to the expressive and presentational mode of the recent painting and sculpture I mostly admired. And that led to a further claim that the present moment in advanced art was marked by an irreconcilable conflict between the 'theatrical' work-in-situations of the literalists and the 'anti-theatrical' painting and sculpture of the radically abstract artists I championed.[3]

Fried's claim that the worst aspect of minimalism is the manifestation of unlimited durationality and his binarism between modernist presentness and minimalist real time in 'Art and Objecthood' was bound to be controversial, but few could have anticipated the full extent of the notoriety that was in store; this notoriety is describable only in retrospect.[4] Fifty-five years on since the 1960s and the art world has clearly taken a performative and durational turn. Jacki Apple, who organised the exhibition 'Alternatives in Retrospect: An Historical Overview, 1969–1975' at the New Museum in 1981, argues about the late 1960s and mid-1970s New York art scene, that the majority of the works were process oriented and situationally specific, involving a relationship between materials, concepts, actions and locations. They were sometimes spontaneous, improvisational, open-ended and often collaborative. The works existed within a given time and then ceased to exist. As a result much of this work, according to Apple:

> was labelled 'ephemeral', the intent being to create an experience rather than a product, and new terms were devised to describe it, such as 'installation' and 'performance' [. . .] During the period in which this exhibition deals, artists out of necessity created and took control of their own contexts.[5]

Fried defines the contours of late modernism in the visual arts and describes the 1960s, especially in 'Art and Objecthood', as 'the last great moment in modernist art'. Further analysis is required regarding the theorist's account of the visual arts and the theatre as problematic.

He tends to concentrate on the historical contexts of painting and frequently employs general notions of theatricality as a way to explain the frameworks that establish those contexts. Among the theorists who influenced Fried were Greenberg, whom he regarded as the foremost art critic of the twentieth century, and also the philosophers Stanley Cavell, J. L. Austin and Ludwig Wittgenstein.

Fried's criticism is marked by philosophical inconsistencies and, in the field of theatre and art theory, his discourse provokes various and intense critical responses, as a distinctly restricted, reductive and decidedly negative view of theatricality. These critical inconsistencies are based on the inability to determine what constitutes the specificity of the medium. Elkins wonders if this appears as a betrayal of modernist faith in media-specificity:

> if that isn't because modernist criticism has a structural inability to determine what constitutes the specificity of a medium. Medium specificity is either presented as a given – an inherent set of properties comprising 'all that [is] unique in the nature' of each medium – or else as a historical fable, now jettisoned in the 'age of the post-medium condition'.[6]

INSTALLATION ART AND AVANT-GARDE PRACTICES

Processes of boundary dissolution internal to the arts, instances of hybridisation or 'cross-over', mutual processes of importation between the arts and the extra-artistic sphere and cross-disciplinary approaches are certain of the most significant aspects of recent aesthetics and cultural production. Contemporary art contextualises the radical shift in art's boundaries that began in the last century and the art world has increasingly assimilated artists' experiments with new media and new contexts. Longstanding sites of production, consumption and display of art – such as the theatre, the museum and the gallery – are being challenged by new methods and media.

Crucial to this process has been the redefinition of the relationship between works and their surrounding space, the concept of the work of art and the spectator's mode of reception (diverging receptions) in terms of presence, embodiment and representation. Both the development of visual culture and the proclamations of the performative turn confirm the belief that the relationship between spectator and artwork is tangled.

Accordingly, the practice of installation art (that developed into a genre in its own right during the 1960s) incorporates all kinds of media and techniques by combining them in many different ways. Installation art is situated on the threshold between the visual arts and the stage, having both performative and static features. As a genre, installation art is associated with the structuring of various objects and materials to create a complex spatial environment within the exhibition space, and does not entail unique formal and technical qualities believed to be intrinsic to this particular type of work. The site of meaning in these works shifts from an inner, formal structure to the shared presence of work and beholder. Installation art is also associated with the creation of an almost architectural construction that the viewer must enter in order to experience its spatiality from within.

The viewer is therefore aware that the installation is an artificial construction, not part of a 'life world' and there is a theatrical side to this awareness that is emphasised. As Ilya Kabakov argues, 'the viewers should not forget that before them is deceit and that everything has been made "intentionally", specially, in order to create an impression. Everything should remind him of the stage in a theatre [. . .]'.

> this 'social recognisability' by the viewers of the place where they find themselves is extraordinarily important for the total installation because they know how to behave in it, where and how to move in such an interior. It is this movement, this travel in the 'social' medium of the installation that is one of the most important artistic means in working with the total installation [. . .][7]

The artwork's 'lived physical perspective'[8] describes its spatial orientation to the viewer's body. As Aristotle states, the mimetic arts differ from one another in three respects: 'by producing mimesis in different media, of different objects, or in different modes'.[9] However, the physical materiality of the artwork, namely, the 'thinghood' of the work of art and the notion of mimesis are reconsidered by modernist theorists as inevitable and at the same time as that which art must always turn against.

According to this reading, the modernist work aspires to defeat or suspend its own objecthood, whereas the minimalist work (art object) becomes and projects its own objecthood. The notion of 'thinghood' has been predominant in the theory of art, as Adorno argues in his *Aesthetic Theory*,[10] 'the perennial revolt of art against art has its fundamentum in re'.[11] Adorno suggests that if it is essential to artworks that they be things, it is no less essential that they negate their own status as things, and thus art turns against art. The totally 'objectivated' artwork, he says, 'would congeal into a mere thing, whereas if it altogether evaded objectivation it would regress to an impotently powerless impulse and flounder in the empirical world'.[12] And he adds 'what appears in artworks is neither to be separated from their appearance nor to be held simply identical with it – the nonfactual in their facticity – is their spirit':

it makes artworks, things among things, something other than thing. Indeed artworks are only able to become other than thing by becoming a thing, though not through their localization in space and time but only by an immanent process of reification that makes them self-same, self-identical.[13]

The 'avant-gardes'[14] of the earlier twentieth century have succeeded in significantly modifying the notion of artwork and its 'thinghood' by opening up new contents and forms against aesthetic formalism. The artists challenge the boundary between artwork and its presentational situation and attempt to change art's social reality and autonomy with temporal and body-based practices, by dematerialising the art object or by emphasising its 'thinghood' to the extent of eliminating the boundary between art and 'non-art'. The concept of autonomy is used in an institutional sense; the avant-gardist movements criticise the functioning of autonomous art and attack the institution of Art [die Institution Kunst],[15] while they disclose the interdependence of art and society.

The mimetic economy of these late avant-garde[16] art practices often differentiate the 'visible' elements of representation (in the classic sense of the word) from the 'invisible' (elements of abstraction). Western avant-garde art practices aim to distance themselves both from the static objects of the visual arts and from the dramatic, text-based theatre of the stage,[17] through a process of juxtaposition of multiple registers of sensory experience – the spatial and the temporal, the textual and the imagistic – into pieces that were intentionally disjunctive and lacking in unity. This practice questions the nature and specificity of the artistic medium (and discipline), its place within artistic modernism, the institutions through which work is presented and the possible modes of spectatorial engagement in order to articulate a vision of intermedia assemblage. These late avant-garde practices establish an aesthetic and conceptual framework that developed further.

Recent developments in the visual arts and the theatre have resulted in increasing overlap, mutual infiltration and obliteration of boundaries. Diverse artistic phenomena are referred to as 'theatre' and many disciplines of art, such as performance and installation art, are making use of theatrical conventions. Artistic practice involves considerable 'theatricalisation' and theatrical productions employ new media and other artistic activity, thus triggering concerns regarding the subjugation of one art form by another.

These developments illustrate the ways in which art practice has undergone a 'performative turn'.[18] Both the development of visual culture and the proclamations of the performative turn confirm the belief that the relationship between spectator and work of art is complex. The performative turn is linked to a critique of the textual culture and theorists have called for a new performative turn, one that will transform the solid and fixed textual culture of the past, as Erika Fischer-Lichte argues,

> into a fluid, ever-changing performative culture of the future that will grant the missing dimensions. Theatre can contribute to the performative turn required when it sets out to treat the text as if it were part of an oral tradition. The fixed text has to be dismembered in order to allow the ever-changing performance to emerge.[19]

The performative turn from a textual to a performative culture points to new possibilities for the theatricalisation of politics, economics, law, arts and everyday life, establishing theatre and performing arts as a cultural mode (from a perspective of culture as performance). This turn that is specific to the 1960s has determined the way art is received and has altered the interaction between spectators and works of art.

Artworks and installations experiment with the theatrical, the spectacular and the scenic and share certain performative qualities and the ability to activate the spectator in a phenomenological and bodily manner. The performative turn draws on a shift from the paradigm of 'representation' to techniques of art/performance and focuses on the exercise of a bodily expounded, 'performative approach'.[20] Julia Walker interprets performance as modernism's 'return of the repressed', and it is against the background of the text/performance split that she wishes to understand the past fifty years' renewed interest in 'performance' as a term of critical analysis. For if, as she says,

> the performative dimension of language was repressed by a certain influential strain of literary modernism, then perhaps this postmodern turn to performance is simply a case of modernism's 'return of the repressed'. Think, for example, of Futurism, Dada, Surrealism, Absurdism, Artaudian cruelty, Happenings, Body Art, Fluxus, political street theatre, feminist performance art, and the experimental 'theatre of images' where performance has often been the avant-garde's favourite mode of resisting the status quo. Whether understood as abstract reason, the law, the law of the father, narrative logic, or conventional forms of representation, that status quo has often been figured as language – the defining limitation that performance strains against and seeks to explode.[21]

Walker highlights the linguistic referent implicit in avant-garde performances such as 'F. T. Marinetti's "onomatopoetic artillery", Hugo Ball's "sound poems", Andre Breton and Philippe Soupault's "automatic writing", Antonin Artaud's "animated hieroglyphs", Carolee Schneemann's "Interior Scroll", Yvonne Rainer's "non-verbal theatre", Ntozake Shange's "choreopoem", or Richard Foreman's "aural tableaux"'. Nevertheless, while the visual arts and the theatre share 'performative' as a common lexical term, this term often has polar associations in these different contexts.

The rhetoric of an isolated and purified opticality appeared in mid-century aesthetics[22] but other forms of aesthetics that oppose this opticality were also in use at the time.[23] Rather than cohering into medium-specificity these art practices challenge the nature and specificity of art, its place within modernism and the possible modes of its spectatorial engagement while they attempt to 'open' the work, to juxtapose multiple media – the spatial and the temporal, the textual and the imagistic – into pieces that are intentionally disjunctive and lacking in autonomy. Both aesthetically and conceptually, these practices established an early foundation for the post-war tradition of expanded art and intermedia practice that would emerge and develop internationally over the quarter century to come.

During the 1970s, according to Fried's reconsideration of his theory, evaluative art criticism no longer mattered as it previously had; with the ever-growing eclipse of high modernism in the later 1960s and the 1970s (and after) the role of criticism became transformed. Fried's criticism is intimately linked with the values, qualities and aspirations of the high-modernist art he found so compelling, while the theorist's evaluative art criticism marked one of the most vexed points of intersection of critical discourses in the theatre and the visual arts.[24]

AESTHETICS OR ONTOLOGY

Fried's criticism, the binary structuring of his themes and the evaluative hierarchy he sets up between theatrical and anti-theatrical art is considered by critics as reductive, but also as anachronistic and conservative, due to its formalist and idealist approach. The cardinal problem is that Fried did not acknowledge the heterogeneity of minimalism and excluded the broader contextual considerations. Parallel to this, his discourse is based on ideological assumptions, platitudes (art and 'non-art' dichotomy) and philosophical inconsistencies. These aesthetic value judgements received rigorous criticism, especially by theorists who supported the 'performative turn' in the visual arts.

Amelia Jones attempts to expose what she considers as the hidden assumptions that underlie his criticism of minimalist art, by criticising Fried's work as an important object of analysis precisely because it stages so obviously, and with such rhetorical style, the oppositional logic and lack of self-reflexivity that continues to characterise the practices of art history and art criticism. Ironically, as Jones argues, Fried's essay, which excoriates the theatricality of minimalist art, is highly theatrical and thus 'exposes, while it attempts to veil, Fried's investment in closing down the engagements that these works so aggressively solicit'. The theorist interprets such works as paradigmatic of a debasement of the pure aesthetics of modernism, a debasement that, not incidentally, takes place precisely through the objects' supposed evacuation (again Bourdieu's terms) of both ethical resistance and, as Jones argues:

> aesthetics neutralization [. . . of] the essentially human power of suspending immediate, animal attachment to the sensible [. . .] It is these objects and their kind, then, that Fried, with a startling lack of self-awareness differentiates from modernism, which he positions as both 'good art' and 'art' tout court Minimalist works (which he labels 'literalist') are 'ideological' (as opposed to the wholly manifest objects of modernism); anthropomorphic (versus the putative self sufficiency of 'good', that is modernist, art); corrupted and perverted by theatre, and, ultimately antithetical to art.[25]

Jones focuses on certain key moments of Fried's critique in order to uncover the assumptions (that she considers) he cleverly covers over with the veil of authority, provided by a loosely Kantian structure of aesthetic judgement. She argues that in order to stage this oppositional hierarchy of good and bad, 'art and non-art', and so as to naturalise it as compelling and truthful, Fried explicitly conflates ontological questions with aesthetic ones, namely, that modernist discourse leads to the problem that what constitutes the art of painting and what constitutes good painting are no longer separable. According to this reading, Fried's discourse strategically conceals his own assumptions about the value of art, by implying that the value is somehow inherent in the ontological structure of the works themselves. This aesthetic 'value' (that, again, Fried conflates with the very art status of the work) is assigned to works of art on extremely tenuous ground. Jones characterises the texts as inflated rhetoric and authoritative posing and suggests that Fried's only argument is that the sole criterion of a work's value is whether or not it is capable of compelling conviction. In Fried's 'tendentious' view, she argues, 'literalist works fail to compel conviction, while the literalists have largely avoided the issue of value or quality'.[26]

TONY SMITH'S RIDE: THE CONTROVERSIAL BINARY BETWEEN ART AND NON-ART

Greenberg is the first art theorist of the modern movement to draw the borderline between "art and non-art', paving the way with his critique of what he calls the look of 'non-art'. The look of machinery, he explains, is shunned now because it does not go far enough towards the look of non-art, 'which is presumably an inert look that offers the eye a minimum of "interesting" incident – unlike the machine look, which is arty by comparison. Still, no matter how simple the object may be, there remain the relations and interrelations of surface, contour and spatial interval'.[27] And he argues that minimal works are readable as art, 'as almost anything is today – including a door, a table, or a blank sheet of paper [. . .] Yet it would seem that a kind of art nearer the condition of non-art could not be envisaged or ideated at this moment'.[28]

If the aim of the modernist work is to explore its medium, be it paintings, sculpture or poetry, minimalist art has taken this investigation too far; it has blurred the boundaries between art and the everyday. Somehow lacking in the aesthetic qualities that art is normally expected to reveal, minimalism undervalues the art object, thus lessening the experience of the viewer. Therefore, there is a disparity between the minimalists' claims about their work and the actual experience of the viewer in looking at it. Similarly, by referring only to itself, the minimalist work undermines the distinction between art and 'non-art'. The meaning in this context of the distinction between art and 'non-art', as explained, is what Fried called 'objecthood'.

Fried suggests that the literalist projection and hypostatisation of objecthood amounted to a new genre of theatre; in contrast to the modernist imperative that seeks to negate objecthood and expresses a fundamental hostility to theatre in all its manifestations. Moreover, the dematerialisation of art into theatricality, even more importantly, because of the emphasis it placed upon reception, is held responsible for what seemed the imminent end of art. Tony Smith's account of his experience on the turnpike (see below) provides the ideal evidence for the imminent end of art, thus to what Fried is trying to prove, notably the threat from the imminent end of art.

However, there is an inconsistency in the understanding of the 'end of art', given that there is an underlying assumption and a restricted notion of what art 'should be'. The ambiguity and sterility of such pronouncements becomes apparent. As Huberman notes, 'the end of art' is a strange expression, with equal aptness:

> one can readily imagine it serving as a rallying cry for the heralds (or heroes, I don't know which) of postmodernism and as the frantic shout of those who are, overall, horrified by contemporary art [. . .] It is as if the affectation of a value, positive-inflamed in one sense and negative-frightened in the other, were not enough to reduce the irony of one and the same phrase being brandished by two rival factions: which evokes a dialogue of the deaf (one party yelling: 'The end of art!'; to which the other retorts: 'Not at all! The end of art!!') – even of an absurd battle in which two armies would hurl themselves at each other while waving the same flag and sounding the same charge.[29]

According to this reading, the thought of the 'end' belongs to a thought of 'ends', or rather of

> their definition, of their categorical identification starting from an act of birth and an idea of their development. So the 'modern' notion of the

end of art is actually as old as the history of art itself: not the history of art in the genitive subjective sense, for a practice need not be enlightened about its end to be efficacious and to develop in the historical element in general.[30]

Fried translates Smith's experience[31] on the turnpike as being the experience of what he is calling theatre: 'it is as though the turnpike, airstrips, and drill ground reveal the theatrical character of literalist art, only without the object, that is, without the art itself – as though the object is needed only within a room (or, perhaps, in any circumstances less extreme than these)'.[32]

Fried considers that Smith's account of his experience on the turnpike bears witness to theatre's profound hostility to the arts, while it discloses, precisely in the absence of the object and in what takes its place, what might be called the theatricality of objecthood. By the same token, however, 'the imperative that modernist painting defeat or suspend its objecthood is at bottom the imperative that it defeat or suspend theatre'.[33]

Moreover, Fried rhetorically asks about Smith's experience on the turnpike, while he describes these artworks 'as abandoned and empty situations'. He wonders if the turnpike, airstrips and drill ground were not works of art, what were they? What, indeed, if not empty or 'abandoned' situations? Smith describes a situation where experience becomes the object of art; with his observation, it is as if he foretells the future of art, namely a long tradition of types of art that are not concerned to produce a singular, tangible artifact (a painting, a sculpture, a print work), but that promotes an encounter with 'objecthood' during which experience becomes the object.[34]

The notion of the 'object' seems to slip from view, as though it has been dematerialised as an experience. Smith's account became a most notorious passage, for it provided a dramatic illustration of what Fried identified as the theatricality of objecthood. Precisely since Smith's experience barely registered as art, it required considerable justification. The view of art as part of its physical or intellectual surroundings was in opposition to the self-contained art and medium specificity that Fried envisaged.

Smith's account raises philosophical issues concerning the reception of the artwork, since it seems that his rejection of medium-specificity is based on the perception that conventional forms have limited life spans. However, an appraisal of Smith's narrative primarily as an account of minimalism or as a defence of anti-art, is reductive. Fried's criticism of Smith's experience seems to project an anti-theatrical prejudice and to use a singular idea of minimalism as a way to enable this critique.

One of the focal points of George Didi-Huberman's deconstructive reading of Fried's theories is that the former has reinscribed within reception aesthetic approaches the psychoanalytic slight against the subject; and that the processes of 'meaning making' do not fall under the recipient subject's authority; that they can never be completely controlled; that the objects sometimes look back in an uncanny way.[35] As Rebentisch argues,

> because what the beholder of Minimalist object sees – what shows or presents itself to him, approaches him – simultaneously distances itself and becomes alien in this approach, perception opens up, according to Huberman, to a process that necessarily includes the work of meaning, which is also always unconscious. The ostensible closure of the minimalist object relates to the openness of its presentation.[36]

Smith's statement resists interpretation because it seems to claim that it meant nothing at all; therefore, like the minimal work, he vexes those viewers who demand more from the work of art, namely, more content, more 'complexity', more clues of the artist's presence. In this context, Sayre demonstrates the ways Fried's articulation of the problem violates the aesthetic position of the avant-garde and reveals the depth of his misunderstanding. As he argues, when Fried says that minimal art is 'incomplete' without the audience, he assumes that it is somehow when and if the audience is engaged. However, the art of the avant-garde is never complete, as Sayre claims:

> determined, as it is, by the local and topical, the events of history itself, and by such things as the forms and operations of mechanical reproduction, from photography to television, that record this history, the art of the avant-garde is always in process, always engaged. It is, furthermore, purposefully undecidable. Its meanings are explosive, ricocheting and fragmenting throughout its audience. The work becomes a situation, full of suggestive potentialities, rather than a self contained whole, determined and final.[37]

In line with Fried's critique, minimalism has been charged with being anti-art, because the way in which minimalism operates is one that takes relationships out of the work and makes them a function of space, light and of the viewer's field of vision. Therefore, in asserting their objecthood, these art pieces begin to operate not internally, but instead resonate with those things and even those people around them. The process that occurs is one that is akin to theatre, but rather than being the weakening force that Fried sees it as, 'theatricality' seems to be stressing the unavoidable object value of art.

In actual fact, Fried's critique represents a last attempt to stem that tide of 'three-dimensional work' and 'generic art' (by which its authority was finally to be swept away). As he underlines, in a historical retrospect of his earlier criticism, his essay is nowhere near as 'pessimistic as future events would warrant' from his point of view. As he said he didn't imagine the possibility that within a few years the art he admired 'would be all but submerged under an avalanche of more or less openly theatrical productions and practices as proved to be the case'.[38]

It is true that since the 1960s, visual art practices, from body art to minimalism, have opened themselves to the dimension of theatricality, as analysed by Fried. Within the art world during the 1960s modernist theoreticians were involved in a search for the 'essence' of art, a kind of authentic 'self' for each art and each work of art and for them the 'theatrical' was seen as inimical to this project. This account both supports and is demonstrated by a canon of 'authentic modernist art' that tends to exclude those Dadaists, Futurists, Constructivists and Surrealists, whose work slips out of the categories of painting and sculpture into the fields of the ready-made, of performance, of poetry or of agit-prop.[39]

In many ways, these fabrications involving the choreography of large and small-scale architectures, artifacts, pseudo-fictional narratives, urban landscapes and even ineffable 'materials', such as light and mist, shift the audience's reception beyond the third dimension and into the fourth (that of time), in contrast to the conditions modernism sought. Amelia Jones attempts to uncover the structure of Fried's ideological thrust by focusing on the transcendental structure of his argument: since she argues, whether consciously or not Fried has signalled that his critical authority in debasing minimalism as 'non-art' is shored up by a tenuous logic whose truth claims rely ultimately on a blind belief in the speaker's singular access to transcendent meaning:

> I see the world as new; I believe God creates the world as new; therefore, God exists. For Fried this would translate as: [I say] theatricality is bad or non-art because it engages the spectator rather than being wholly manifest; [I say] therefore, minimalism is non-art. Fried's logic which is predicated on the veiling of the 'I' of his assertions so as to naturalize them as transcendentally, universally true, is based entirely on his responses – highly invested and specific in relation to New York politics and art world of the 1960s.[40]

These transcendental aspects uncover the ideological and philosophical inconsistencies of Fried's discourse and the extent of abstraction in his theory. Adding to this, Caroline Jones[41] goes beyond the mainstream criticism and focuses on the lesser-known ways in which Fried's articulation of Greenberg's modernism is indebted to the matrix of ideas circulating around Kuhn's *The Structure of Scientific Revolutions*, many of them mediated by the cogent philosophy of Stanley Cavell. Kuhn's philosophy of science was applied by art historians and critics during the late 1960s, to enforce a particular reading of modernism and to protect that reading from the attacks of those who would be celebrated as postmodernists in the decades to come.

Cavell addresses elliptically the emergent crisis in the definition of modernism and the notion of 'successions of art', while Jones argues against the customary reading of Kuhn's theories as instigators of postmodernism. She attempts to demonstrate the ways in which Kuhn, despite the care he took to describe multiple modes of doing science (while shielding himself from charges of relativism), became associated in the art world with a narrow view of artistic practice that held modernist painting to be not one among many paradigms, but the only viable paradigm governing contemporary art.

In part, Jones historicises the word and the concept of the paradigm, so that its continued deployment today may be informed by some knowledge of the role it has played in modernist polemics since the 1960s. The concept of modernist art (as distinct from 'the modern' or 'modern art' or 'the avant-garde') during the sixties became the subject of particular anxiety and heated debate and Fried, according to Jones, 'held modernism to be an inexorable progression toward the irreducible essence of all painting'.[42] Jones argues that Fried is ambivalent in his most recent writings[43] about 'whether there was, or was not, a 'sense of crisis' at the time; that perhaps 'one can understand Fried (in 1998) to view the crucial essays ("Shape as Form" and "Art and Objecthood") as being beset by internal crises in a world that appeared, on the surface, to be otherwise sunnily at peace'.[44]

THE ENCROACHMENT OF POSTMODERNISM AND THEATRICALITY

Art and theatre pose interesting challenges to the legacy and specificity of 'theatricality', but the term cannot be amenable to the reductions of theorists, in particular to those who do not acknowledge the heterogeneity of minimalist art or who use a singular notion of theatre as a way to enable their historical narratives. Theatre theorists such as Martin Puchner and Michael Weber consider as noteworthy that the anti-theatricalism of Fried, Adorno and Benjamin is based not on an external attack on the theatre but on the modernist theatre itself. And so Brecht and Beckett keep coming up in these polemics, not as examples of what is wrong with the theatre but as solutions to theorists' objections to theatricality.

These approaches can serve as an indication of the formative productive role of anti-theatricalism for modern drama and theatre. As Puchner argues, modern drama and theatre did not endure their modernist enemies and avant-garde enthusiasts; as an alternative, they internalised both their critique and their enthusiasm for the purpose of a far-reaching reform of the dramatic form and of theatrical representation. Drama, like Hitchcock's film (*Stage Fright*), has always recorded and responded to the arguments of its detractors.

Modern drama continues to record anti-theatricalism – nowhere more obsessively than in the *oeuvre* of Luigi Pirandello – but it allows itself to be shaped by anti-theatricalism as well. Puchner sites the example of Euripides' *The Bacchae* that personifies the dangerous actor in the Asiatic Dionysus and anti-theatrical stage fright in the moralist Pentheus. As he argues, Brecht mistrusted the theatre:

> Yeats' tirades against the actors, Stein's nervousness in the presence of live actors, and Mallarme's rejection of the theatre are varieties of a resistance to the theatre that are structural and fundamentally formative, shaping these writers' use of the dramatic text, of dramatis personae and of actors.[45]

And he adds that modernist anti-theatricalism is no longer interested in bashing actors or closing down theatres and does not remain external to the theatre, but instead becomes a productive force responsible for the theatre's most glorious achievements.

Fried didn't expect that his theory would facilitate the encroachment of postmodernism and theatricality in the visual arts, given that he established a discourse that made it possible to theorise postmodern performance, a phenomenon that is in effect, as Philip Auslander argues, the antithesis of the hermetic modernist abstraction Fried sought to protect.[46] This discourse, especially his account of presence and theatricality, is instrumental for the analysis of artworks such as *Breath*, regardless of the fact that Fried's treatise was not originally intended to examine the aesthetic assumptions of performance.

Auslander refers to two treatises that appeared in *Modern Drama* in 1982, one by Josette Feral and another by Chantal Pontbriand, both of whom use Fried as a point of departure for efforts to distinguish performance from theatre. Auslander's work concentrates on the common ground that these essays have with each other and with Fried. Even though Feral and Pontbriand are talking about theatre in a more literal sense than Fried, they use the term 'theatre' in much the same way – one more indicator of how firmly ensconced in the Friedian discursive field their commentary is. Auslander argues that Fried's use of a theatrical vocabulary has proved to have a decisive effect for critical discourses on postmodernism, in both the visual arts and performance, 'even if this victory may have proven Phyrric for Fried'.[47]

Fried's 'theatricality' is a term that denotes what we now identify as 'postmodernism', hence Fried's statements are seen as prophetic. According to Auslander, his account of the conflict and his metaphor between modernism and theatricality is revealing about the polemics between modernism and postmodernism. The list of artists that Fried links with the minimalists as partaking in the theatricalist sensibility could stand as a partial genealogy of the postmodern, particularly in the visual arts, including the surrealists and John Cage, Kaprow, Cornell, Rauschenberg, Oldenburg, Flavin, Smithson, Kienholz, Segal, Samaras and Christo. To put it differently, as Auslander argues, whereas colour field abstraction is the modernist response to a certain problematic in the history of painting, minimalism is the postmodernist response to that same problematic. Implicit in Fried's essay is an account of postmodern-ism, as Auslander writes, 'that suggests that postmodernism arose within the problematic of late modernism not somehow after modernism or as a result of a rupture with modernism. Fried gave a name to the preference shared by many modernists, for reading over watching and for text over theatre, namely absorption'.[48]

A critical overview of Fried's problematic approach concerning the relation of the theatre with the visual arts, by considering the ironies and limitations of his approach, is presented in the context of an innovative reconsideration of the conceptual and aesthetic fields with which the visual arts and theatre are inextricably linked. The following chapters (6 and 7) apply features of Fried's discourse on presence and theatricality so as to analyse and comprehend works that share performative qualities.

Fried's theory has been applied by prominent theatre theorists to assess the differences between performance and theatre, despite the fact that his treatise was not originally intended to examine the aesthetic assumptions of perfor-mance. Thus, this chapter integrates the analysis of breath-related works by visual artists who experiment with performance in an attempt to examine the durational and 'experiential' turn in contemporary art and the dispari-ties between the theatre and the medium of performance, in conjunction with the ways that performance merges with politics and feminism in the works of Marina Abramović and Ulay *Breathing In/Breathing Out*, Janez Janša's *Something's in the Air* and the Feminist Art Workers' (FAW) *This Ain't No Heavy Breathing*.

Performing Breath: Marina Abramović (with Ulay) *Breathing In/ Breathing Out*, Janez Janša *Something's in the Air* and Chris Burden *Velvet Water*

Marina Abramović's *oeuvre* focuses on the relationship between the physi-cal body, respiration, expansive space and the transformative relationship between 'space', 'viewer' and 'performer', as well as on the transitory objects that trigger experience and engage the audience in live situations. An impor-tant aspect of her practice is the performer's consistent concern with spatial and architectural experience that is primarily focused on creating a performa-tive interrelationship between artist and audience. The performer asks what is the definition of 'performance' and considers that performance is some kind of mental and physical construction into which an artist steps, in front of the public. As she states, 'performance is not a theatre piece, is not something that you learn and then act, playing somebody else. It's more like a direct transmis-sion of energy [. . .] The more the public, the better the performance gets, the more energy is passing through the space'.[49]

Shared space and closed circuit experience is the focus of works that challenge

Figure 2.1: MARINA ABRAMOVIĆ (WITH ULAY). *Breathing In/Breathing Out.*
Performance, nineteen minutes. Student Cultural Center, Belgrade, April 1977
© Marina Abramović and Ulay. Courtesy of the Marina Abramović Archives

the public to be in control rather than the performer, like the pieces that she
developed and performed with Ulay.[50] Their first performance, *Relation in
Space*, took place at the Venice Biennale in 1976, where two bodies ran at and
smashed into each other for an hour, mixing male and female energy together
into a third component that they called 'that self'. In *Interruption in Space*,
the two performers ran at each other from different directions. As Abramović
describes:

> we ran to each other with our full force, we ran against the wall between
> us. *Expansion in Space* took place at Documenta in Kassel, in 1977: we
> tried to expand our bodies in the space by moving two large columns
> of 140 and 150 kilos respectively, twice the weight of our own bodies.
> The piece was very important because there was an audience of almost
> one thousand people. It was the first time that we experienced what the
> energy of the audience means and we went over our limits – physically
> and mentally.[51]

The themes of respiration and death recur in Abramović's *oeuvre*, while
with Ulay she worked on performances (from 1976 to 1988) exploring the psychological and physical limits of personal identity and the tense relationship

they established with the audience. Their first performances were governed by a three-fold principle. They were to have no predetermined purpose, no repetition, and no possible reproduction. Subsequently, their work developed and became intermedial with the use of various media, including photography, film and video. The body is both the subject and medium for these works that pioneered the use of performance as a visual art form. Exploring the physical and mental limits of their being, they withstood pain, exhaustion and danger. During the performance of *Breathing In/Breathing Out*, Marina Abramović and Ulay, with their mouths clamped tightly together and microphones taped to their throats, breathed in turn the air from each other's lungs, until – almost to the point of suffocation – they were exchanging only carbon dioxide.

The artist's work is based on the idea that what is important is less what you do, than the state of mind in which you do it. This state of mind is interconnected with the immaterial and the emptying of the body. As Abramović states, boat emptying, stream entering, 'this means that you have to empty the body/ boat to the point where you can really be connected with the fields of energy around you. I think that men and women in our Western culture are completely disconnected from that energy, and in my new work I want to make this connection possible'.[52] According to the artist, art will become intangible and will surpass the art object in the future; and the art of the future will be an art without objects, because in the communication of pure energy, the object appears as an obstacle.

Performativity in Abramović's work involves the participation of the viewer while she focuses on the creativity of the recipient of the work. She has been influenced by Duchamp who says that the artist is not the only one who should be creative, the public should be creative too. According to Abramović, art has changed a lot, but the spectators haven't changed that much; the viewers should constantly transform themselves like the artists who are preparing, by the way they live and transform themselves, an art that could focus on the mental/spiritual/intellectual/mindful. Death is usually performed in Marina's *oeuvre* as the interrogation of life, since 'live' performers move through 'real time' toward their deaths as they perform. As Blau asks 'What is the theatre but the body's long initiation in the mystery of its vanishings?'[53]

Artists Janša, Narat, Preda and Tomažin's piece *Something's in the Air* draws from Marina Abramović's *Breathing In/Breathing Out* so as to investigate the notion of collective breath, the relationship between the physical body, respiration, expansive space and the transformative relationship between space, viewer and performer, as well as to experiment with the notion of a life subjected to merely biological functions. The ensemble is 'breathing as one', as a community that, as Robert Bobnič states, in the 'company of a person whose breathing is loud or noticeable, we soon realise that our personal line has been crossed and that we can't resist the other person's affecting us'.[54]

Figure 2.2: JANEZ JANŠA, BOŠTJAN NARAT, IRENA PREDA, IRENA TOMAŽIN.
Something's in the Air: 2015. Production: Maska. Co-production: Mladinsko Theatre.
Photo by Nada Zgank

The performance attempts to blur the boundaries between life and art and explores the merging of the two in a similar way to Chris Burden's *Velvet Water* (1974), a performance that shows the artist repeatedly dunking his head in a sink filled with water, doing so again and again, trying to inhale the oxygen-rich water, until he collapses on the floor, chocking, spluttering and gasping for breath. The entire time, there is a camera fixed on him, relaying a live video feed of the action to an audience sitting in adjoining space, until the monitor goes dark. At the start of the piece, Burden addresses the cameras, announcing to the audience, 'Today I am going to breathe water, which is the opposite of drowning, because when you breathe water, you believe water to be a richer, thicker oxygen capable of sustaining life.'[55]

THE POLITICS OF BREATH: THE FEMINIST ART WORKERS (FAW) *THIS AIN'T NO HEAVY BREATHING*

The collaborative performance art group Feminist Art Workers, established in 1976 by Nancy Angelo, Candace Compton, Cheri Gaulke and Laurel Klick, and that later included Vanalyne Green, also draws from everyday life so as to address issues of violence against women, politics, collective action and labour. Emerging from the educational programmes at the Woman's Building in Los

Angeles, the group incorporate techniques of feminist education into participatory performance structures in the public sphere: in buses, protest rallies, the street and the museum.

The performance piece *This Ain't No Heavy Breathing* took place in Pasadena, California, for a total of five days in 1978, as a response to the 1970s' focus on sexual violence against women. Members of the audience are brought into a grimy phone booth, like the ones obscene callers might use. In this case they are used for the audience members to listen to audiotapes of women describing their experiences of receiving obscene phone calls: 'I think that someone is watching me because it never happens when someone else is in the house with me. And that's what frightens me. It's usually in the evening when I'm alone.'[56]

PERFORMING TEXTUALITY, BREATH AND PROJECTIVE PROSE: VALIE EXPORT *BREATH TEXT: LOVE POEM*, NANCY SPERO *WOMAN BREATHING*, GIL JOSEPH WOLMAN *MEGAPNEUMES*, CHARLES OLSON'S BREATH-INSPIRED PROJECTIVE VERSE

VALIE EXPORT's practice is often expressed as a political and cultural manifesto that includes digital technologies, cinematic and video work, photography, text and performance. The artist goes beyond the pictorial surface and thus experiments with 'expanded cinema', an invented medium that incorporates real bodies and objects. EXPORT employs detailed linguistic analysis of image policies as one of her distinctive techniques. As de Certeau argues, 'EXPORT develops her tactics that move within the visual field of the "enemy". These tactics enable EXPORT to participate in certain political discourses, to appropriate them for herself and at the same time to subvert them, to make herself understood through language and its grammar [. . .]'[57] The artist examines the relationship between a constructed body language and the surrounding urban space and experiments with audience reception.

Breath Text: Love Poem is a video poem showing VALIE EXPORT from the front behind a glass plate, on which she breathes 'I love you.' The plate in the video and the plate of the monitor suggest a corresponding surface, so that there is an impression that the breath is in direct contact with the set. EXPORT directs herself in an experiment that researches the limits of cinema, and in her cinematic actions she challenges realism and representation, as well as the passive reception that is characteristic of the medium of cinema. This embodied intermedial experience entails a politics of spectating in contrast to a modernist purified opticality. By shaking up the notion of a unified and 'disembodied' visual field, EXPORT motivates the spectator into making connections between the different elements and media comprising the work.

Textuality is also the primary medium in *Woman Breathing*, the minimalist piece by the feminist artist and activist Nancy Spero, that consists solely of

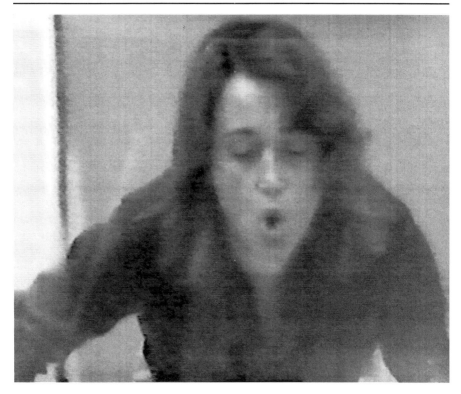

Figure 2.3: VALIE EXPORT.*Breath Text: Love Poem*: 1970. 1970/1973Video-Poem/
video poem.Videostill© VALIE EXPORT, Bildrecht Wien, 2017. Courtesy of VALIE
EXPORT

words printed along the undulating creases of paper, mirroring the action of
breathing that is described in the text. Using the 'hand-stamping technique',
that she began to employ in the mid-1970s, the artist varies the pressure as
she prints each individual letter. Spero deliberately attempts to distance her
art from the Western emphasis on the 'subjective portrayal of individuality
by using a hand printing and collage technique utilizing zinc plates as an artist's tool instead of a brush or palette knife'.[58] The artist stopped painting on
canvas in 1966, opting instead for the 'freer, more temporal, ephemeral' material of paper – on which she would produce her most critically acclaimed work.
Created the same period (1976–9) that Spero was exploring the protagonistic
role of women in history (Notes in *Time on Women* series), *Woman Breathing*
is not as politically charged as the pieces that explore acts of war, violence,
torture and aggression, but the artist examines the methodical act of formalisation in the medium and the progressive aesthetic abstraction in her attempt to
depict the minimum condition of existence, namely, breathing.

Breath and the voice are considered as the core of bodily processes for sound poetry similarly to performance practices that emerged within Fluxus and actionism. In his *Megapneumes* (1967) Gil J. Wolman captures the artist exhaling and inhaling into a microphone to a point of tactile abrasiveness, so as to illuminate poetry's return to primary origins, and to focus on the 'hyper expression of breath', while the American modernist poet Charles Olson published his influential breath inspired *Projective Verse* in 1950, and argued that poetry should embody the rhythms of natural breath, while he claimed that a poem, if it is to be of essential use, has to put into itself certain laws and possibilities of the breath. Breath is all that is left after theatre is stripped to its absolute essentials. The persistent search for irreducible essentials that scholars find evidenced in the minimalist progressive simplifications and reductions are the result of a self-reflexive concern with genre and the creative act that often approaches the state of non-art.

Embodied presence and social participation is the focus of performative practices that seek to exceed the limits of representation. The depiction of formless visual shapes (respiration) that become a metaphor for conceptual forms is always a mediated act like any form of representation, even in performative art practices that involve the immediacy of the body. Detached from established aesthetic norms, the selected corporeal and intermedial art pieces offer an alternative to a particular history of modernism identified with the idealisation of forms and with the tendency by revered figures within the modernist tradition to evaluate artists based on media specificity and autonomy. The artworks highlight not the efficacy, but rather the limits of the medium, in the face of attempts to understand, represent or emulate the properties of breath. The intermedial methodological challenge of converging different mediums and of working in-between the boundaries of artistic media is manifested in these works, as well as the critical attempt to engage the perceptual and political imaginary of the beholders.

NOTES

1. Samuel Beckett. *Worstward Ho*. London: John Calder, 1983: 13.
2. Potts, Alex. 'Installation and Sculpture', *Oxford Art Journal*, 24.2 (2001): 6.
3. Fried, Michael. 'An Introduction to my Art Criticism'. In *Art and Objecthood Essays and Reviews*. Chicago: University of Chicago Press, 1998: 2.
4. See Auslander, Philip. 'Presence and Theatricality in the Discourse of Performance and the Visual Arts'. In *From Acting to Performance: Essays in Modernism and Postmodernism*, London and New York: Routledge, 1997: 49–57.
5. Apple, Jacki. 'Introduction'. In *Alternatives in Retrospect: An Historical Overview, 1969–1975*, exhibition catalogue. New York: New Museum, 1981: 5–7. See http://archive.newmuseum.org/index.php/Detail/Occurrence/Show/occurrence_id/39
6. Elkins, James. 'What Do we Want Photography to Be? A Response to Michael Fried,' *Critical Inquiry*, 31 (Summer 2005): 941. In Costello, Diarmuid. 'On the

Very Idea of a Specific Medium: Michael Fried and Stanley Cavell on Painting and Photography as Arts', *Critical Inquiry*, 34 (Winter 2008): 274–312.

7. Petersen, Anne Ring. 'Between Image and Stage: The Theatricality and Performativity of Installation Art'. In Rune Gade and Anne Jerslev (eds), *Performative Realism*. Copenhagen: Museum Tusculanum Press, University of Copenhagen, 2005: 209.

8. See particularly Krauss, Rosalind. *Passages in Modern Sculpture*. New York: Viking Press, 1977.

9. Aristotle. *Poetics 1*, 1447a. In Stephen Halliwell (ed. and trans.), *Poetics*. Cambridge, MA: Harvard University Press, 1999: 29.

10. The book was written in the 1960s.

11. Adorno, Theodor W. *Aesthetic Theory*, trans. Robert Hullot-Kentor. Minneapolis: University of Minnesota Press, 1997: 230.

12. Ibid.: 230.

13. Ibid.: 114.

14. The avant-gardist movements of the early twentieth century and the material and discursive legacies of the avant-gardes are differentiated from the later avant-garde movement of the sixties.

15. Peter Bürger in his influential analysis of the avant-garde in his book *The Decline of Modernism* discusses and questions the formal relationship between art and life that had dominated the eighteenth and nineteenth centuries, while he charts the establishment of literary and artistic institutions since the Enlightenment and their apparent autonomy from the prevailing political systems. Bürger addresses the relationship between art and society, from the emergence of bourgeois culture in the eighteenth century to the decline of modernism in the twentieth century. In analysing this relationship, he draws on a wide range of sociological and literary critical sources: Weber, Benjamin, Foucault, Diderot, Sade, Wyndham Lewis, Peter Weiss and Joseph Beuys, among others. Bürger, Peter. *The Decline of Modernism*. Cambridge, MA: Polity Press, 1992.

16. Goldberg, Roselee. *Performance: Live Art since 1960*. New York: Harry Abrams, 1998. See especially her discussion of avant-garde practices.

17. See Goldberg, RoseLee. *Performance Art: From Futurism to the Present*. New York: Harry Abrams, 1988.

18. Erika Fischer-Lichte, in *Astetische Erfahrung*, describes how cultural studies have undergone a so-called 'performative turn' during the 1990s that can be traced back to the end of the seventeenth century. The concept of performance received a reconceptualisation in the 1970s, in what is now known as the 'performative turn' in anthropology and sociology, and scholars such as the cultural anthropologists Victor Turner and Clifford Geertz, theatre director and theorist Richard Schechner, and later, performance studies scholar Dwight Conquergood and sociologist Erving Goffman,

> attempted to wrestle performance away from its purely artistic-bound connotations. As early as 1973, Schechner already called for using the theories and methods of the social sciences to understand the nature of performance, and not only the kind occupying the traditional stage environment or the avant-garde of the art world.

Quoted in Salter, Chris. *Entangled: Technology and the Transformation of Performance*. Cambridge, MA and London: MIT Press, xxiv.

19. Fischer-Lichte, Erika. *Theatre, Sacrifice, Ritual*. London and New York: Routledge, 2005: 224.

20. Contemporary works trace, re-enact and reappropriate basic postulates of the 'performative turn'.

21. Walker, Julia A. 'Why Performance? Why Now? Textuality and the Rearticulation of Human Presence', *The Yale Journal of Criticism*, 16.1 (Spring 2003): 149.
22. According to Fried's claims, nothing in Greenberg's art criticism (or in his own) has come in for more sustained assault in recent years than the claim that modernist painting posits or privileges or establishes the illusion of a purely visual or 'optical' space, one addressed to eyesight alone. I have no wish to defend that claim here, but it should at least be noted that the idea of opticality (and related notions) plays a double role in Greenberg's criticism of the early 1960s.
23. See Introduction to this book.
24. See Fried, Michael. 'An Introduction to my Art Criticism': 15 and Auslander, Philip. 'Presence and Theatricality'.
25. Jones, Amelia and Stephenson, Andrew (eds). *Performing the Body/Performing the Text*. London: Routledge, 1999: 45.
26. Ibid.: 50.
27. Fried, Michael. 'An Introduction to my Art Criticism': 152.
28. Ibid.
29. Didi-Huberman, Georges. *Confronting Images: Questioning the Ends of a Certain History of Art*, trans. John Goodman. University Park: Pennsylvania State University Press, 2005: 37.
30. Ibid.: 43 and 44.
31. Smith refers to an episode in his life and to the effect it had on his views about art. The episode took place when he was teaching at Cooper Union in the fifties and someone told him how he could get onto the unfinished New Jersey turnpike. He took three students and drove from 'somewhere in the meadows' to New Brunswick. The drive was a revealing experience for Smith. It was a dark night and there were no lights or shoulder markers, lines, railings, or anything at all except the dark pavement moving through the landscape. The road and much of the land-scape was artificial, and yet it couldn't be called a work of art. And he writes, 'on the other hand it did something to me that art had never done'. At first, he said,

> I did not know what it was but its effect was to liberate me from many of my views I had about art. It seemed that there had been a reality there that had not any expression in art. The experience on the road was something mapped out but not socially recognized. I thought to myself it ought to be clear that that's the end of art. Most art looks quite pictorial after that.

Smith, Tony. 'Interview with Samuel Wagstaff Jr', *Artforum*, 5.4 (December 1966): 14.
32. Fried, Michael. 'An Introduction to my Art Criticism': 159.
33. Ibid.: 160.
34. Ibid.: 159.
35. Didi-Huberman, Georges. *Ce Que nous yoyons, ce qui nous regarde*. Paris: Les Éditions de Minuit, 1992: 33. Translated in Rebentisch, Juliane. *Aesthetics of Installation Art*. Berlin: Sternberg Press, 2012: 63.
36. Rebentisch, Juliane. *Aesthetics of Installation Art*. Berlin: Sternberg Press, 2012: 63.
37. Sayre, Henry. *The Object of Performance: The American Avant-Garde since 1970*. Chicago and London: University of Chicago Press, 1989: 7.
38. Fried, Michael. 'An Introduction to my Art Criticism': 43. See also Hal Foster, Rosalind Krauss, Yve-Alain Bois and Benjamin Buchloh. *Art since 1900: Modernism, Antimodernism, Postmodernism*. New York: Thames and Hudson, 2011.
39. See Foster, Hal, Krauss, Rosalind, Bois, Yve-Alain and Buchloh, Benjamin. *Art*

since 1900: Modernism, Antimodernism, Postmodernism. New York: Thames and Hudson, 2011.

40. Jones, Amelia and Stephenson, Andrew (eds). *Performing the Body/Performing the Text*: 45.
41. See Jones, Caroline A. 'The Modernist Paradigm: The Artworld and Thomas Kuhn', *Critical Inquiry*, 26 (Spring 2000): 488–528.
42. Ibid.: 495.
43. Fried, Michael. 'Critical Response to Caroline A. Jones' *Critical Inquiry*, 27.4 (Summer 2001): 703–5.
44. According to Jones, Fried's anxious efforts in 1966 to extricate himself, via Kuhn, from charges of reductivism came too late. As she puts it,

> Fried wielded Kuhn in order to fend off the accusation that what he was proposing was in some way a reductionist conception of Modernist painting. But it was manifestly too late. That reductionist enterprise was one in which Fried was already mired – an interpretation that held Modernism to be an inexorable progression toward the irreducible essence of all painting (a phrase I use [. . .] to encapsulate the view of modernism I claim is wrong).

In Fried, Michael. 'Critical Response to Caroline A. Jones', *Critical Inquiry*, 27.4 (Summer 2001): 703.

However, Fried replied to Jones' criticism by arguing that her article operates from first to last on a mistaken and prejudicial premise, namely, that the footnote to his 1966 article, 'Shape as Form: Frank Stella's New Paintings', in which he alludes to Thomas Kuhn's *The Structure of Scientific Revolutions*, is an 'anxious' attempt to defend himself – 'which is to say my previous writings against the charge of reductionism'. She uses the adjective 'anxious' twice (pp. 488 and 523), and introduces the noun 'anxiety' in a related context (p. 489).

45. Puchner, Martin. *Stage Fright*: 12.
46. See Auslander, Philip 'Presence and Theatricality'.
47. Ibid.: 55.
48. Ibid.
49. Abramović, Marina and Ratti, Antonio (eds). *Body Art*. Milan: Charta, 2002: 27–39.
50. German artist, Abramović's partner in life and co-performer for thirteen years.
51. Abramović, Marina and Ratti, Antonio (eds). *Body Art*: 33.
52. Abramović, Marina. 'Interview', *Journal of Contemporary Art* (June 1990). In http://www.jca-online.com/abramovic.html [accessed 1/11/16].
53. Blau, Herbert. *Take up the Bodies: Theatre at the Vanishing Point*. Urbana: University of Illinois Press, 1982: 299.
54. In *Radio Student*.
55. In https://artandcultureinchicago.wordpress.com/tag/chris-burden/ [accessed 1/11/16].
56. In https://feministartworkers.wordpress.com/ [accessed 01/11/2016].
57. In http://www.valieexport.org/ [accessed 01/11/2016].
58. Spero, Nancy. Courtesy of Nancy Spero, from an unpublished 1989 statement by the artist entitled 'The Continuous Presence'. In http://www.artnet.com/awc/nancy-spero.html [accessed 1/11/16].

PART II
(RE)PRESENTING BREATH

3

SHORTNESS OF BREATH: BECKETT'S *BREATH* IN CONTEXT

Air as a part of the body's sensorial sphere[1]

Beckett's work is sustained upon an imagination of air[2]

Though Beckett's work is less well-ventilated than that of almost any other writer, air and breath are still everywhere in it, as they must be for any kind of life to be sustained. In its enterings into air, Beckett's work seems to define for itself and work within the terms of an extreme materialism. My concern with air forms part of an exercise in understanding what Gaston Bachelard calls the 'material imagination' in Beckett, a phrase which names not only the way in which the material world is imagined, but the materiality of imagining itself, the way in which materiality must continue however obliquely and tenuously it may be to insist, through every effort to imagine what it would be like to be.[3]

I have come to the conclusion it is almost impossible to do *Breath* correctly in the theatre so I must ask you to decline this request and all future ones for the play.[4]

The historical context of the writing and staging of *Breath* is pivotal in approaching the ultimate reduction of Beckett's life-cycle theme and his ultimate anti-theatrical statement. Beckett once commented to his favourite actress, Billie Whitelaw, 'I don't know whether the theatre is the right place for me anymore,' and as Whitelaw attests, she knew what he meant: 'I thought, well perhaps he should be in an art gallery or something. Perhaps I should be pacing up and down in the Tate Gallery [. . .]'[5]

The playlet was written in response to Kenneth Tynan's request[6] for a short piece that he could include in an erotic review he wanted to produce in New York, and it became the opening sequence of *Oh! Calcutta! An Entertainment, with Music,*[7] devised by Tynan and directed by Jacques Levy. It proved very controversial, since the British theatre critic and director changed the stage directions by adding naked bodies to the rubbish heap as the play's props. It is reported that Beckett was appalled by this version of the play, especially as the revue's programme attributed the work to him.

The play moved to Broadway on 26 February 1971, where it continued to be produced, with only one short interruption, until the 6 August 1989. Eighty-five million people saw 1,314 performances, and so *Breath* is probably the most viewed Beckett play ever, a record unlikely to be broken.[8] However, according to John Calder, in Tynan's production[9] the philosophical point is lost by the addition of the bodies and an ambiguity is introduced that can only mislead the audience. Because of this unauthorised addition, Beckett did not allow *Breath* to be included in the first London production of Tynan's review *Oh! Calcutta!* at the Roundhouse (on 27 July 1970). The unaltered version of the playlet was given its British premiere at the Close Theatre Club in Glasgow in October 1969 produced by Geoffrey Gilham, while the unaltered text was originally published in *Gambit*.[10]

Late Beckett: Shorts, Fragments, Playlets, Pieces

Breath is one of Beckett's shortest texts, known as 'dramaticules' or 'residua', terms that the writer uses to describe them, or according to Ruby Cohn 'lyrics of fiction'. These works stretch the meaning of the word 'play', thus other terms have been invented to describe them, such as 'fragments of theatre', 'ends and odds', 'shorts', 'playlets' and most commonly 'pieces'. These works, that critics often refer to as the 'mature' plays, register a new phase in Beckett's development.[11]

A new kind of critical vocabulary is necessary in order to understand the writer's later style in the theatre. Lyons argues that Beckett's plays are often discussed inter-textually, given that the late plays are seen as a developing sequence of dramas that are related to each other and not so much to other dramatic works. As Lyons suggests, they are marks on a continuum, which are characterised by a progressive economy of dramatic images and distillation of character and plot.

The progressive experimentation with dramatic form and the exploration of genre is traced in the Beckettian maxim that 'the artistic tendency is not expansive but a contraction'.[12] In his late stage and 'televisual' plays, action, dialogue, language, length, setting and characters are subject to a process of reduction and contraction. Moreover, these small-scale dramatic forms are characterised by simplicity of the dramatic situation, concentration, visual, aural and textual fragmentation. The technical exploration in style and content discloses their experimental nature. Condensed as well as contracted, these pieces share the same 'savage economy of hieroglyphics',[13] and, as Brater argues, this contractive tendency was further elaborated in *Breath*.

As one of the shortest stage pieces ever written and staged in the history of the theatre, and in view of its formal characteristics, the playlet can be described as a sound installation, a sound art piece, or a sound tableau that Lyons calls 'the minimalist absolute of *Breath*'; as Paul Keller reviews, 'Blink and you will miss it!'[14] Beckett once told Alan Schneider that he would make *Waiting for Godot*, *Endgame* and *Happy Days* shorter[15] pointing to his desire to reduce his plays to the bare minimum.

Regardless of its shortness, it is difficult to situate *Breath* in the context of a particular art movement, and theorists such as Enoch Brater argue that the playlet goes beyond minimalism. Given that the late plays establish a genre of their own, by moving on from 'the old shorter', his own as well as others, the form that Beckett chooses for his valedictory, according to Brater, becomes 'a genre of its own, a genre that makes us recognize, finally, a new possibility for drama and poetry in that visionary realm that will always come to rest somewhere beyond minimalism'.[16]

According to this view, theatre expresses a new level of minimalism in theatrical language, dramatic form and staging technique that goes beyond length. Alan Schneider responds to the statement that *Rockaby* is an 'one actor play' by arguing that 'all of Mr Beckett's plays are full length; some of them are longer than others, that's all, but they are all full length'[17] and Brater considers that the late plays belong to a new kind of drama (in the scale of fragment)[18] that generates a genre of its own (despite the minimum size). According to Brater, by dramatising moments of radiance rather than transcendence, the spectacle of Beckett's images and sounds, his spectral shapes and his melodic lines, continues its assault against clearly impossible odds.[19] In this process Beckett creates a new kind of drama in the scale of fragment that 'carries beneath its amorphous texture the density and complexity of experience itself. It is Beckett's raid on the inarticulate, but it is also a challenge in the theatre for transformation and renewal in a world of ever-shrinking possibilities'.[20]

The dynamic interface between the theatrical and the visual in the later work, and in particular in *Breath*, challenges conventional representational strategies, and becomes expressive of the transformational theatre that Brater describes, while it challenges the relationship between theatricality and textuality, actuality and theatrical representation, as well as the nexus between the concept of mimesis and theatrical practice. Drawing from Gilles Deleuze's taxonomy *Quad* is space with silence, *Ghost Trio* is space with voice and music, *but the clouds ...* is image with voice and poem, and *Nacht und Träume* is image with silence, song and music.[21] Moreover, in *Ping* (1967) Beckett is attempting to move from an alphabetical language to a 'language of the image', and in *Lessness* (1970) (both these are examples of longer pieces) he presents a colour-scape that is dominated by white. Jeffers observes:

> a text marked by the suffix 'less' maps its coordinates carefully onto a white topography of would-be stillness and silence – both 'less' sound and 'less' movement. Words function like the still, flat tints of an abstract painting: colour escapes from a chromatic spectrum into a fresh and unique achromatic realm.[22]

Beckett's representational mechanism is formed with principles prevalent in the visual and plastic arts. Condensed and highly elliptical on first encounter, Beckett's 'dramaticules', Brater argues, appear to haunt us with surreal landscapes divested of all recognisable proportions, a nightmare vision that reminds us of the practice of visual artists like Giacometti, Tanguy, Dali and de Chirico.[23] According to Brater,

> Beckett's persons, places, and things are transmuted into a bold orchestration of shape, texture, and tonality, a highly imaginative synthesis of the constructivist and surrealist modes. A Beckett 'dramaticule' confronts the spectator with an embodiment of elusive incongruities, like a Joseph Cornell box. Every attempt to penetrate the mysteries of these 'anxious objects' is, in one form or another, the same 'raid on the inarticulate' that T. S. Eliot saw in poetry.[24]

Yet, as he adds:

> in Beckett's hands tiny bits and pieces acquire ambiguous meaning and a scale – the scale of miniaturized grandeur – are removed from their modest physical size. And the actual brevity of these plays – the creation of a compressed and very empty space by means of elaborate but minuscule dimensions – affords these works a 'world' in which they achieve the kind of imaginative harmony associated with the larger canvases of *Endgame* or *Waiting for Godot*.[25]

THE LIGHTING FIELD AS A VISUAL FIELD

Breath's visual articulation is based on lighting, and the primary articulation of the *mise en scène* is the lighting design. Stage light is a determinant of shape, visuality and visual form; it establishes (through illumination) the spatial presence of the visual object, or its non-presence, given that no light is indexical of non-location. The visual field is composed with sharp dichotomies of light and dark, while darkness represents a 'non-space', a 'non-seen' space. The stage becomes visible in a light that starts faint, becomes less faint, and then fades to black, while the props are a pile of rubbish dispersed on the stage, lit by a light that begins dim, brightens (but never fully) and then recedes to dimness.

The playlet consists solely of scenic directions based on a pattern, the interplay of silence and sound, light and darkness, time and space, covering timing for sound and lights, level and intensity of lights. This composition is founded on precision and exactitude (if 0 = dark and 10 = bright, 'light should move from about 3 to 6 and back' is typical),[26] set dressing and a description of the sound cues. The only aspect not contained in the stage directions is the sound level of breathing; the note on breath is simply 'amplified recording'.

Theatre theorists like Marvin Carlson argue about the significance of stage directions, and critics such as Martin Puchner also draw attention to the fact that few have acknowledged the central shift taking place in modern drama:

> a shift is based on the growing importance of stage directions. Stage directions enfold a universe parallel to, and thus at all times compete with, the drama of speech. Reading the plays of Beckett requires a double reading of direct speech and stage directions, as he argues, his plays are therefore split between a theatre of dialogue and a theatre of objects and gestures, the latter captured by the descriptive diegesis of stage directions.[27]

The principal aim in reviewing these hermeneutic perspectives is the comprehension of the formal principles that underlie its structure and pattern; the dramatist calls *Breath* 'a farce in five acts', and Ruby Cohn argues that these acts form a symmetrical whole: Act I is repeated by Act V – the cry; Act II is repeated by Act IV[28] and, according to Cohn, the apex Act III is unique and the playlet's context is metaphoric rather than metonymic. The play etches human life against infinity:

> a voice against the void, breath-light against the classico-Christian tradition, against the expanding space of modern science. The brief play contains Beckett's staples – symmetry, repetition, inversion, the wresting of sound from silence, a flicker of light against the dark, dying but not definable death.[29]

Beckett's archetypal use of cyclic form is to be found in *Breath*. Symmetry, repetition and inversion form a cyclic structure. Rosemary Pountney, in the book *Theatre of Shadows,* investigates the cyclical structure of *Breath* and argues that the playlet is the ultimate reduction of Beckett's life-cycle theme, while she analyses the piece as structured in circles. She writes, it is 'a sigh lasting thirty seconds. It begins and ends with an identical birth cry, and encompasses between the two the pangs of birth, followed by the death rattle'.[30]

Beckett experiments with form and pattern as well as with the structure of the 'well-made' play, since *Breath* constitutes an inversion of the 'traditional well-made play' with a remarkable precision, to the pyramidical structure.[31] As we have already seen, these Acts form a symmetrical whole.[32]

The piece shares all the elements of the 'well made' play: the 'rising action' of the second 'act', the pause, the climax: the third act, the culmination, the apex, the exhalation (advancing) and death (declining) (i.e. complete exhalation) that represents the 'falling action': and the fourth act that is followed by the reiterated cry, the 'resolution'; and the final silence before the curtain descends.[33] Its formal structure shares the classic Aristotelian narrative technique of tumescence and detumescence (namely a dialectics of inflation and deflation). However, Beckett employs this classic form in its complete reduction, with no overtones; he calls the play 'a farce in five acts' and refutes any formal and contextual interpretations of the playlet.

Breath challenges the 'well made' structure through a highly articulate process of erasure and constant disruption of the processes and the kinds of terms that surround representational theatre. According to William Hutchings' analysis, the formal aspects of the playlet are based on the dramatic technique postulated by Gustav Freytag in *Die Technik des Dramas* in 1863. Firstly, the initial pause and the first cry, representing birth, constitute the introduction and 'inciting moment' of life in general and of this play in particular; secondly, the inhalation, a symbol of growth and development, is clearly, as he writes:

> a 'rising action' (of the thorax and diaphragm as well as of the play), which is appropriate of the second 'act'; The pause while the breath is held is the climax and the third 'act', the culmination of growth and maturation, the apex of the vital capacities of the lungs and hence of life. Finally the exhalation – a metaphor of the entropic decline of the body with advancing age, a declining 'vital capacity', and death (i.e., complete exhalation) – constitutes the 'falling action' of the thorax and the fourth act of the play, which is followed immediately by the reiterated cry, the catastrophe or 'resolution' of the play, and the final silence before the curtain descends.[34]

Breath reorients reflections concerning the formation of genre, character, place, action, situation and language, turning towards processes and contexts, through which the limits of the work are yet to be defined.[35] Herbert Blau attempts to explain this process by focusing on *Breath*'s reception, and argues that the theatrical event 'hangs perceptually on our breath at the edge of what is possible, at the edge of representation. He writes: 'what moves in performance is always thought, which plays upon the body and is never still, even when the body is absent, as it is in the "recorded vagitus" of Beckett's *Breath*.[36] We might have expected from Beckett the last syllable of recorded time, but what appears in the vagitus is more like the last minimal mediation of the birth cry of ancient drama. As Blau notes,

> With dim light and synchronized breath, there is nothing to this play but the brief repetition of a faint, brief cry, but it is sufficient to remind us that what can never be represented (or can only be represented) is no less moving in thought: that the body in performance is dying in front of our eyes. Unceasing process is out there in the flesh. Or hangs, perceptually, on the audience's breath. No one sees the motion but the motion, but it is thus that performance remains – through the appearance of the invisible or the ghost of a rigor mortis ontological model of an encounter with the unforeseen.[37]

The playlet evades human and corporeal representation; the body is missing both as an object and as an image, and human agency is made present through its absence while, as Blau concludes, the privilege of the dramatic stage is 'its very corporeality being the basis of its most powerful illusion, that something is substantially there, the thing itself, even as it vanishes'.[38]

PRODUCTION HISTORY. THE LEGACY OF *BREATH*'S STAGINGS: S. E. GONTARSKI, BARBARA KNEZEVIC, FERNANDO AND ADRIANO GUIMARÃES, DAMIEN HIRST

The legacies of *Breath*'s 'stagings' by prominent and emerging visual artists, performance practitioners and theatre directors from different cultural and national backgrounds illustrate the controversial reception of the text. In particular, Kenneth Tynan's production reveals the tension regarding the interpretation and the 'readings' of the playlet. In 1969, *Breath* made its debut in Kenneth Tynan's bawdy revue *Oh! Calcutta!* Infuriated by this staging, which ignored a typically specific set of stage instructions, Beckett removed the work and the play became a shadowy chapter in his back catalogue. This incident with Tynan's addition forms the crux of Barbara Knezevic's exhibition at the Joinery, 'Breath and Other Shorts', in which a framed programme of *Oh! Calcutta!* is set beside an old library copy of *Breath* and a red-bound book, entitled *Beckett: An Exercise in Omission*. This last piece contains Knezevic's account of *Breath*'s ill-fated debut. Inside, the text is repeated hundreds of times, each page a copy of the one before, until its image fades and becomes skewed. A metaphor for the changes that occur when a work is restaged, 'this piece establishes a thread for the rest of an exhibition which abounds with duplicates'.[39]

Theorists draw attention to the necessity of periodic reinvention of Beckett's *oeuvre*, in particular the theorist and director Stanley Gontarski points out the significance of the play's avant-garde potential and its unconventional context, and attempts to direct and present *Breath* in a framework that he considers is more appropriate to the writer's initial objectives. The director tries to negotiate the complexity of the interface between a theatrical performance and a purely visual representation by directing and 'presenting' the work in a visual art context, and attempts to resolve the problems involved in the staging of *Breath* that are essentially related to its 'anti-theatrical structure'.

Gontarski argues that it was the clamour over Tynan's excesses that kept him thinking about how a director could solve the problems of staging *Breath*, thus he decided to resolve the problem by not 'staging' the playlet. The director aspired to present a performance closer to Beckett's rather than Tynan's; as an autonomous entity and not as part of an evening's theatrical sequence. He attempted to foreground what he considers as the play's avant-garde potential, the play of memory, its power to subvert or defy conventions and expectations and to shock its audience into thinking, at very least, about performance itself; thus he realised that the sort of performance he envisioned[40] did not require a theatrical venue.

In 1992 Gontarski was invited to participate in an evening of visual art and performance at Florida State University Gallery and Museum. It was in such a "fragile" and "ephemeral" artistic environment that he decided to present *Breath*. The project's curatorial approach was to use the gallery as a de-centred theatre space with events performed in several spaces of the gallery and the audience would wander or drift from one to the other with only the slightest prompting. Instead of adopting the structure of an outdoor fair, where simultaneous performances are offered to a roaming audience, the gallery evening features sequential performances without overlap. The evening as Gontarski describes, would comprise readings and other theatrical performances and environments among the gallery's various nooks and rooms and 'his offering was, then, in keeping with the hypertext theme, or rather to present versions of digital or telereality'.[41]

Breath, similarly to the majority of Beckett's later plays, requires a different frame, beyond the traditional proscenium arch, that was unavailable in the theatre, and Gontarski realised this fact, acknowledging that the playlet raises issues concerning the space of its production, reception, presentation, venue (gallery or theatre), but also of viewing and audience response. Consequently he decided to present it in an ambiguous context by highlighting its hybrid and technological implications. Gontarski calls the performance 'A Simulated Television Production' and rather than constructing a proscenium, he built an oversized prop television, through the absent screen of which *Breath* was performed 'live', thus this version was framed by an almost clownish simulated television screen. This was the continued development of the hybrid art that he considered to be Beckett's late theatre and as he describes it, it was 'an art of icons, images and afterimages, ghosts of memories – as closely related to sculpture as to what we have traditionally called theatre'.[42] The pile of 'miscellaneous rubbish' was physically present with the other installations in the gallery and he intended to show that Beckett's 'play' should be indistinguishable from the other art objects on display or from the gallery's refuse outside the service entrance.[43]

The director intended to stress the different features of *Breath*, namely its 'hybridity' and theatricality, in contrast to the other exhibits. Gontarski's production focuses on the primary articulation of the *mise en scène* that is based on the lighting design as well as on the presence of the rubbish, so as to differentiate the subtext of *Breath* in relation to the other gallery artworks. The 'performance' of *Breath*, as opposed to the gallery's other sculptures, is 'announced' by the light's fading up on the set, that is, on the heap of rubbish some ten feet behind the television screen, as the gallery lights simultaneously (but only slightly) dimmed. The brief cry (vagitus) and amplified inspiration would sound for some ten seconds and after the prescribed five-second pause, the expiration and identical cry for some ten seconds. Fade down the stage; fade up the gallery. The playlet was repeated several times during the evening, interspersed amid other performances, and the director hoped that such repetition might suggest the regenerative element he saw as implicit in the play.

As he mentions, he couldn't foresee the audience's response. The context of the gallery and the fact that the viewers were not manipulated into seeing *Breath* as an ordinary theatrical piece, with the rise and fall of the curtain, led to an 'open response' that blurred the distinction among artistic forms. This reception pleased Gontarski, who felt that the production was like an invisible theatre that took place in a gallery; he deliberately chose to associate Beckett's 'play' with the visual arts, and that was the reason that he 'staged' this performance in an art gallery context.

He was not surprised that the viewers never seemed to understand that they were watching what he considered live theatre, since the performance lacks what had heretofore been deemed an essential ingredient of theatre, namely, actors. The audience, deprived of its standard ambience and cultural cues, failed to applaud at the fade down, but neither did they applaud the viewing of other sculptures as they departed, even when the gallery lights dimmed as they did to announce another *Breath*.

Counter to Beckett's stage directions, the production includes no curtain and no curtain call. Gontarski considers that the lack of audience response is a measure of the success of this production, since the project blurs the distinction among artistic forms and becomes, almost, invisible theatre. But, 'while I may have saved the play from being lost amid a sequence of other plays as planned, I may also have lost it to a neo-Dadaist revival of found sculpture'.[44] This statement reveals that the director intended to reinvent and experiment with *Breath*, only to the extent that the piece would not approximate a ready-made structure that shares structural affinities with anti-artistic approaches. Therefore, the piece's complex relationship between a visual art piece (found sculpture, readymade piece) and the theatre challenged the director.

Fernando and Adriano Guimarães' staging of *Respiração* + (2002–7) involves the staging of Beckett's playlet along with the installation entitled *Breathó*. The artists are interested in the different representations of respiration and often work with the notion of respiration and on Beckett's plays. Adriano Guimarães sees in *Breath* a 'life in 35 seconds, and what you have is rubbish, organic material, what the human being is made of'.[45] The artists, however, consider as vital the presence of the human figure in this work (like Tynan). *Breath* is the centrepiece of the exhibition, one version of which features a live, naked actor in an embryonic sac. The performance takes place in two transparent tanks filled with water, where the fully-clothed performers dive, as they hold their breath. The installation consists of living people, who are forced to stay under the water, where they are unable to breathe. Their work focuses on the human body and according to the art critic, Vitoria Daniela Bousso, they engage directly 'the cultural games of regulation and control that are played upon it. The body is less ancillary in the artists' work, as Bousso argues, than it might generally be in Beckett and instead becomes the seat of the struggle of power relationships – if not overtly expressed, certainly a subtext of Beckett's work as well'.[46]

The Guimarães' brothers reinvent the context in which *Breath* is presented by offering a new poetic interpretation of the Beckettian *oeuvre*, on the threshold between the visual and the theatrical. According to Gontarski, who reviewed the piece, the artists create something like their own Beckett archive: 'Beckett in or as a cabinet of curiosities, a Beckett made up of cultural shards. Their antiphonal use of Beckett's works and words is a case in point.'[47] According to the director and theorist, their performances are less critiques of Beckett's work, than reinventions of it:

> these works are Beckett's afterimages and hence in no need of serious revision or renovation, since they are already preceded and followed, as they are, by images of the Guimarães brothers' re-imagining of Beckett afterimages, of Beckett's texts.[48]

This version of the playlet disregards *Breath*'s anti-theatrical features as well as its minimal context and the writer's intention to expose the components of the medium in skeletal form. According to Gontarski, the rubbish is seen as a metaphor for the human body, which is finite and disposable, a similar approach to Damien Hirst's allusion to medicine as a reflection of the human organism. However, the decision to present the human body in these works disregards the writer's central premise that eradicates the body/subject from the stage. Consequently, the installation fails to convey the existential and ontological importance of Beckett's decision to present the 'absence' of the human subject.

Damien Hirst,[49] the director of *Breath* for the Beckett on Film project, mentions that when he was asked to direct the film, he read the text and thought it was incredibly precise and strict. As he was preparing to shoot, he read the text over and over, and what really impressed him was Beckett's direction 'hold for about five seconds'. That was when he realised that the writer had 'this massive sense of humour'.[50]

Hirst attempted to direct his version of the playlet based on this enormous and idiosyncratic sense of humour, alongside Beckett's meticulous and rigorous artistic practice and the visual artist's own saturated aesthetics. In his attempt to negotiate the complex interface between the theatre and the visual arts, Hirst designs a 'controversial' scenery that consists of an installation of medical waste. This additional component does not necessarily contribute to a critical conceptual framework or enhance and develop the playlet's meaning and humour. Hirst's staging is a version of the playlet seen as a 'Vanitas', that doesn't discover new aspects or place the playlet in a new context; one that relates to the original and current context. The visual artist reproduces his own preoccupations with the saturation of culture with commercial imagery.[51] As Claire Lozier argues, there is in Beckett a desire to write a 'Vanitas' and she attempts to explore Beckett's debt to the genre of painting known as the 'Vanitas', and more specifically to its reworking in *Breath*. Lozier argues that 'the pictorial tradition of the baroque genre debt (the seventeenth-century Dutch genre of painting known as the "Vanitas") informs the play's aesthetic, to the point where *Breath* can be described as a transcription of the older genre'. The play inflicts a postmodern ironical twist upon the moral of the *contemptus mundi* and *memento mori* expressed by the 'Vanitas' tradition, and Lozier examines this contradictory use of the 'Vanitas' in the stylistic features of the writing, while she draws her argument from a comment made by Beckett in a 1973 interview with Charles Juliet. The writer mentions that he would like to be able to say death and life in an extremely reduced space, and Juliet reports that Beckett 'refers to the seventeenth-century Dutch paintings which serve as memento mori and that, like those painters, il aimerait pouvoir dire la vie et la mort en un espace extrêmement réduit'.[52]

By and large, the YBA interest in respiration lies in their involvement with the themes of life and death, 'Vanitas' and the brevity of life. Marc Quinn's *You Take My Breath Away* (1992) is a thin skin bearing the imprint of his body that is exhibited hanging like a discarded condom, while Tracey Emin's

You Left Me Breathing (1992)[53] includes a series of early drawings and mono-prints, from diminutive stitched texts to monumental and hand-embroidered textile assemblages. *You Left Me Breathing* has diverse undertones, as the artist argues 'the obvious is half-dead, but also, when someone leaves you standing – crying – as you sob and inhale the air you realise how important breath is. The same as when making love with uncontrollable passion, when there are no thoughts but just breath and the sound of a beating heart'.[54]

The ideological guise of the YBAs is revealed when compared to Beckett's *oeuvre* , since these works are immersed in the culture they criticise. On the contrary, Beckett's *Breath* resists recuperation and can be seen as a critique of the conditions of art making, display, marketing and interpretation, in con-trast to the YBA movement that became dependent on these processes. The analysis of *Breath*'s stagings by visual artists such as Damien Hirst, Nikos Navridis, Adriano and Fernando Guimarães and by theatre directors including Stanley E. Gontarski, Kenneth Tynan and Amanda Coogan shows the impact of Beckett's work on contemporary art practice and the ways in which the interface between staging performance and displaying art can create a new intermedial 'genre' that can suit the purposes and approaches of both Beckett's *Breath* and contemporary art. The artists decide to transform and reinvent the context in which *Breath* was written by opening the work in a spatially expanded situation. Chapter 6 examines, in particular, Navridis' version of the piece that offers an experiential and intermedial context by projecting an image of waste above ground, so that the spectators can walk on the surface and become immersed in this environment.

The artist challenges the solid and fixed context and ascribes interme-dial qualities to the work, thus activating the viewers in a bodily manner. Nevertheless, the majority of the above-mentioned versions disregard Beckett's intention to reveal the fundamental ontological emptiness on *Breath*'s dis-embodied stage. The following chapter examines in detail the existential, as well as the aesthetic ramifications of Beckett's ultimate decision to present the 'empty figure' on this shattered scenery.

NOTES

1. Bruno Latour. 'Air'. In Caroline Jones (ed.), *Sensorium*. Cambridge, MA: MIT Press, 2006: 104.
2. Samuel Beckett. *Murphy*. London: Calder, 1993: 5.
3. Ibid. Connor, Steven. 'Beckett's Atmospheres'. In S. E. Gontarski and Anthony Uhlmann (eds), *Beckett after Beckett*. Gainesville: University of Florida Press, 2006: 52.
4. Beckett wrote to agent Jenny Sheridan on 27 April 1972. See S. E. Gontarski, 'Reinventing Beckett', *Modern Drama*, 49. 4 (Winter 2006): 428.
5. Quoted in Kalb, Jonathan. *Beckett and Performance*. Cambridge: Cambridge University Press: 235.
6. Ruby Cohn remarks that,

although a fair copy of *Breath* has been widely reproduced, no holograph is extant. In the summer of 1966 Beckett recited to me in response to my question about what he had written and had sent to Kenneth Tynan for his revue of *Oh! Calcutta*. The staging became the most notorious deviation of Beckett's text first published as the prologue of *Oh! Calcutta*, New York Grove, 1969. It was printed correctly in the second impression (1970) and then by Calder in Gambit 1970. It is found in CDW and in Beckett's French in *Comedie et Actes Divers* 1972. Cohn, Ruby. *A Beckett Canon.* Ann Arbor: University of Michigan Press, 2001: 298

7. This collection of short plays by a variety of authors included a prologue by Samuel Beckett, which he had originally written under the title of *Breath*, was finally staged after thirty-nine preview performances, on the 16 June (17 according to Gontarski), 1969 at the Eden Theatre in New York City.
8. See Stanley Gontarski. 'Reinventing Beckett', *Modern Drama*, 49.4 (Winter 2006): 439.
9. According to Gontarski,

Breath's most memorable performance was its first, as the opener, called *Prelude*, to the Jacques Levy-directed and Kenneth Tynan-conceived sextrava-ganza, *Oh! Calcutta!, Calcutta!*, the image and title adapted from the painting of Camille Clovis Trouille's posterior odalisque, with its pun on the French 'O quel cul t'as [O what a lovely ass you have],' said 'cul' being prominently dis-played. As an opener to an evening of shorts, by Beckett or a variety of artists, as was the case with the Tynan-Levy production and as it is most frequently performed, the play is inevitably lost. Tynan drew attention to the playlet by adding three words to the opening tableau. To Beckett's 'Faint light on stage littered with miscellaneous rubbish,' Tynan added, 'including naked people' [. . .] Leading off with Beckett. Bruce Williamson, who introduced the work for a 'pictorial essay' in Playboy billed as 'A Front – Row – Centre Look at Oh! Calcutta!' Calcutta! (known by some wags [so to speak] as Jingle Balls), was as he wrote the only show in town that has customers piling into front row-centre seats armed, by God, with opera glasses. But Tynan was called a literary pimp, and his stable of authors, Beckett included, 'a pack of whores' [. . .] As the Playboy feature suggests, the musical spawned something of an industry, reflecting the era's sexual revolution and its commodification of sex. A book version of the play was issued by Beckett's American publisher, Barney Rosset of Grove Press, who published the play as performed in an illustrated edition in 1969, attributing to Beckett alone the playlet – with Tynan's erotic alterations. While only the earliest playbills identified authors, Rosset's volume listed them under a traditional Table of Contents. The musical was subsequently issued as an LP, was made into a Hollywood film, and is still currently available in CD, VHS, and DVD formats. The enterprise may have been Beckett's sole entry into the Age of Aquarius, certainly his only appearance in Playboy. Despite such phenomenal success and unprecedented exposure, drama reduced to its bare necessities, one might say, most respectable critics have generally joined Beckett in the condemnation of at least his contribution to the production.

Gontarski, Stanley. 'Reinventing Beckett': 439.
10. *Gambit*, 4.16 (1969): 5–9.
11. A chronological scope of the late plays: *Act Without Words I* and *II* (1959), *Embers* (1959), *Words and Music* (1962), *Cascando* (1963), *Play* (1963), *The Old Tune* (adaptation of *La Minivelle*, by Robert Pinget) (1963), *Come and Go*

(1966), *Eh Joe* (1967), *Breath* (1969), *Not I* (1973), *Footfalls* (1976), *Ghost Trio* (1976), *Rough for Radio I* and *II* (1976), *Rough for Theatre I* and *II* (1976), *That Time* (1976), ...*but the clouds* . . . (1977), *Ohio Impromptu* (1982), *A Piece of Monologue* (1982), *Rockaby* (1982), *Catastrophe* (1984), *Nacht und Träume* (1984), *Quad* (1984), *What Where* (1984).

12. Brater, Enoch. 'Fragment and Beckett's Form in *That Time* and *Footfalls*', *Journal of Becket. Studies*, 2 (Summer 1977): 70; and Beckett, Samuel. *Proust*. London: Chatto and Windus, 1931: 64.
13. See Brater, Enoch. 'Fragment and Beckett's Form': who mentions that Beckett used the phrase 'savage economy of hieroglyphics' to describe Joyce's work. In http://www.english.fsu.edu/jobs/num02/Num2EnochBrater.htm
14. Keller, Paul. 'Feature – Londoners gasp at Beckett's 30-second play' London: Reuters, 11 Feb. 1999.
15. See Harmon, Maurice (ed.). *No Author Better Served: The Correspondence of Samuel Beckett and Alan Schneider*. Cambridge, MA and London: Harvard University Press, 1998: 24.
16. Brater, Enoch. *Beyond Minimalism: Beckett's Late Style in the Theatre*. Oxford: Oxford University Press, 1987: 177.
17. Harmon, Maurice (ed.). *No Author Better Served*: 24.
18. The mimes *Kilcool* and *J. M. Mime* were described by Beckett as 'fragments of theatre' and they were contained in a notebook given by Beckett to the Trinity College, Dublin.
19. In https://www.badnewdays.com/beckett-s-dramaticules
and http://www.english.fsu.edu/jobs/num02/Num2EnochBrater.htm See also Beckett, Samuel. *Ends and Odds*. New York: Grove Press, 1976:
20. In https://www.badnewdays.com/beckett-s-dramaticules and http://www.english.fsu.edu/jobs/num02/Num2EnochBrater.htm
21. See Deleuze, Gilles. *Cinema 1: The Movement-Image*. Minneapolis: University of Minnesota Press, 2006; and *Cinema 2: The Movement-Image*. Minneapolis: University of Minnesota Press, 2007.
22. Jeffers, Jennifer M. 'The Image of Thought: Achromatics in O'Keefe and Beckett', *Mosaic*, 29.4 (December 1996): 74.
23. Brater adds, 'in his earlier plays there is more attention on representational detail, and these details are constantly and eloquently subjected to correction, revision, based on the shifting ambiguities of audience perception, especially in Beckett's *Fizzles*'. Brater, Enoch. 'Fragment and Beckett's Form in *That Time* and *Footfalls*': 71.
24. Brater, Enoch. 'Fragment and Beckett's Form in *That Time* and *Footfalls*', *Journal of Beckett Studies* (Summer 1977): 70–81. In http://www.english.fsu.edu/jobs/num02/Num2EnochBrater.htm [accessed 1/11/16].
25. Ibid.
26. Beckett, Samuel. *Breath and the Complete Dramatic Works*. London: Faber and Faber, 1986: 209.
27. In Puchner, Martin. *Stage Fright: Modernism, Anti-Theatricality and Drama*. Baltimore, MD and London: Johns Hopkins University Press, 2002: 26.
28. Cohn, Ruby. *Just Play Beckett's Theatre*. Princeton: Princeton University Press, 1980: 4.
29. Ibid.
30. Pountney, Rosemary. *Theatre of Shadows: Samuel Beckett's Drama: 1956–76*. Gerrard's Cross: Colin Smythe Ltd, 1988: 42. However, the idea of the 'death rattle' is often disputed, see Hutchings, William. 'Abated Drama: Samuel Beckett's Unabated Breath', *ARIEL: A Review of International English Literature*, 17.1 (1986): 88.

31. See Hutchings, William, 'Abated Drama': 88.
32. Cohn, Ruby. *Just Play Beckett's Theatre*. Princeton: Princeton University Press, 1980: 4.
33. See Hutchings, William, 'Abated Drama': 88.
34. Ibid.
35. See ,Kalb, Jonathan. *Beckett and Performance*.
36. Blau, Herbert. *The Audience*. Baltimore: Johns Hopkins University Press, 1990: 365 and 366.
37. Ibid.
38. Blau, Herbert. *Blooded Thought: Occasions of Theatre*. New York: Performing Arts Journal Publications, 1982: 132.
39. See http://www.barbaraknezevic.com/ [accessed 1/11/2016].
40. According to Gontarski, Deborah Warner shared the same intentions, as she wanted with the staging of *Footfalls* to provoke the Beckett estate. Gontarski, S. E. 'Reinventing Beckett', *Modern Drama*, 49. 4 (Winter 2006): 441.
41. Gontarski, S. E. 'Reinventing Beckett'. *Modern Drama*, 49.4, University of Toronto Press, (Winter 2006): 441.
42. Ibid.
43. Ibid.
44. Ibid.: 442.
45. Ibid.: 441.
46. Bousso, Vitória Daniela. 'Interstice Zone in Adriano and Fernando Guimarães'. 'Todos Os Que Caem / All That Fall' catalogue. Rio de Janeiro: Centro Cultural Banco do Brasil, 2004: 97–9.
47. Gontarski, S. E. 'Reinventing Beckett': 451.
48. Ibid.
49. Hirst is a representative artist of the new British art of the 1990s, 'Young British Art' (YBA): Damien Hirst, Tracey Emin, Jake and Dinos Chapman, Marcus Harvey and Sarah Lucas, among others. YBA obsessed with commerce, mass media and the cult of personality, a movement that proved to have 'avant-garde pretensions'. Julian Stallabrass analyses all aspects of this young generation of British artists and their environment from a critical perspective, and places it in the broader context of contemporary art. Stallabrass, Julian. *High Art Lite: British Art in the 1990s*. London: Verso, 1996.
50. See http://www.beckettonfilm.com/plays/breath/synopsis.html [accessed 1/11/2016].
51. See Derval Turbity's extended criticism of Hirst's version of the playlet. Turbity, Derval. 'Beckett's Spectral Silence: *Breath* and the Sublime', *Limit(e) Beckett*, 1 (2010): 102–22.
52. Lozier, Claire. 'Breath as Vanitas: Beckett's Debt to a Baroque Genre'. In Erik Tonning, Matthew Feldman, Matthijs Engelberts and Dirk Van Hulle (eds), *Samuel Beckett: Debts and Legacies*. Amsterdam and New York: Rodopi, 2010: 241. Charles Juliet's translation into English of the phrase 'évoque ces tableaux hollandais du XVIIe siècle faisant fonction de memento mori'. 'Breath as Vanitas: Beckett's Debt to a Baroque Genre'. In Erik Tonning, Matthew Feldman, Matthijs Engelberts and Dirk van Hulle (eds), *Samuel Beckett: Debts and Legacies*. Amsterdam and New York: Rodopi, 2010: 41.
53. Gagosian Gallery in Los Angeles in 2007.
54. Emin, Tracey. 'My Life in a Column', *The Independent*, Friday, 3 August 2007.

4

EMPTIED OF THEATRE: BREATH AND THE PHENOMENOLOGY OF DISEMBODIMENT

The empty page defended by its own whiteness[1]

If there ever was a kenotic writer, the writer of the utter self-emptying of subjectivity, of its reduction to a minimal difference, it is Beckett.[2]

Art can only be reconciled with its existence by exposing its internal emptiness.[3]

There is something about void and emptiness which I am personally very concerned with. I guess I can't get it out of my system. Just emptiness. Nothing seems to me the most potent thing in the world 1968.[4]

In the theatre, the human figure is represented, both verbally and visually, by means of the physical presence of the performer. The actor enters the empty stage and becomes the performative agent who introduces theatricality into the realm of space and time. Temporality and space come together as theatrical presence. Yet, according to Oscar Schlemmer, the history of the theatre is the history of the transfiguration of the human form[5] and Beckett's anti-theatrical project integrates strategies in order to diminish the presence of the character.

This chapter examines the variety of means that the writer deploys so as to generate that lack of the subject.

The evasion of figuration, the withdrawal from representation and the abeyance of the mimetic are related facets of Beckett's method of representational reduction. As Lippard pronounces,

> Morris has projected a sculpture of steam jets; Andre made a monument out of sand dropped into a conical pile from one floor above; Le Witt has hidden elements of his serial projects within other elements where their existence must be taken completely on faith, as will his buried cube at the airport mentioned above. Hermeticism, dematerialization, total intellectualization has an increasing appeal. The complex concept buried in an impressive mass of purely physical bulk or else dispersed into thin air, but remembered, related to the idea of archaeology itself. The pyramids started out as architecture, but once the tombs were closed, they became sculpture. Over the ages they have become objects rather than functional enclosures, but a part of their fascination lies in their unseen cores, in the uses for which they were originally intended. Someone defined the major characteristic of sculpture as 'Just Being there'[6] a statement also made by Robbe-Grillet about Samuel Beckett's plays.[7]

The body of the actor has a privileged status in theatrical representation; it introduces presence and actuality on stage; it also constitutes the subject, as the experiencing agent of the dramatic phenomenon. The human figure becomes the principal architectural space of the theatre; it is the centre point from which the other elements – setting, lighting and sound – are oriented. The performer incarnates the character. The human figure in its physiology and materiality constitutes the form of the subject, the site and sign of the subjectivity of the character. It contributes to the composition of the character and orients at once theatrical empty space and the subjective, corporeal awareness of the spectator.

Beckett's decision to eradicate the stage of the figure might be received as inconsistent in relation to the prominence of the body in his theatre, but it is imperative to focus on the reflective emptiness of the dramatic character and not only on its physical presence. As Drew Leder stresses, while in one 'sense the body is the most abiding and inescapable presence in our lives, it is also essentially characterized by absence'.[8]

DISEMBODIED SPACE

Attitudes towards the staged body – its corporeality, subjectivity – and towards the aesthetic union between stage and the human figure that is delineated by the term 'bodied spatiality'[9] as the agent of the dramatic structure, and the primary element in relation to character formation, determine the context of dramatic writing and practice and define the work of dramatists and theatre practitioners. Peter Brook's (often cited) analysis of 'empty space'[10] unveils this process, by demonstrating the importance of the presence of the performer for the realisation of the theatrical event when s/he enters the empty theatrical space and this emptiness becomes an essential part of the performance.

Theatre and performance are associated with diverse modes of presence. The 'live' immediacy of the performer, the unmediated unfolding of dramatic action and the 'liveliness' generated through an actor-audience relationship are among the notions frequently used to explain theatrical experience, and are all underpinned by a specific understanding of 'presence'.[11] Following the dominance of realism, the 'present-ness' of theatre and literalness became important concerns of the 1950s and 1960s, when aesthetic concerns shifted to a theatre interested in staging the real by focusing on presence.

Theatrical experience draws from the interplay of affirmation or negation of presence and on the interplay of absence and presence. Yet, as Jon Erickson asks, 'what happens to the specific pleasure that theatre affords if presence is to be evaded, eliminated or deconstructed [. . .]?'[12] The above issues are addressed by analysing attitudes towards the absence of the character (of the subject and the body), the formation process of absence and presence in their complex and elusive modes of disclosure, and the theatrical implications of emptiness in Beckett's late dramatic works, and predominantly in *Breath*, by focusing on incorporeality as a component of essential emptiness on stage.

Incorporeality, emptiness and the nexus of materiality and 'incorporeal immateriality' are intimately related in specific art practices. Theatricality, according to Foucault, is the expanding domain of intangible objects that must be integrated into our thought so as to articulate a philosophy of the phantasm that, as he argues, cannot be reduced 'to primordial fact, through the intermediary of perception or an image but that arises between surfaces [. . .] in the temporal oscillation that always makes it precede and follow itself – in short, in what Deleuze would perhaps not allow us to call its incorporeal materiality'.[13]

THE PHENOMENOLOGICAL BODY: INTERFACES OF ABSENCE AND PRESENCE

Beckett experiments with human perception, subjectivity and embodiment, notions identified with the phenomenology of performance. The phenomenology of drama is principally concerned with the phenomenological body that is characterised by a decentred field of subjectivity, and by the polysemous modes of absence and presence. As Garner suggests, the Husserlian tradition relinquishes its hold on the stable subject, which is bound on an ideal self-givenness. It opens, as he argues, 'its domain to experience as we are learning to see it in its dislocations and ambiguities, its variable modes of embodiment, its traces'.[14] The disembodiment and not the dismembering (fragmentation) of the body in *Breath* produces an 'incorporeal spatiality', while Beckett draws from these diverse modes of embodiment and foregrounds on stage a 'trace of presence', since the body is removed from the theatrical space.

Therefore, the aesthetic union and dialectic between theatrical space and human body on stage is simultaneously ruptured and established. The term used to describe this union is 'bodied spatiality' and, according to Garner, 'bodied space' is designed to evoke this 'twinness' of performance when subjected to specifically phenomenological attention. Theatrical space is 'bodied' in the sense of 'bodied forth'; oriented in terms of a body that exists not just as the object of perception, but as its originating site, its zero-point. As Garner argues, 'To stage this point in space before the witness of other bodies is to engage with the complex positionality of theatrical watching.'[15]

The corporeal, as a significatory medium, is essential for the analysis of Beckett's late plays that express 'a writing of the body itself'.[16] The naturalistic body is replaced by the intermedial body which operates in-between live and mediated performance, namely, in-between liveness and technology. The enduring binary between live and mediated performance, as well as the binary between the theatre and the visual arts, is principally founded on different representational attitudes towards the live body, the human figure, corporeal presence, subjectivity/subjecthood and agency. The human body is either physically present or technically represented/mediated in video, film, television and digital media. Intermedial exchange (in the theatre and the visual arts) manages to reconcile this binary by integrating a variety of technical media into a large medial framework.

Notwithstanding the significant presence and materiality of the miscellaneous rubbish as the protagonistic element of the stage design (their literal use – objecthood) and the interplay between light and darkness, the stage is empty of subjectivity in *Breath*. There is an essential absence and lack of the subject, theatrical character and subjecthood. The play opens with a recorded cry that Beckett calls an 'instant of recorded vagitus'. The 'vagitus' is an organic sound, intentionally amplified, yet it is not produced by a present body on stage. The spectator listens to the sound that the body produces on a stage deprived of the presence of an actual body. The auditory frames of representation are extralinguistic and sound alone represents/produces presence, while respiration is not 'visible'; there is almost nothing to see, no mirror image.

The act of listening and sound plays a protagonistic role and, as Enoch Brater suggests, in Beckett's work 'sound literally makes sense'.[17] The playlet's intermedial inquiry into the range of processes, revealing the in-between of theatrical languages, as Dorothee Ostmeier suggests, could be called in acoustic terms silence and in visual terms invisibility.[18] Beckett's intention is 'to force the fundamental invisibility of exterior things till that very invisibility becomes itself a thing, not just awareness of limits but a thing that can be seen and made seen'.[19] The writer delves into the visual image in order to uncover its perceptual 'invisibility' and devises perceptual fields based on theatre's dual status as a visible and invisible space. From a theatre of activity Beckett shifts to a theatre of perception that explores 'the activity lodged within stillness and to sound the depths of visual latency. The result [. . .] is to etch the contours of performance even more within the spectator and to replace a theatre of activity, with a theatre of perception, guided by the eye and its efforts to see'.[20]

The 'visual field' becomes a 'perceptual field' and, like language that has the potential of pointing beyond itself to the unsayable, the visual becomes a screen for the unseeable. Beckett's ultimate objective is not to eliminate either visual image or language, but, as Essif argues, 'to discover images, as well as utterances, that, instead of telling a story, would convey to the spectator a profound and complex sense of emptiness and silence'.[21]

From the emptiness of the stage – whether ostentatious (empty space) or discreet (realistic or even naturalistic set) – the actor's body began to emerge along with every component of theatre – the costumes, scenic elements, lighting, sound and music. Beckett's theatre is a theatre of corporeality, but in *Breath* the writer designs a space emptied of the presence of the subject and the body. Paradoxically though, as Essif insists, 'emptiness is a primary presence; only its absence, one found in realist forms of theatre, could set the stage for a perception of a presence'.[22] The human icon and body is emptied and is placed beyond the visual spectrum, but respiration is produced by the body and entails presence. According to the critic Antony Kubiak, by postulating a theatre that is at the edge of appearance and disappearance, Beckett produces *Breath*: a 'Post Apocalypse with Out Figures'.[23] Kubiak argues that Beckett brings us to the most fundamental moment of theatrical perception, the moment in which one asks what it is that makes 'it' theatre, the moment in which the mind's eye perceives itself seeing, and thinks itself thinking the *mise en scène*. He adds,

> lacking any quality that consensus might declare 'real' performance – devoid of actors, speech and plot. Seemingly devoid of the very theatre that gives it birth. *Breath* invokes an imaginary theatrical apocalypse, the final movement of the performative erased of everything but its own scene.[24]

In the late plays, Beckett simultaneously establishes bodied and disembodied spaces while he designs two spatial fields: the seen and the unseen, the visible and the invisible. In *Breath*, presence is generated, despite the fact that the referent is materially absent; and it is this absence 'in which all presence is announced'[25] as Jacques Derrida remarks. Theorists have been preoccupied with the notion of absence in art, but to posit the concept of an absent signifier is not to reverse the semiotic model, as Fuery notes, 'nor is it to abide by some binarism of the sign itself. Rather, the absent signifier represents a typology – a logical type located in the larger class of signifiers (absent or present)'.[26]

Beckett's aim to purge his texts of mimesis and symbolism alike left him with the task of refining the ways in which 'a text can reflect its lack of content, the central absence'.[27] The body asserts itself as a primary field for the play of presence and absence, existence and death, through the respiratory system. Respiration belongs to the body and is produced by it, yet the figure in *Breath* is an absent signifier and the sound of respiration is a present signifier and paradoxically the one generates the other. This paradox can, however, be grasped, given that the only way to represent absence, as Bergson suggests, is 'through some kind of presence, in the sense that one does not so much represent it as point toward its ineluctable presence'.[28]

The conveyance of a sense of absence is one process, whereas the recognition of emptiness is another. The notion of absence implies referentiality and representability in a way that the notion of emptiness does not. In *Breath*, the absence of the body 'co-exists' with the 'emptiness of space'; the body (an absent signifier) generates emptiness on stage. The decision to subtract the figure from the stage evokes the reception of the empty and *Breath* is integral to the space 'it' stages. The impression of emptiness is not an impression that is related to the scenic materiality of the stage (in this case the miscellaneous rubbish), but to the essential emptiness created by the lack of the body/subject. Les Essif formulates a dramaturgical view of the fusion of the 'empty' body of the actor with the material emptiness of the theatrical space, based on the juncture between theatrical space and the body of the actor, that he considers a meta-dramatic fusion. Essif's approach to drama and performance is based on a new poetics of space for the text based on emptiness.

In the book *Empty Figure on an Empty Stage*, Essif examines the theatrical implications of emptiness with reference to actual performances of dramatic works. He considers the ways playwrights draw meaning from emptiness, by focusing on the ways dramatists create an impression of emptiness not only on the stage but also in the body and mind of the central character. He presents an overview of the evolution of 'empty' characters and 'empty' space in Western drama, as well as the dramatist's use of empty space in the theatre and the spectator's perception of it. His primary referent is the meta-physical and 'sur-real' essence of emptiness and its effect on the spectator.

Essif examines drama associated with non-realistic movements, principally through the aesthetics of 'Nouveau Théâtre',[29] a term that describes the avant-garde theatre of the 1950s, 1960s and 1970s in France, that includes movements such as the 'Theatre of Cruelty', the theatre inspired by the writings of Antonin Artaud. The Nouveau Théâtre artists experiment with notions of emptiness and imaginative uses of the effect of emptiness. Yet according to Essif's approach the representative writers of Nouveau Théâtre are not filling emptiness, they design empty space by valorising it as fundamental, non-representational and non-referential.

In this context, Beckett's dramatic works are characterised by Essif as the quintessential paradigm of 'Hypersubjective Nouveau Théâtre', given that Beckett is more interested in the ways the stage is essentially emptiable instead of essentially fillable. The writer approaches 'empty space qua empty space' and the ways in which it impacts theories of the dramatic subject, the concept of the marionette – like dramatic character and the concept of death for this theatre. Essif examines unrealistic empty space with the aim of re-evaluating theatrical concepts, such as the subjective status of the dramatic character. Beckett, in the late plays, explores and refines the material meaningfulness of the human figure set in emptiness and, like Beckett, dramatists and directors write and direct, as Langbaum argues, 'from the complete emptiness of the stage towards a visual image, that points to the idea of emptiness, as the common denominator between the inside and the outside. The visual image that provides the link between empty stage and empty mind is the human body on stage'.[30]

Nevertheless, Essif claims that Langbaum, like many other theorists, does not acknowledge the essentialist perspective that operates this image on stage, and he appraises the hypothesis that 'metatheatricality' and the existential void that surrounds the mind is duplicated within the mind by producing a double referent that invokes metatheatricality in a profound way. According to this view, Beckett brings the concepts of stage and mind closer together and makes the connection between the exterior and the interior, as Essif argues, 'the head of the dramatic character becomes the central self-referential icon or mise en abyme of theatrical empty space'.[31]

The aesthetic and self-referential nature of Beckett's concentrated (empty) image and this Artaudian metaphysical approach to his theatre – an approach that reveals rather than impedes our awareness of the void of the hypercorporeal, of the extralinguistic – fundamentally prioritises the visual image over narrative story and concentration over fragmentation, as well as emptiness over fullness. This analysis differentiates signs from signals; signs are replaced and signals are introduced, given that signals are considered to be broader than the semiotic message. Phenomenological signals are essentially signifiers that signify extra-referentially and by so doing they point to non-referentiality, thus they are more pertinent for the analysis of emptiness in the theatre, in tandem with Essif's extra-physical, hypercorporeal, metaphysical and phenomenological approach to the empty theatrical space and character.[32]

THE MISSING CHARACTER

The emptiness of space can have a great effect on our perception of the human figure. It is awkward for spectators to imagine a stage without actors, laid out to an empty auditorium. Moreover, it is difficult to perceive the material emptiness of the theatrical space, to perceive 'empty space qua empty space'. The term 'empty' is interpreted as a potentially fillable space, both visually and acoustically. The stage is filled with the actor's presence, even without a setting; the isolated human form, the solitary human figure on the empty stage represents the figural image of the character. The separation of the image of the theatrical space from the image of the character seems unrealistic, since the two are directly aligned and the spectator perceives the dramatic character within space. We need to confront the fact, as Charles Lyons argues, that 'the image of the character in space and time constitutes an irreducible aesthetic unit. No critical system can erase the presence of the human image that occupies the space of the stage'.[33]

Character and its spatial surroundings are conjoined, since the perceptual nature of the theatre is dependent on the stage presence of the human figure, on its phenomenal existence. Scenic and textual levels of representation shape the form of the character as a corporeal presence and visual image on the stage. At the same time, the dramatic text emerges from the performer. As Bruce Wilshire suggests, in a theatrical event, 'an actor must stand in for a character; his image is one that links text and stage space'.[34]

The status of presence becomes problematic in relation to the dramatic text when we consider the written text as something separate and distinct from its staging. Corporeal presence and liveness are often differentiated from the text's verbal language and articulation. Two attitudes are observed in relation to this differentiation. On the one hand, even though non-textual elements generate meaning on the stage, dramatists attempt to preserve the primacy of the word in the theatre. On the other hand, textual representation is subsumed in scenic representation and the dramatic text is treated as the opponent of theatrical presence. This differentiation is expressed as the dichotomy of mimetic space and diegetic space (as proposed by Michael Issacharoff's semiotic analysis of textual space). The mimetic space is that which is made visible to an audience, represented on stage and not conveyed by verbal language.

Issacharoff suggests that dramatic tension in contemporary drama stems from the antinomy between visible space represented and invisible space described. The diegetic space is 'described [. . .] referred to by the characters [. . .] mediated through the discourse of the characters, and thus communicated verbally and not visually'.[35] The visible space is the visual image presented on stage that constitutes the theatrical and the scenic frame of representation, and is considered as multi-layered in comparison to narrative space that is invisible and is generated by the spoken text.

The auditory dimensions of theatricality, even beyond textual representation, foreground sound as stage presence, while the articulation of the body concentrates on the performative. The theatrical body becomes an image produced, signifying and perceived. The notion of the double nature of the human figure, as both living and formal,[36] can be surveyed both in the context of the experiencing body and of the body as it is given to external observation.

The body is treated as an individual, a human subject and a character, or it can be dissociated from its usual function of indicating an individual identity or a character, and can become an object, a mannequin. The human figure introduces a fundamental, vital and intrusive actuality into the field of dramatic representation, an actuality that charges even verbal reflections (and evocations) of bodily presence that Garner sees as a point of independent sentience; the body represents, as he states, 'a rootedness in the biological present that always, to some extent, escapes transformation into the virtual realm'.[37]

Different accounts of the relationship between actuality and theatrical representation, the concept of mimesis and theatrical practice, textuality and theatricality (speech, voice, language and non-linguistic processes of signification), become the backdrop of dramatic writing and practice, and indicate the interface between literary drama and non-textual performance. McLuhan makes an analogy from the world of physics, arguing that two cultures or technologies can, like astronomical galaxies, pass through one another without collision; but, as he writes, 'not without a change in configuration. In modern physics there is similarly, the concept of "interface" or the meeting and metamorphosis of two structures'.[38]

This formative process generates an inter-generic treatment of text and performance. The interactive dynamic between text, performance and theatricality is seen as the interplay of auditory and scenic frames of representation (rather than a term which merely indicates a clash between the visual image presented onstage and the verbal image created by the spoken word). In Beckett's later theatrical works, and in particular in *Breath*, this dynamic interface generates a 'new type of text', that is intrinsically intermedial, given that it operates in-between auditory and scenic frames of representational practices. Beckett, being both the writer and the director of his work identifies the literary text with its performative realisation (focus on stage directions), while he expands the literary genre and defies literary and dramatic conventions. 'Text', as Beckett has been redefining it (since *Not I*), disintegrates the conventional way of thinking about drama as something separate and distinct from performance. The absence of any acceptable boundaries distinguishing play from performance reality signals the breakdown of other generic distinctions.

The Beckettian text challenges the genre of a unified dramatic form, and proposes a significatory practice that includes but also goes beyond the centrality of language (as a system of meaning). This unified dramatic form becomes the centre of action in these plays and the writer's attempt to relyricise the genre is, as Brater states, 'the only way the voice of the would-be poet can open the constraints of a performing arts medium'.[39] The inter-generic nature of Beckett's 'fabricated' language expands the limits of language by providing an alternative that also unsettles views about the nature of language. Beckett's ultimate aim is to express being without words, beyond our linguistic set-up.

Faced with the paradoxical nature of his artistic endeavour, Beckett pursues his assault on language in the hope of finally achieving the 'literature of the unword' (a term that Beckett used to describe his work). This assault is identified as 'indeterminacy' by Marjorie Perloff, 'decreation' by Ruby Cohn, and as 'the syntax of weakness', 'the point zero of language', 'arts of impoverishment' and 'literature of silence' by other commentators.

The rejection of any attempt at writing is analysed thoroughly in 'The German Letter' (1937), that is a part of a correspondence between Beckett and Alex Kaun (a friend whom he met in Germany). It was becoming more and more difficult, even senseless, for Beckett to write in an official English and progressively his own language appeared to him like a veil that, as he writes:

> must be torn apart in order to get at things (or the Nothingness) behind it. Grammar and Style. To me they seem to have become as irrelevant as a Victorian bathing suit or the imperturbability of a true gentleman. A mask. Let us hope the time will come, thank god that in certain circles it has already come, when language is most efficiently used where it is being most efficiently misused. As we cannot eliminate language at once, we should at least leave nothing undone that might contribute to its falling into disrepute. To bore one hole after another in it [language], until what lurks behind it – be it something or nothing – begins to seep though; I cannot imagine a higher goal for a writer today.[40]

According to Brater, Beckett's drama is not a 'drama in the shape of poetry but poetry in the shape of drama', since the experience for the audience in the theatre is like the experience of reading a poem, except that in this instance the poem has been staged. Language art and theatre art draw together, he suggests, progressively validating through stage time and our own time the purity of the writer's voice, as Beckett builds a sustained dramatic metaphor. In his late plays, Beckett pursues the limits and possibilities of such unified dramatic form even further by challenging his audience to analyse and, as Brater argues, 'to encounter with him the special effects of a stage situation, when one genre breaks into another'.[41] However, Brater and Esslin share different perspectives concerning language and visual imagery. Esslin points beyond language: he considers that the visual frames of representation are primordial to the textual; the late plays represent a wholly new genre; they are poems without words, visual poetry and according to this view Beckett reaches the 'point zero of language'.[42]

Esslin highlights the visual and aural disposition of Beckett's art and its relationship to some types of contemporary performance art. The metaphor and the poetics have been freed from the word altogether:

> It is not drama any more, it is poetry, wordless poetry. Nor is it strictly speaking cinema: it lacks the epic quality, the storytelling element of

cinema; it is most akin to some types of contemporary performance art, where also, often, two distinct phases are distinguishable: firstly the ritual of building the image, secondly the display of the image. In some sense this is a kind of painting, the creation of an 'emblem' to be deciphered by the viewer, except that the image moves and has sound.[43]

The interchange between non-textual frames of representation in performance and text oriented drama leads to a redefinition of the concept of the character in contemporary performance and a gradual revision of character representation.[44] The dramatic character holds a problematic status on the contemporary stage. This destabilisation leads to the fragmentation of the textual and visual frames that are used to figure the subject and to the displacement of the figure within the narrative. Character dissolves into the flux of performance elements and, as Gruber argues, 'the idea of character haunts us in the theatre like the absence of some pictorial metabolism in a colour field. Playwrights have abandoned many elements long thought essential to drama, including plot, action and character'.[45] Thus it is essential to contextualise this process in terms of art theory and discourse on aesthetics, where there is also a tendency to move away from the human subject.[46] The move away from the human subject (in cubism, futurism and other art movements) is foreshadowed by other 'advanced' theatre artists at the end of the nineteenth century, thus it is often believed that owing to the live actor, dramatic character survived what we think of as the particular modern dis-assemblage of the concept of the character.

Elinor Fuchs relates the ontological issue of 'the character's desubstantiation' in the theatre to the crisis of representation to discourses and ideas that derive from French critical postmodern discourses. In critical theory the subject is put in question. From Lacan's insight into the symbolic construction of subjectivity, as he states regarding Foucault's announcement of the 'end of man' to Derrida's attack on the 'metaphysics of Presence', Roland Barthes' 'Death of the Author', Baudrillard's shattering 'precession of the simulacra', Deleuze and Guatari's 'schizoanalysis' and Lyotard's collapse of the 'grands récits' of modernism.[47] Nevertheless, as a rule, we examine strategies that are employed in order to diminish the presence of the character, but not the total abstraction that left behind the human form. *Breath* pursues this course even further, by illustrating Beckett's project to create a text devoid of character and actors.

The human figure in performance is not a representation of something spoken, but rather speaks itself. The body introduces a radical actuality on stage that surpasses linguistic signification. The human body as a working material goes beyond the representational role-playing of theatre and generates 'the dramaturgy of the organic'. The best possible play is one in which 'there are no actors, only the text', Beckett told Deidre Bair, 'I am trying to find a way to write one.'[48] Moreover, Beckett's ultimate aim is to express being without words, beyond our linguistic set-up. It is equally interesting to bring to mind Beckett's desire 'to create a blank or white page'. Esslin mentioned half-jokingly after meeting Beckett for the first time, 'he was trying to become more and more concise so that he could perhaps produce a white page in the end'.[49] The blank spaces between each paragraph offer a constant reminder of this paradoxical goal. Words only serve to dim the images he is laboriously constructing or rather deconstructing:

> Till blank again . . . No words again . . . Then all dimmed . . . That words had dimmed. The trouble is that without words there is no form: What when words gone? None for what then . . . For what when nohow on. Somehow nohow on. Faced with the paradoxical nature of his artistic endeavor, the narrator can only pursue his assault on language in the hope of finally achieving a literature of the unword.[50]

The body in performance can either displace or be a supplement for the character and according to Pierre Chabert,[51] the body is always present in those forms of theatre that use actors, but it may be present and active in many different ways. In theatre based on characters (the majority of existing plays) the actor's figure is subjugated to psychological factors: the actor must incarnate different character types and express different psychological states. In this context, the body is a means, entirely subordinated to the plot and to psychological description. It is not approached for and in itself. As Chabert suggests, 'it supports the action and acts as a relay for bringing the character to life'.[52] Beckett's later plays reveal an increasing dispossession within bodied subjectivity, and the gradual abandonment of the naturalistic body. The writer employs strategies to diminish the presence of character, and evolves techniques of concentration on the body, on aspects of the physical and the corporeal.

The figure/character becomes fragmented, dehumanised, spatially restricted, and it is drawn towards 'invisibility' and 'immobility'.[53] Beckett's process of reduction removes the context for the narrative and presents merely the figure and the text, and, as Lyons argues, the recited discourses in these later plays overpower the dramatised action and they provoke us to re-examine the conventional relationship between narration and enactment in drama:

> whereas *Waiting for Godot* (1953/55) consists of two acts, five characters and the length of a 'well-made' play, Beckett's *Endgame* (1957/58), consists of two pairs of actors, one pair confined to waste bins, and one act, *Act Without Words I* and *II* (1957/59) are mime plays for one or two characters, *Krapp's Last Tape* (1958) did with one actor, on the verge of extinction, and could easily be produced for the radio, because action there is reduced to changing spools and satisfying basic human needs, such as to eat and drink.[54]

Furthermore, *Krapp's Last Tape* was inspired by a voice Beckett had heard on BBC during the period he was in Paris and the text written especially for this 'voice'. *Happy Days* (1961) features two actors, but Winnie, the female and the only speaking character in the play, is 'embedded up to above her waist [. . .] in a mound'. In *Breath* this process of reduction reaches its climax; narrative, text and figure are removed from the stage; the triptych of character, body and actor has vanished. Johanneke van Slooten discusses these later works in terms of the reduction of the visual frames used for the representation of the body:

> in the course of Beckett's dramatic work a phased reduction of the body can be observed. In *Waiting for Godot* two complete men walk in circles. In *Eh Joe*, the protagonist is reduced to sitting on the edge of his bed, while listening to a woman's voice. By the slightest movements of his back, we get to know his emotions. In *Happy Days*, Winnie's movements are restricted to her upper body, because the lower part is locked up in a sandhill. She is left with only the ability to gesticulate. The bodily function is even further reduced in *Play*, where only the heads remain: their bodies are stowed away in urns. They merely have the command over their mimics and the ability to (literally) change their point of view. *Not I* leaves us with nothing but a mouth that keeps talking until breath, the vehicle of the voice, is all that remains. A breath moves through its extreme life story in *Breath*. After its birth from the dark acoustics of the head, it emerges and comes to life in the light for a brief contact with the outside world, then withers away in the twilight – until the last breath is exhaled and darkness falls.[55]

In view of the increasing dispossession within bodied subjectivity and the eradication of the body in *Breath*, it is inexplicable that stagings of the playlet overlook or intentionally disregard Beckett's central premise, namely, the absence of the subject. Thus, the artists and directors do not acknowledge the writer's aesthetic decision to stress the significance of the lack of the human figure and character. Rather than highlighting this fundamental emptiness, the artists aim to unveil an essential subjectivity by adding the human figure in various forms, thus associating *Breath* with the human body, despite Beckett's manifest desire to distinguish the two.

Amanda Coogan's *Breath*

The Beckett Centenary presentation of *Breath* by Bedrock Productions in Dublin, directed by performance artist Amanda Coogan, also includes human bodies. Plastic figures are the protagonistic element of the set design. The bodies of mannequins are lying shattered amongst Beckett's miscellaneous rubbish. The bodies become a pile of rubbish illuminated by 'faint light'.

Figure 4.1: AMANDA COOGAN. *Breath*: 2007 design and direction for the Samuel Beckett play. Bedrock Production for the Beckett Festival at the Project Arts Centre, Dublin

Coogan, according to Turbity, 'in what might be considered an ironic gesture to Kenneth Tynan's production, includes a scattering of mannequin limbs amongst the detritus barely visible under the dim light, evoking also the prosthetic element of Beckett's work within the context of a very characteristic aesthetic of debilitation, dismemberment and decay'.[56] Rather than focusing on the implications of the emptiness that is produced by the presence of the empty figure on stage and the dialectics of presence (liveness) and absence, the artist substitutes the miscellaneous rubbish with plastic human figures, and instead of alluding to the fundamental existential emptiness, the body multiplies and becomes a stage prop.

This directorial vision shows the limitless enlargements of Beckett's *oeuvre* , since the writer has been made the centrepiece of what might be called a contemporary aesthetics of the inexhaustible that, as Connor argues:

> assumes the sovereign value of endless propagation and maintains a horror of any kind of limit. Having perhaps helped in some of my previous work to recruit Beckett to this aesthetic, I would like now, in this talk, to argue that Beckett is in fact a writer who is governed by the principles of limit and finitude, principles that are in fact both philosophically

more provocative and politically more responsible than the cult of endless exceeding that has attached itself to Beckett.[57]

The decision to include a body on *Breath*'s set stresses the significance of the representation of the body on the stage, but Coogan approaches this aesthetic issue only from a 'physical' point of view, since she overlooks the reflective emptiness of the dramatic character and the self-referential and meta-theatrical nature of the piece. *Breath*'s 'emptiness' is not incorporated in the dramatic subject because the dramatic subject is absent.

The stage, moreover, is empty of the presence of the human figure, hence the treatment of 'empty space' is associated with *Breath*'s emphasis on the actual, its modes of presence and its resistance to being transformed into the virtual realm. As Timothy Wiles reveals, the value of 'empty space' is a value that he believes is implied by Peter Brook's notion of the empty space. Wiles argues that Brook points to a phenomenon of theatre architecture that has broader implications for our understanding of the poetics of space in dramaturgy and in aesthetics. For Wiles, the concern with empty space suggests the disavowal of an autonomous site of theatrical activity – a rejection of both the stage setting and of the auditorium (if the setting is understood as an assembly hall that is set apart from the world and has no other function than that). Instead of this separation, Wiles argues that:

> the empty space asks for continuity between theatre event and life event – that is, it claims that the theatre event is a kind of a life event, not a copy of one. And its more general aesthetic implication is to require us to pay as close attention to the empty space surrounding and shaped by the art object, as we pay to the object itself.[58]

This hermeneutic approach attempts to cancel out the aesthetic and the non-aesthetic dichotomy by providing a certain integration of the aesthetic with everyday life. Respiration on stage originates directly from everyday life, from the individual's concrete life experience. Wiles' approach acknowledges the tension between the representational and the non-representational aspects of theatrical reality, and the challenge Beckett poses to the limits of the art object, while it focuses on the spatial, gestural and durational extensions of artistic innovation. Space and time are primary materials, while the viewer is aware of her/his presence during the theatrical process. This process is affected by the 'contextual' elements whose expanded engagement eventually unhinges medium purity.

The concept of aesthetic autonomy as the very condition of the possibility of 'art' itself is re-evaluated or even abandoned, and the notion of context-independent art is impossible even in Beckett's abstracted imagery. The fundamental ontological emptiness of *Breath*'s disembodied stage has political and ideological underpinnings. Beckett's decision to eradicate the subject is not only a formal decision, nor is it only an allegorical statement about the human condition, it is a critical response to a post-Holocaust reality that is depicted on stage as a stagnant landscape filled with waste.

NOTES

1. Stéphane Mallarmé. 'Brise Marine' [1887]. In Anthony Hartley (ed.), *Mallarmé*. Baltimore: Penguin Books, 1965: 29.
2. Žižek, Slavoj. 'Beckett with Lacan'. See http://www.lacan.com [accessed 1/11/2016].
3. Adorno, Theodor W. *Aesthetic Theory*, trans. Robert Hullot-Kentor. Minneapolis: University of Minnesota Press, 1997: 230.
4. Robert Barry. In Lippard, Lucy R. (ed.), *Six Years: The Dematerialization of the Art Object from 1966 to 1972*. London: Studio Vista, 1973: xx.
5. Oscar Schlemmer. In Gropius, Walter (ed.), *Oscar Schlemmer, László Moholy-Nagy, Farkas Molnar, The Theatre of the Bauhaus*. Baltimore: Johns Hopkins University Press, 1996: 17.
6. Alain Robbe-Grillet writes about Beckett's drama, citing Heidegger, that the key to his work is to be there, to be present on the stage. As he argues,

> the condition of man, says Heidegger, is to be there. The theatre probably reproduces this situation more naturally than any of the other ways to represent reality. The essential thing about a character is that he is on the scene: there. Thus once more, right up to the final image, we have the essential theme presence. Everything that is here; off the stage there is nothing, non-being.

Robbe-Grillet, Alain. 'Samuel Beckett or Presence on the Stage'. In *For a New Novel: Essays on Fiction*. Evanston: Northwestern University Press, 1989: 111.
7. '10 Structuralists in 20 Paragraphs' was written for the catalogue accompanying the exhibition 'Minimal Art', organised by Enno Develing at the Haags Gemeentemuseum, The Hague, The Netherlands, in 1968, that was one of the major exhibitions on this subject put on by a European Institution. Harald Szeemann's 'Attitudes Become Form' followed in 1969, as a tribute to conceptual art. The emergence of conceptual art is considered by art theorists as minimalism's avant-garde successor. In Lippard, Lucy R. (ed.), *Six Years*: 31.
8. Leder, Drew. *The Absent Body*. Chicago: University of Chicago Press, 1990: 1.
9. A term introduced by Stanton Garner who applied a phenomenological method of analysis to performance. Garner, Stanton. *Bodied Spaces: Phenomenology and Performance in Contemporary Drama*. Ithaca, NY: Cornell University Press, 1994.
10. See Brook, Peter. *The Empty Space*. New York: Atheneum, 1984.
11. See Power, Cormac. *Presence in Play: A Critique of Theories of Presence in the Theatre*. Amsterdam and New York: Rodopi, 2008.
12. Erickson, Jon. *The Fate of the Object: From Modern Object to Postmodern Sign in Performance, Art, and Poetry*. Ann Arbor: University of Michigan Press, 1995: 216.
13. This review essay originally appeared in *Critique*, 282 (1970): 885–908. The translation, by Donald F. Brouchard and Sherry Simon, has been slightly amended. Murray, Timothy (ed.). *Mimesis, Masochism, and Mime: The Politics of Theatricality in Contemporary French Thought*. Ann Arbor: University of Michigan Press, 1997.
14. Garner, Stanton. *Bodied Spaces: Phenomenology and Performance in Contemporary Drama*. Ithaca, NY: Cornell University Press, 1994: 230.

15. Ibid.
16. See the works of Derrida and Chabert generally.
17. Enoch Brater quoted in Buning, Marius (ed.). *Historicising Beckett: Issues of Performance*. Amsterdam: Rodopi, 2005: 212.
18. See Ostmeier, Dorothee. 'Dramatizing Silence: Beckett's Shorter Plays'. In Lois Oppenheim and Marius Buning (eds), *Beckett On and On ...* Madison and London: Associated University Presses, 1996: 187.
19. Essif, Les. *Empty Figure on an Empty Stage: The Theatre of Samuel Beckett and his Generation*. Bloomington: Indiana University Press, 2001: 58.
20. Garner, Stanton. 'Visual Field in Beckett's Late Plays', *Comparative Drama*, XXI.4 (1987–8): 371.
21. Ibid.: 60–1.
22. Ibid.
23. Kubiak, Anthony. 'Post Apocalypse with Out Figures: The Trauma of Theatre in Samuel Beckett'. In Joseph H. Smith (ed.), *The World of Samuel Beckett*. Baltimore: Johns Hopkins University Press, 1991: 107.
24. Ibid.
25. Derrida, Jacques. *Writing and Difference*, trans. Alan Bass. Oxford: Routledge, 2008: 7.
26. Fuery, Patrick. *Theory of Absence: Subjectivity, Signification, and Desire*. Westport, CT: Greenwood Press, 1996: 25.
27. Albright, Daniel. *Beckett and Aesthetics*. Cambridge: Cambridge University Press, 2003: 13.
28. Quoted in Essif, Les. *Empty Figure on an Empty Stage*: 27.
29. See Serreau, Geneviève. *Histoire du Nouveau Théâtre*. Paris: Galimard, 1966.
30. Langbaum, Robert. *The Mysteries of Identity: A Theme in Modern Literature*. London and Chicago: University of Chicago Press, 1982: 137.
31. Essif, Les. 'Introducing the Hyper Theatrical Subject: The Mise en Abyme of Empty Space', *Journal of Dramatic Theory and Criticism*, 9.1 (1994): 69.
32. Phenomenology in performance is seen as a term of fundamental complementarity. As Garner states, 'phenomenology complements the always already of signification with the always also of the subject's corporeal fields'. Parallel to this, what the text loses in significative power in the theatre, he says, 'it gains in corporeal presence, in which there is an extraordinary perceptual satisfaction. Hence, the need for rounding out a semiotics of the theatre with a phenomenology of its imagery or if you will, a phenomenology of its semiology'. Garner, Stanton. *Bodied Spaces: Phenomenology and Performance in Contemporary Drama*. Ithaca, NY: Cornell University Press, 1994: 230.
33. Lyons, Charles. 'Character and Theatrical Space'. In James Redmond (ed.), *The Theatrical Space*. Cambridge: Cambridge University Press, 1987: 28.
34. Wilshire, Bruce. *Role Playing and Identity: The Limits of Theatre as Metaphor*. Bloomington, IN: Bloomington University Press, 1982: 42 and 43.
35. Issacharoff, Michael. 'Space and Reference in Drama', *Poetics Today*, 2.3 (1981): 210.
36. A comparative analysis of the chapters on 'The Grain of the Voice' and 'Baudelaire's Theatre' shows the significance Barthes attributes to corporeal presence. As he writes, authentic theatricality, in Baudelaire's plays is 'the sentiment, indeed one might say the torment, of the actor's disturbing corporeality'. According to Barthes, 'Baudelaire's theatre: had an acute sense of the most secret and also the most disturbing theatricality, the kind which puts the actor in the centre of the theatrical prodigy and constitutes the theatre as the site of an ultra incarnation, in which the body is double, at once a living body deriving from a

trivial nature, and an emphatic, formal body, frozen by its function as an artificial object.' Barthes acknowledges a disturbing theatricality with the actor as its centre and with various implications for the representation of the body in the theatre'. Barthes, Roland. *Critical Essays*. Evanston: Northwestern University Press, 1972: 28.
37. Garner, Stanton. *Bodied Spaces*: 44.
38. Quoted in Heuvel, Michael Vanden. *Performing Drama/Dramatizing Performance: Alternative Theatre and the Dramatic Text*. Ann Arbor: University of Michigan Press, 1991: 20.
39. Brater, Enoch. *Beyond Minimalism*: 17.
40. Beckett, Samuel. 'German Letter'. In Ruby Cohn (ed.), *Disjecta: Miscellaneous Writings and a Dramatic Fragment*. London: Calder: 172.
41. Brater, Enoch. *Beyond Minimalism*: 17.
42. See Esslin, Martin. 'A Poetry of Moving Images'. In Alan-Warren Friedman, Charles Rossman and Dina Sherzer (eds), *Beckett Translating/ Translating Beckett*. University Park: Pennsylvania State University Press, 1987: 74.
43. Ibid.: 47.
44. Modern playwrights and theatre practitioners are critical of realistic forms of representation and reconsider conventional structures of identity, the official presence of the character on stage, and stable constructions of plot and language.
45. See Gruber, William. *Missing Persons: Character and Characterization in Modern Drama*. Athens: University of Georgia Press, 1994: 5.
46. As José Ortega y Gasset argues, in his study about the 'dehumanization of art'. Gasset, José Ortega y. *The Dehumanization of Art, and Other Writings on Art and Culture*. Ann Arbor: Doubleday Anchor Books, 1956.
47. Fuchs, Elinor. *The Death of Character: Perspectives on Theater after Modernism*. Bloomington: Indiana University Press, 1996: 1.
48. Bair, Deidre. *Samuel Beckett: A Biography*. London: Cape, 1978.
49. Esslin, Martin. *Une Poesie d' images movantes, Beckett's revue d'esthetique, numero hors-serie*. Prépare par Pierre Chabert. Paris: J-M. Place, 1990: 403. Gontarski notes

> the quotation anticipates the paradoxical self-canceling nature of Beckett's art, it focuses on his continuing attempts to write the vanishing self-destructive text, and further anticipates the Beckettian aesthetic axiom on the impossibility of expression 'there is nothing to express nothing with which to express, nothing from which to express together with the obligation to express'. Beckett's oft-quoted statement deserves a gloss. 'Nothing to express' is also an active phrase: what remains to be expressed is nothingness, primary absences, even though that needs to be done with the faulty system of language, a system whose referential quality is in serious question. There is 'nothing from which to express' because self is not a unity, not a coherent entity, but itself an interplay of presence and absence, a dialectic of the one and the other. There is no power to express because author and narrator, characters and language itself are impotent.

Gontarski, Stanley. *The Intent of Undoing in Samuel Beckett's Dramatic Texts*. Bloomington: Indiana University Press, 1985: 81.
50. Beckett, Samuel. *Worstward Ho*. London: John Calder, 1983: 13.
51. The actor and Beckett's close friend who wrote about *Beckett and the Body*. See Pierre Chabert. 'The Body In Beckett's Theatre', *Journal of Beckett Studies*, 8 (Autumn 1982): 23–8.
52. Ibid.: 24.

53. Ibid.
54. Lyons, Charles. 'Character and Theatrical Space'. In James Redmond (ed.), *The Theatrical Space*. Cambridge: Cambridge University Press, 1987: 28.
55. Quoted in Oppenheim, Lois and Marius Buning (eds). *Beckett On and On . . . .* Madison and London: Associated University Presses, 1996: 59–60.
56. Coogan, Amanda. 'Performance Art' *IGNITE*. Science Gallery, Trinity College, Dublin, 14 April 2010. Quoted in Turbity, Derval. 'Beckett's Spectral Silence: Breath and the Sublime', *Limit(e) Beckett*, 1(2010): 102–22.
57. Connor, Steven. 'On Such and Such a Day . . . In Such a World: Beckett's Radical Finitude'. 'Borderless Beckett'. International Samuel Beckett Symposium in Tokyo, 29 September 2006. See http://www.stevenconnor.com/finitude/ [accessed 1/11/16].
58. Wiles, Timothy. *The Theatre Event: Modern Theories of Performance*. Chicago: University of Chicago Press, 1980: 114.

PART III
THE EXHALED FIELD

5

WASTE OF BREATH:
THE READYMADE AS A STAGE SET

in the insomniac dream, it is not a question of realising the impossible,
but of exhausting the possible.[1]

any spatial relations and material forms one might still experience
outside [the] registers of overproduction of objects and of electronic
digitalization now appear as mere abandoned zones, as remnant objects
and leftover spaces . . ." In such a context, is there a limit to recycling
and representation? Or is there a point at which waste cannot become
art (or anything else)?[2]

The relationship between objecthood and art shifted in the 1960s, from the
'readymade' and standardised units to the utilitarian objects and the materials
of impoverishment, including waste matter. Waste, that is represented by a pile
of scattered and lying rubbish, becomes the protagonist on *Breath*'s set, akin to
the installations and contemporary visual art pieces by artists such as Thomas
Hirschhorn, Mark Dion, Mierle Laderman Ukeles, Abraham Cruzvillegas,
Andreas Gursky and Vik Muniz, Surasi Kusolwong and Santiago Sierra who
employ debris as a material and sculptural element. Detritus, as Benjamin
Buchloch argues, is an inevitable consequence of 'the incessant overproduction
of objects of consumption and their perpetually enforced and accelerated obso-
lescence [that] generate a vernacular violence in the spaces of everyday life'.[3]
Thus, the representation of waste exposes the logic of excess in our society.

The significant presence and materiality of the miscellaneous rubbish as the protagonistic element of the stage design (their literal use – objecthood) is not so much sculptured as assembled and arranged. However, the interplay between light and darkness and the sound of inhalation and exhalation is strictly orchestrated in *Breath*. Beckett opens the pictorial (found objects) and sculptural to actual space in the same way that minimalists and conceptual artists experiment with these transpositions. This chapter attempts to further illuminate *Breath*'s complex relationship between a visual art piece and the theatre by examining Beckett's choice to fill the stage with scattered and lying rubbish as an effort to escape 'aesthetisised automatism', and by arguing that the presence of rubbish is related to Beckett's 'anti-aesthetic' and 'aesthetics of failure', as described in his final piece of discursive criticism the 'Three Dialogues', that implies the failure to represent (to fail means to fail to represent) and the state of artistic impotence.

The history of painting, according to Beckett, is the history of 'its attempts to escape from this sense of failure, by means of more authentic, more ample, less exclusive relations between representer and representee, in a kind of tropism towards a light as to the nature of which the best opinions continue to vary [. . .]' The methodological challenges of converging the relational with the non-relational in art are very demanding, however Beckett considers that the fidelity of failure becomes a new term of relation and aims to 'endorse disjunction' and to 'exhaust possibilities' by insisting that 'all that is required now, in order to bring even this horrible matter to an acceptable conclusion, is to make [. . . of . . .] this fidelity to failure, a new occasion, a new term of relation [. . .] I know that my inability to do so places myself and perhaps an innocent, in what I think is still called an unenviable situation, familiar to psychiatrists'.[4]

The fidelity of failure becomes for Beckett a new occasion, a new term of relation intrinsically related to the decision to depict waste on the stage. The depiction of waste and Beckett's attempt to escape 'aesthetisised automatism' are but a further extension of the desire for an art autonomous from the aesthetic. The resistance to representation is fundamental for understanding artistic impotence and Beckett's decision to stage a pile of rubbish is one that alludes to the failure which perhaps has to be endorsed.[5] This anti-aesthetic approach and the 'art of the non-relational' opens new relations and opportunities for art, the first to submit, Beckett says:

> wholly to the incoercible absence of relation, in the absence of terms or, if you like, in the presence of unavailable terms, the first to admit that to be an artist is to fail, as no other dare fail [. . .] to make this submission, this admission, this fidelity of failure, a new occasion, a new term of relation, and of the act which, unable to act, obliged to act, he makes, an expressive act, even if only of itself, of its impossibility, of its obligation

[. . .] for what is this coloured plane, that was not there before. It seems to have nothing to do with art, in any case, if my memories are correct (prepares to go).[6]

THE POLITICS OF FORM AND THE ANTI-AESTHETICS OF WASTE: THOMAS HIRSCHHORN, MARK DION, ANDREAS GURSKY, VIK MUNIZ, MIERLE LADERMAN UKELES, SANTIAGO SIERRA, SURASI KUSOLWONG AND ABRAHAM CRUZVILLEGAS

Visual artists employ disposable objects and discarded elements as materials through which they construct their work, and as metaphors that allude to the disparity between poverty and wealth, encroaching commercialism and its consequences, but also to the precarious and ephemeral conditions of contemporary life. The plasticity of waste is prevalent in the installation pieces by Hirschhorn, Dion, Sierra, Kusolwong and Cruzvillegas, but is also represented in the medium of photography and photographic assemblage in the works of Gursky and Muniz.

The assemblage of installation elements and oversized objects produces a still image that resembles a temporalised contemporary art installation (tableau) depicting a moribund environment. The tableau of assemblage and readymades produces a spatial collage that is reduced in time and space to the point where it becomes static and frozen, both temporally and spatially, while the actual stage becomes an element of this three-dimensional composition.

Beckett designs and controls even the slightest detail of the set and in particular, in *Breath*, he employs a sculptural process that is similar to the ways in which assemblage is applied to the visual arts. The piece integrates the theatrical and the visual into a large medial framework, but also into a single visual experience that opens up to extra-theatrical forms including installation art, readymade and assemblage. The assemblage of installation elements and oversized objects shows structural affinities with the visual arts.

Assemblage is not a separate medium but is based on media formations that are intermedial, in the sense that they share basic properties; assemblage combines syntactical elements that come from more than one medium but are combined into one and are thereby transformed into a new entity. Spatial collage has structural affinities with assemblage, given that both techniques oscillate between the pictorial and the three-dimensional. As Paola Ibarra points out, assemblage at a tangible level (that is, of actual physical objects) became evident with the transformation of visual representation introduced by collage in 1912.[7] According to Ibarra, Clement Greenberg, in his essay *Collage*,[8] argues that Picasso and Braque incorporated, for the first time, extraneous materials into the surface of a picture in search for 'sculptural results by strictly non-sculptural means'. In turn, cubist collage gave way to what Greenberg refers to as the 'new sculpture' or 'construction-sculpture' that revolutionised the medium – from its materials to the techniques and compositional methods. The new sculpture, Greenberg writes:

> tends to abandon stone, bronze and clay for industrial materials like iron, steel, alloy, glass, plastic, celluloid, etc., etc., which are worked with the blacksmith's, the welder's and even the carpenter's tools. Unity of material and color is no longer required, and applied color is sanctioned. The distinction between carving and modeling becomes irrelevant: a work or its parts can be cast, wrought, cut or simply put together; it is not so much sculptured as constructed, built, assembled, arranged.[9]

Cubist collage displays concern with the pictorial or structural elements contained within works of art, in contrast to minimalist works that are based on additive components and on the inclusion of the viewer. The collage, therefore, has an inherent structure and is appreciated by Greenberg as an independent entity that shows that the artwork attempts to locate the essence of its medium through a process of immanent self-criticism.

The representation of waste, sanitation and maintenance labour raises aesthetic, conceptual and formal questions that challenge the status of the aesthetic object and that contextualise domestic economy and broader urban and ecological processes. In contrast to modernist discourse and aesthetic modernity, artists who investigate the materiality of waste and its readymade status regard formalist concerns as predominantly ideological. Thomas Hirschhorn's spatial collages challenge the artwork's status as an object and its relationship to the viewer, while it stresses the social ramifications of the work and the social reality of production, consumption and excess. As the artist states, 'I make poor art, but no Arte Povera [. . .] I don't make installations, I make sculptures [. . .] energy yes, quality no [. . .] I don't want to make political art, but I want to make my work political.'[10] Santiago Sierra's work is also political and reflects on the humanist ramifications of waste picking, while Abraham Cruzvillegas' and Mierle Laderman Ukeles' work focuses on environmental politics.

Ukeles' post-minimalist *oeuvre* investigates the sanitation system and ascribes value to maintenance over creativity. She says, in the *Manifesto for Maintenance Art*, 'the sourball of every revolution: [. . .] who's going to pick up the garbage on Monday morning?'[11] Ukeles' first project with the Department of Sanitation, *Touch Sanitation Performance* (1979–80), is a work of performance and process art. The artist's research is based on every aspect of the Department of Sanitation's facilities, employees and routes. Cynthia Deitering argues that the 1980s marked a shift from a culture defined by its production to a culture defined by its waste, and that this shift showed our own complicity in post-industrial ecosystems, a statement that shapes Ukeles' work. As Mark B. Feldman argues:

this ecological perspective lets or perhaps forces one to see the city as a complex, interrelated, and dynamic living system. It also encourages a view of the city as embedded within a larger economy, calling attention to asymmetrical divisions of labor and wealth. Ukeles' sanitation art projects seek to bestow dignity on a typically undervalorized sector of the economic labor market – the men and women who pick up our garbage.[12]

The figure of the contemporary waste-picker stresses the role that maintenance labour plays in sustaining the post-industrial ecosystem of the urban centres, as well as the consumer's implication in the work of sanitation. By focusing on forms of labour that represent radical limitations on personal freedoms, Kusolwong and Sierra invite their audiences to consider which social groups are included in, or excluded from, narratives of urban modernity (or to use Amartya Sen's word, social 'development') in local and international contexts. These artists ask viewers to question the constituent elements of urban modernity both from a local and a supranational perspective. As Kathryn Brown argues:

> the transposition of such labor practices to cities that have been viewed as quintessential sites of urban modernity (New York and London) prompts reflection not only on the political and economic discrepancies in the societies within which such labor takes place, but also on the conflicting narratives that have informed the history of modernity itself.[13]

Apnoeic Detritus: The Exhausted Project of Modernity

Political engagement in works that reflect on the accumulation of waste is implicit since the works problematise modernist aims and concerns by taking the pieces to new levels of complexity, beyond aesthetic autonomy. Utilitarian objects such as debris, in contrast to aesthetic objects, fail to manifest implicitly their unique medium shape. According to modernist discourse shape is 'the essence of the pictorial' and the means by which it would defeat art's objecthood. Modernist theorists would argue that the representation of waste, like the readymade and brute objects, has the look of 'non-art' and evokes 'presence' – as opposed to the presentness of modernist art. The miscellaneous rubbish engenders a powerful physical immediacy, yet because of its human scale and hollowness it simulates the presence of another person, albeit a mute, identity-less person.

Moreover, the spectator stands in an open-ended, indeterminate and wholly passive relation to these works as a detached subject. Interaction, engagement and response – the characteristics of aesthetic experience – are turned into isolation, passive reception and domination. The 'theatricality/objecthood' of waste creates an over-awareness of the situation in which the object stands, and a heightened sense of the object as an obdurate entity, thus the experience is one of indefinite duration or endlessness; there is no meaningful dimension to the work, that stimulates a momentary epiphany of understanding within our experience of it. Modernist art, conversely, is characterised by its 'instantaneousness', its meaningfulness is made wholly manifest in our momentary experience of it.[14]

Nevertheless, the selected artificial landscapes and installations of waste resist aestheticisation and distinctly allude to the exhausted project of modernity that is identified with a particular modernist commitment to the work of art as an object detached from the world. The attempt to exhaust the art object and to exhaust the constant endeavour to create meaning is linked to an inherent criticism of the work of art and to the social implications of any formalist quest.

Beckett's relentless negations of meaning and alleged nihilism appear as antisocial and anti-political. However, as Simon Critchley claims, it is precisely in their abstention from political engagement that Beckett's works point towards 'the creation of a just life' with ramifications that are ethical and political alike. Critchley cites a passage from *Aesthetic Theory*, where Adorno writes that 'The Greek military junta knew why it banned Beckett's plays, in which there is not one political word. Asociality becomes the social legitimation of art.'[15] And Beckett achieves this through a conception of form or worklessness, but a work which is a determinate negation of meaning, a narrative against narrative.[16]

Beckett's negation of meaning and the dialectics of 'positive' and 'negative' representation unfolds in the interplay of birth (inhalation) and death (exhalation). The life-giving force of respiration co-exists in *Breath* with the perplexing 'terror' caused by the decay of humankind, as it is 'signified' by the presence of waste. The notion of terror is in 'all cases whatsoever, either more openly or latently the ruling principle of the sublime',[17] as Edward Burke puts it, and both notions (terror and the sublime) are connected with the magnitude of nature to overwhelm humans. Technology, however, subsumes, according to Gilbert-Rolfe, the idea of the 'sublime because it, whether to a greater extent or an equal extent than nature, is terrifying in the limitless unknowability of its potential'.[18] The following chapter investigates the potentiality of Beckett's media environments and the writer's experimentation with technology in *Breath*.

NOTES

1. Deleuze, Gilles. *L' Épuise*. London: Faber, 1973: 100–1.
2. Buchloh, Benjamin. 'Detritus and Decrepitude: The Sculpture of Thomas Hirschhorn', *Oxford Art Journal*, 24.2 (2001): 55.
3. Ibid.
4. See 'Three Dialogues with Georges Duthuit'. In Martin Esslin (ed.), *Samuel Beckett: A Collection of Critical Essays*. New York: Prentice-Hall, 1965: 21.

5. Ibid.
6. Cohn, Ruby (ed.). *Disjecta: Miscellaneous Writings and a Dramatic Fragment.* New York: Grove Press, 1984: 145.
7. Ibarra, Paola. 'Beautiful Trash: Art and Transformation', *Revista Harvard Review of Latin America*, 14.2 (Winter 2015): 41–3.
8. Greenberg, Clement. *Art and Culture: Critical Essays.* Boston: Beacon Press, 1961: 58.
9. Greenberg, Clement. 'The New Sculpture', in ibid: 58–9.
10. See https://www.museumdd.be/en/verleden/t4 [accessed 1/11/16].
11. Ukeles, Mierle Laderman. *Manifesto for Maintenance Art 1969! Proposal for an Exhibition Care.* See http://www.arnolfini.org.uk/blog/manifesto-for-maintenance-art-1969/Ukeles_MANIFESTO.pdf
12. Feldman, Mark B. 'Inside the Sanitation System: Mierle Ukeles, Urban Ecology, and the Social Circulation of Garbage', *Iowa Journal of Cultural Studies*, 10/11 (Spring/ Fall 2009). In http://ir.uiowa.edu/cgi/viewcontent.cgi? article=1082&context=ijcs [accessed 15/7/17].
13. See Brown, Kathryn. 'Undoing Urban Modernity: Contemporary Art's Confrontation with Waste', *European Journal of Cultural Studies*, 65.1 (July 2013): 134.
14. Vickery, Jonathan. 'Art and the Ethical: Modernism and the Problem of Minimalism'. In Dana Arnold and Margaret Iversen (eds), *Art and Thought.* Oxford: Blackwell, 2002: 111–28.
15. Adorno, Theodor W. *Aesthetic Theory.* Trans. Robert Hullot-Kentor. Minneapolis: University of Minnesota Press, 1997: 343.
16. Critchley, Simon. *On Humour.* London: Routledge, 2010.
17. Burke, Edmund. *A Philosophical Enquiry into the Origin of Our Ideas of the Sublime and Beautiful.* London: R. and J. Dodsley, 1761. http://academic.brooklyn.cuny.edu/english/melani/gothic/burke2.html [accessed 1/11/2016].
18. Gilbert-Rolfe, Jeremy. *Beauty and the Contemporary Sublime.* London: Allworth Press, 1999.

6

INTERMEDIAL BREATH: DEFYING THE BOUNDARIES BETWEEN DISPLAYING AND STAGING

> Intermediality should not be misunderstood as evidence either of ignorance regarding the specificities of various aesthetic media or, on the other hand, of mere ignorance regarding conventions of formal creation within the traditional genres. Instead, the specificities of each medium become the object of an artistic production that confronts these conventions freely – but not from a position of simple ignorance.[1]

> Intermedia is not performance, but performative action.[2]

Contemporary discourses on intermedia are describing the phenomenon of crossing the borders between traditional media (painting and photography), contemporary media (cinema, television, video, computer and other hyper-media), and live and animated stage production. This process investigates the methodological challenges of converging different mediums, live performance, animation, film, music and design. Beckett's media environments and his experimentation with technology in relation to the complex contemporary media culture is contextualised within the intermedial cultural discourse. The writer explores certain cardinal aspects of technology and writes texts that deploy media so as to create dramatic effects and simultaneously challenge the limitations of the artistic medium.

As mentioned, *Breath* is intrinsically intermedial, given that it operates in-between realities, in-between the boundaries of artistic media, the verbal and the visual, the audible and the scenic, in-between visibility and invisibility, absence and emptiness, embodiment and ambiguity of corporeal experience. Artistic experimentation includes shifts of art practice into non-artistic fields, as well as exploration of technological and scientific innovations. Respiration presupposes a relation to found biological phenomena that doesn't operate in the domain of cultural and art production. However, artists formulate various means of presenting breath in art. Breathing is considered as an intermedium, in a twofold sense. The first suggests the breach between art and life and the interest in non-art, and the other the breach between different artistic media.

The term intermediality is directly related to the concept of the medium (and its essential components), from a perspective that takes into consideration the far-reaching transformations of aesthetic experience (and of the arts) that have been effected through recent and contemporary developments. Both of the constituent parts of the term 'intermediality', 'inter-' and 'media', designate 'between-ness'. The many interrelated aspects of the multifaceted concept of the medium generally include several types or levels of mediality that have to be correlated with each other. This condition can also be described as 'inter-medial', 'multi-modal' or even 'post-medial'.[3] Intermedia appears in the form of conceptual art, performance art, video art, new dance, graphically-notated music and music involving theatrical activity, a 'new' theatre based on extra-theatrical sources, visual poetry and phonetic poetry.[4]

The theorist Oleg Gelikman places the concept of intermediality in the context of the unresolved conflict between philosophical aesthetics and aesthetic theory. The conflict originated in the response of an influential generation of thinkers to the crisis of the neo-Kantian schools and the emergence of modernism in the 1910s. As Gelikman supports, despite the relatively new usage of the term it presses into service an old, indeed archaic, argument for the centrality of the medium to representation. It can be found, as he states, in Aristotle's *Poetics*, Lessing's *Laocoön* and the newer versions that proliferated in the twentieth century.[5] Gelikman sketches a transition other than the one from the mono-medial to inter-medial production, namely, from 'aesthetics' to 'aesthetic theory'. However, when he proposes to relate 'intermediality' to the transition from aesthetics to aesthetic theory, he does not mean to suggest that we are free to go back to the historical context in which the distinction between the two appeared.[6]

Intermediality as a conceptual framework is further developed by the Theatre and Intermediality Working Group. The Group draws not only from the interaction of technology and the convergence of live and mediatised performance, but also from intermediality as the interaction of media; they argue that intermediality is not reliant on technology but on the interaction between performance and perception. Nevertheless, Chapple and Kattenbelt offer a broader definition of intermediality as 'a powerful and potentially radical force, that operates in-between performer and audience; in-between theatre, performance and other media; and in-between realities – with theatre providing a stage space for the performance of intermediality'.[7]

BECKETT'S TECHNICULE

By contextualising Beckett's experimentation with media and technology in the multifaceted contemporary media culture, we observe that the writer explores certain cardinal aspects of technology and writes texts that both deploy media to generate dramatic effects and simultaneously comment on each medium's limitations. The innovative use of medium, technology and the apparently simple staging of his plays is one of the reasons that artists continue to produce his works in new media[8] and formats. In particular, *Breath*, as Ruby Cohn suggests, might be called a 'technicule', dependent as it is on technology. The scenic directions, she writes, stipulate that the two recorded cries 'be identical and that the light and amplified breath be strictly synchronized. The elemental symmetries of life on earth rely upon sophisticated theatre electronics'.[9]

Beckett's late stage plays foreground the notion of changing media environments and technology, so as to draw attention to the artifice of the dramatic form itself. Adding to that, the continuity with his writing for the stage, radio and television, as well as the use of theatrical language suggest a certain variability or doubling of medium, as though the texts include within themselves the possibility of their staging in some other form.[10] Beckett's dramatic works assert the specificity of their media; they are placed at the representative edges of those media rather than at their centres. It is these boundaries, as Steve Connor suggests, that 'constitute the specificity of their medium, even as they mark the dubious place where they touch and perhaps cross into different media'.[11]

Beckett's relationship to technology and television, in particular, receives the attention of writers including Linda Ben-Zvi, Eckhart Voights-Virchow, Gilles Deleuze, Graley Herren and Daniel Albright. Albright argues that, while Beckett (like surrealist artists) is 'doting on technique', he does so not to show technology's potential and power but, rather, its 'muteness, incompetence, non-feasance of transmission', the medium is allowed 'to dwindle before the stress that Beckett places on it'.[12] Beckett uses technology to indict itself, as Linda Ben-Zvi argues, 'I agree that – just as he uses language to reveal its own paucity – creating a technology of the unworkable just as he committed himself at the beginning of his career to write "a literature of the unword".'[13] His texts change in different technological environments and experiment with the convergence of old and new technology formats. The writer embraces the challenges of new media and technology provides more possibilities, as Albright writes, 'for unfiguring more things than words ever could'.[14] His work for film, radio and television is not merely plays written for different media, but rather explorations of the potential and limits of each medium to express Beckett's aesthetics. Media are stripped down as far as possible to let the technology show. And although the technique probably derives from the writer's tendency toward simplicity, as Linda Ben-Zvi writes, 'its effect is to reveal the nature of the medium to show what it doesn't do and provide clarity and wholeness to "the mess" of life or the world itself'.[15]

Theorists like David Saltz[16] explain the ways in which Beckett develops multimedia stagings of *Ohio Impromptu*, *Eh Joe*, *Not I*, *Play*, *Come and Go*, *Breath* and *Quad*. Sean McCarthy argues that these plays allow the audience to engage more closely with the texts, and highlight the texts' cyclical quality, as he writes, 'to explore the interaction between live performance and technology inherent in them; and, most important, to test [his own] contention that Beckett's short plays redefine in a very specific and radical way, the nature of the dramatic text itself'.[17]

The intermedial approach emphasises the dialectic between the media. The term differs from 'multimedia' (a term that correlates different media that are presented together synchronously yet remain distinct), since it goes beyond mixed media. It is a term that incorporates elements of one medium in another (e.g. photography in film, painting in photography.) Adding to that, intermediality denotes that the reference frame of the entire system of art forms (that mediates the intermedial correlation) is itself included in the processes of transformation. As Yvonne Spielmann argues, the definition of intermedia (in relation to visual media) inherently implies that the processes of transformation are reflected in the form of the images. It is through the modes of self-reflection that the structural shifts characteristic of new media images are mediated and made visible. The point is that the transformation of elements of at least two (historically) different media creates a new form of image that, as she writes, 'reveals these differences in a mixed form and mostly reveals the self-reflexivity of the medium in a paradoxical structure'.[18]

The same process is valid in relation to all media. Intermediality is applied throughout the arts; an intermedium can be traced between music and sculpture, between poetry and sculpture. The structure of the intermedium is analysed in relation to theatricality, while the mediums are analysed in the context of the intersection of theatre and the visual arts. Several factors should be considered in attempting to formulate distinctions between these two disciplines. The effects in relation to the theatrical in contemporary art are vast and the comparison of works of several media point to the convergence of the visual arts and the theatre. However, consequential disciplinary boundaries are still detectable in the instances in which one art form conjures another.

The intermedium investigates the ways in which the mapping of one structure, originally composed in one medium, is mapped onto another structure in another medium. In the context of the interface between the theatre and the visual arts, we observe that visual artists are investigating the nature of the medium of theatricality[19] by experimenting with the fundamental registers of the theatre like embodiment, spectacle, ensemble, text, sound, gesture, situated space and re-enactment.

The theatre is related to situatedness, spectatorial encounter, referentiality, literality and extended spatiality that unsettles the circumscribed spatiality of the 'autonomous' art form. Theatre is also durational, an engagement with temporality that violates the juxtapositive immediacy of visual art forms. The selected artworks, which investigate the notion of theatricality, the construction of space, the stage and the duration of the experience, the significance of the text and the need for a new attitude on the part of the audience, are principally interested in the act of perceiving.

In addition to these formal conceptual characteristics and effects of intermedia, intermediality may also be understood as a cultural and ideological positioning and basis for strategy.[20] Beckett's *Breath* displays contemporary investigations of theatrical intermediality seen in relation to the exploration of a wide range of forms, territories, strategies and artistic motivations. The artist's use of technology has lead to a remediation of the interface between the theatre and the visual arts, of a revision of the boundaries of media[21] and of the effects of intermediality that involve innovative modes of representation; dramaturgical strategies; new ways of positioning bodies in time and space; and new ways of creating temporal and spatial interrelations.

Beckett attempts to reconceptualise theatre as a 'hyper-medium'[22] that integrates a variety of technical media into its performance. Theatre, thus, becomes a large medial framework, that incorporates different media without negotiating the assumed live quality of the theatrical body. Visual and theatrical practice are seen as constituting and constructing each other, operating as an axis that allows media relationships to be established. It is significant to note that Beckett's theatre is able not only to represent but also to stage other media. Media therefore become visible as media, as means of communication, each with its own materialities, medialities and conventions of perception. Theatre's medium specificity becomes, with Beckett's manipulations, a field that contains within its phenomena a heterogeneous collection of interdependent media.

NAVRIDIS' INTERMEDIAL STAGING OF *BREATH*

Navridis' 'staging' attempts to re-invent the original context of Beckett's *Breath* by experimenting with the use of new media and intermedial developments. The artist envisages *Breath* as a video installation and invites the audience to experience the work by walking (moving through the piece). Viewers walk into a dark room where eight overhead projectors compose a disorienting, mobile landscape of garbage, making it difficult for them to find their way

Figure 6.1: NIKOS NAVRIDIS. *Breath*: 2005, based on Samuel Becket's playlet *Breath*. Video installation, video projections synchronised in loop, sound. Duration: 35 seconds. Dimensions variable. First installed 51st Venice Bienniale, *Always a Little Further*, Arsenale, Venice, 12 June–6 Nov 2005, curator Rosa Martinez. Courtesy of the Bernier/Eliades Gallery and the artist. Photo: Panos Kokinias

out. Navridis' work extends Beckett's concerns with metaphysics, performance and particularly the human body.

The visual artist adds an experiential and intermedial aspect to the playlet by projecting the image of waste on the surface of the floor so that the viewers can walk on it. Navridis ascribes certain performative qualities to the work and activates the spectator in a bodily manner by challenging the rigid context of *Breath*'s staging. The artist does not include the agency of a human body so as to produce presence; on the contrary the viewers become the participants as leading figures on the 'stage'.

ANTONY GORMLEY'S *BREATHING ROOM II* AND ANTHONY MCCALL'S *BREATH*

The intermedial relationship between the sensuous and the technological and the culture of the technologised body affect the biological process of breathing. The sculptor Antony Gormley revitalises the human image in sculpture through the investigation of the body as a place of memory and transformation, using his own body as subject, tool and material. Since 1990, the artist has expanded his concern with the human condition; and the installation *Breathing Room* is an attempt to make a three-dimensional drawing in space,

Figure 6.2: NIKOS NAVRIDIS. *Breath*: 2005, based on Samuel Becket's playlet *Breath*. Video installation, video projections synchronised in loop, sound. Duration: 35 seconds. Dimensions variable. First installed 51st Venice Bienniale, *Always a Little Further*, Arsenale, Venice, 12 June–6 Nov 2005, curator Rosa Martinez. Courtesy of the Bernier/Eliades Gallery and the artist. Photo: Panos Kokinias

that is both a diagram and an object. It is an instrument that allows the viewers to become the viewed by creating an interpenetrating nest of seven space frames that occupy a central position in the room.

The volume outlined by the frame remains constant whilst being extended in each case on a different axis. A mandala-like drawing on the floor forms the ground plan from which the seven rooms grow. As Gormley states, the object hovers between being architecture and being an image of architecture. It is a contained object in a defined internal space. Electrical lights are removed and

Figure 6.3: NIKOS NAVRIDIS. *Breath*: 2005, based on Samuel Becket's playlet *Breath*. Video installation, video projections synchronised in loop, sound. Duration: 35 seconds. Dimensions variable. First installed 51st Venice Bienniale, *Always a Little Further*, Arsenale, Venice, 12 June–6 Nov 2005, curator Rosa Martinez. Courtesy of the Bernier/Eliades Gallery and the artist. Photo: Panos Kokinias

the frames are painted with two layers of phosphorescent paint that absorb light during the day and emit it at night. The work assumes an unstable position between the virtual and the real when darkness falls. If perspective and orthogonal architecture in the West are the way in which space is described and contained, this is an attempt to open up those limiting characteristics.[23] Similarly to Beckett's *Breath*, in *Breathing Room II* the figure is absent, nonetheless the spectator embodies the human subject by being immersed in the space that the artwork occupies.

Anthony McCall's[24] *Breath I* (2004), *Breath II* (2004) and *Breath III* (2005) are a series of artworks based on projected light that consist of several media (installation art, film, sculpture and performance). The artist is developing architectural installations that explore height and verticality and the way the viewers relate to horizontal and vertical projections. In the horizontal forms one moves within and around every part of the projected object and the source of light is close to eye level. The vertical projections rise to five times the height of the viewers and they can only occupy the lower part of the installation, while observing the tunnel of light above them, meaning, as McCall states, 'the defining membranes of light, together with the chambers they enclose, are made visible by the movement of the mist, with its sometimes spiralling movements, which carry the eye to the vanishing point around the lens of the projector'.[25]

The installations have a sculptural quality of the luminous, volumetric, beam, using digital production techniques rather than film, while they intersect between cinema and sculpture. The forms and the spaces are projected, and gradually change through the passage of time. The projections produce three-dimensional enclosures (darkened spaces filled with mist), based on abstract figures, ellipses and waves that gradually expand and contract in the space like ephemeral architectonic walls. The viewers can be walking around and within the translucent walls and enclosed spaces.[26]

INTERMEDIAL CURATORIAL PRACTICE: KOAN JEFF BAYSA *OXYGEN*

Contemporary curatorial practices draw on dramaturgies of space and on different ideas of the 'exhibition' – of 'presentation', 'showing' or 'appearance' – and focus on intermedial practices as well as on novel treatments of the exhibition medium and notions of the theatrical and dramaturgical structure of exhibitions.

The intermedial curatorial collaborative project *Oxygen* presents the ways in which eleven artists relate to breathing, after the terrorist attacks of 9/11. The medical doctor Koan Jeff Baysa experiments with a combinatory structure of syntactical elements that come from the field of science, sociology and art, but are combined into one and are thereby made into a new entity in the form of an environmental project that addresses, among other things, the heightened

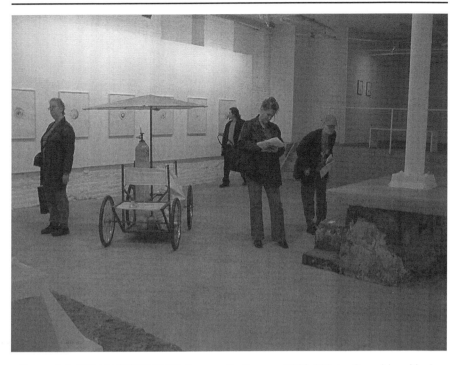

Figure 6.4: KOAN JEFF BAYSA (curated). *Oxygen*: 2002. White Box, New York.
http://www.whiteboxny.org

awareness of matters pertaining to life and death after the 'terror'.[27] Each of these works 'hinges on the nature of breathing as an ever-present memento mori'.[28] The project includes Gordon Matta-Clark's breathing station made out of oxygen bottles with attached masks on a wheeled cart, while Marina Abramović distressingly breathes under the weight of a human skeleton.

The endangered atmosphere of the urban environment is the focal concern of the project that provides a selected visual inventory of (dys)function and topology of respiration, namely, the 'crucial element that comprises 21% of our atmosphere that is extracted by the lungs to sustain aerobic life'. As Anne Filen Honigman writes:

> a paired active inspiration and passive expiration, initiated at birth and terminated at death. This threatened resource and disorders of breathing have become emblematic of the endangered atmosphere and the tenuous balance between the environment and its human habitation.[29]

The exhibition's original title, 'Ondine's Curse', is 'a caveat against taking things for granted, referred to the spell that required conscious thought

Figure 6.5: MARINA ABRAMOVIĆ. *Nude with Skeleton*: 2002. Performance sixteen minutes. Belgrade. Photos Attilio Maranzano. Courtesy of the Marina Abramović Archives

about each breath', and the metaphors and images presented in *Oxygen* are valuations of life framed within the acknowledgement of loss, disease and mortality.[30]

Oscar Muñoz's *Aliento* represents the politically disappeared in South and Central America; the victims' images appear for the duration of the viewer's exhalations, the artist's surfaces are deceiving, similar to daguerreotypes, while the images become apparent only when viewers breathe on the surface. With a breath, sepia photographs of *desaparecidos*, young Colombian men proclaimed 'disappeared' by their government, appear on 'mirror-like metal'. As Amanda Graham notes,

> the condensation fades on the mirror-like metal, so do the images. Here the aesthetic disappearance parallels the corporeal-political one. For a moment, viewers recognize the 'Other' in their own reflections and in so doing begin to comprehend how Muñoz's piece forces the repetition of the moment of encounter and in the process uncovers hidden truths.[31]

Developments in technology and curatorial practices transform the audience into the key site of intermedia art. The embodied intermedial experience entails a politics of spectating in contrast to a modernist purified opticality. The spectator becomes a participant in these intermedia works that not only demand her/his active perceptual engagement, but also generate explicit awareness of this activity. Thus, the spectators are not reduced to a state of unquestioning awareness or a wholly passive relation to the object. Interaction, engagement and response are required for the aesthetic experience of intermedial art, and the artworks on respiration return us to the body of the spectator as a space that is both sentient and active.

The following chapter explores this process even further in relation to the body and its breathing apparatus. The fundamental contribution of breath related artworks is to provide the potential of public engagement with the respiratory system so as to enhance artistic research into the relationship between the material and the 'immaterial'. By encouraging multiple perspectives on health, art and life these art practices contribute to scientific research and offer original methods of understanding the role that respiration plays in our sensory, emotional and spiritual life.

NOTES

1. Krauss, Rosalind. *A Voyage on the North Sea: Art in the Age of the Post-Medium Condition*. London: Thames and Hudson, 2000: 122.
2. Busse, Klaus-Peter. 'Intermedia: The Aesthetic Experience of Cultural Interspaces'. In Hans Breder and Klaus-Peter Busse (eds), *Intermedia: Enacting the Liminal*. Dortmund: Dortmunder Schriften zur Kunst, 2005: 264.
3. A distinction is made between media understood as a means of transmitting signals bearing a written, aural or visual message and mediums as designating the very fabric or substance of which signals and messages are made. Different media borders and multimodalities are analysed as medium/intermediality mode/multi-modality material, sensorial, spatiotemporal modality, semiotic modality, tangible, perceptual, conceptual, basic, qualified, technical media. See Lars Elleström. *Media Borders, Multimodality and Intermediality*. Basingstoke: Palgrave Macmillan, 2010.
4. See Breder, Hans and Busse, Klaus-Peter. *Intermedia: Enacting the Liminal*. Dortmund: Dortmunder Schriften zur Kunst, 2005: 31.
5. Beginning with Irving Babbitt's *The New Laokoön: An Essay on the Confusion of the Arts*. Boston: Houghton Mifflin, 1910.
6. Gelikman, Oleg. 'Intermediality and Aesthetic Theory in Shklovsky's and Adorno's Thought', *Comparative Literature and Culture*, 13.3 (2011): 2–10.
7. Chapple, Freda and Kattenbelt, Chiel (eds). *Intermediality in Theatre and Performance*. Amsterdam: Rodopi, 2006: 12.
8. For the *Beckett on Film Project* (2002), the British visual artist Damien Hirst directed *Breath* using the voice of comedian Keith Allen. In this project funded by the Irish Film Institute, the Irish broadcasting network RTE and Britain's Channel 4, virtually all of Beckett's stage plays were committed to film by a wide range of artists. Certain of the project's artists worked regularly with Beckett texts, such as director Harold Pinter and actors Alan Stanford and Barry McGovern. Other artists involved in the project had not worked regularly with Beckett (Anthony Minghella and Neil Jordan, for example) or the film medium. The series of films was broadcast on television in both Britain and Ireland.
9. Cohn, Ruby. *A Beckett Canon*. Ann Arbor: University of Michigan Press, 2001: 298.

10. See Connor, Steven. *Samuel Beckett: Repetition, Theory and Text*. Oxford and New York: Blackwell, 1988: 167.

11. Ibid.: 167.

12. Moorjani, A., Ben-Zvi, Linda (eds). *Beckett, McLuhan and Television: The Medium, the Message and the Mess in Beckett at 100 Revolving It All*. Oxford: Oxford University Press, 2008: 2 and 3.

13. Ben-Zvi, Linda. 'Beckett and Television: In a Different Context', *Modern Drama*, 49.4 (Winter 2006): 469.

14. See Albright, Daniel. *Beckett and Aesthetics*. Cambridge: Cambridge University Press, 2003: 137.

15. Ibid.: 104.

16. See Saltz, David. 'Live Media: Interactive Technology and Theatre', *Theatre Topics*, 11.2 (September 2001): 107–30.

17. McCarthy, Sean. 'Giving Sam a Second Life: Beckett's Plays in the Age of Convergent Media', *Texas Studies in Literature and Language*, 51.1 (Spring 2009): 102–17.

18. Spielmann, Yvonne. 'Synesthesia and Intersenses, Intermedia in Electronic Images'. *Leonardo*, 34.1 (2001): 55.

19. Weber, Samuel. *Theatricality as Medium*. Ashland, NY: Fordham University Press, 2004: 30.

20. See Busse, Klaus-Peter. 'Intermedia is not Performance': 264.

21. Recent media remediate earlier media (i.e. filmic remediation of theatre; televisual remediation of radio, theatre and film; digital remediation of print, photograph, television etc.). Intermedial dramaturg(ies), intermedial bodies in performance, mixed media, multimedia, crossover and hybrid performances, 'live' performance in virtual space and virtual performance in 'live' space.

22. See Chapple, Frieda and Kattenbelt, Chiel. *Intermediality in Theatre and Performance*. Amsterdam: Amsterdam University Press, 2006: 32.

23. See <http://www.antonygormley.com> [accessed 1/11/2016].

24. Anthony McCall is considered to be one of the prominent representatives of London's avant-garde cinema of the 1970s. He started to work with performance and film at the beginning of the 1970s, initially with a series of open-air performances, in which fire was used as a sculptural element. McCall focuses on the mechanical basis of film projections and treats light beam as a three-dimensional presence, before it is discharged on the two-dimensional screen where the images are formed.

25. Walley, Jonathan. 'An Interview with Anthony McCall', *The Velvet Light Trap*, 54 (Fall 2004): 65–75. In http://muse.jhu.edu/login?auth=0&type=summary&url=/journals/the_velvet_light_trap/v054/54.1walley.html [accessed 1/11/16].

26. See Branden, Joseph. *Anthony McCall: The Solid Light Films and Related Works*. *Artist interview by Jonathan Walley*, ed. Christopher Eamon. Evanston: New Art Trust, Northwestern University Press.

27. Gene, Ray. *Terror and the Sublime in Art and Critical Theory: From Auschwitz to Hiroshima to September 11*, New York and Basingstoke: Palgrave Macmillan, 2005.

28. See Honigman, A. Finel. 'Oxygen', *Time Out*, New York, 2002.

29. Ibid.

30. Ibid.

31. Graham, Amanda Jane. 'Assisted Breathing: Developing Embodied Exposure in Oscar Muñoz's *Aliento*', *Latin American Perspectives* (15 December 2011). In http://0-lap.sagepub.com.opac.sfsu.edu/content/early/2011/12/15/0094582X11 431807.abstract?rss=1 [accessed 1/1/2016].

7

INVESTIGATING THE MATERIALITY OF RESPIRATION IN DIFFERENT MEDIA

The breath was not perceptible[1]

Is air thinkable?[2]

Breathing is a foundational experience. As long as the child is in the womb of the mother the experience of a distinct outside and of an inside is no doubt mediated through a sonorous and primary tactility; the birth of the skin which submits to and provokes movements and the confused sensibility of the edges and limits of the body. Agitations cannot be temporalised in that internal space. Going out into the air suddenly projects the body into a new rhythm, that of breath.[3]

Within the art (as, one suspects, within the artist) form and formless are linked in constant combat.[4]

Science is deeply concerned with its own epistemological limits, the relation between the unknown and the known, the invisible and the visible, the assumed, the proven and the evidenced. Notions of immateriality occupy a complex place in these dynamics as they refer to material affects or dynamics that remain unobservable, immeasurable, sensed or intuited. How can science develop adequate resources, tools or instruments to reach or discover beyond the five senses and to research the influence of the immaterial? How can the discourse of the immaterial in the arts and humanities meet the language of science given its historically distinct understandings? This chapter attempts to offer insights into fields of knowledge that are to a certain extent inaccessible to scientific study, because they break down the long-held dichotomy between the material and the immaterial. The diverse values, methodologies and strategies that underlie current applications of the medical humanities to art are considered in relation to the interface between the material and the immaterial as it is manifested in the biological process of respiration.

Artists attempt to access technical apparatuses and graphic devices that make visible to the eye phenomena that are beyond human vision.[5] Breath, as a measured volume of air that is manifested in the respiratory cycle, is one of these biological phenomena; its 'formless' and 'immaterial' spectrum mediates between the inner and outer space of the material body. The respiratory system is interior and integral to the unseen components of the body, but it also connects to the felt (sensed) exteriority of the body. In the realm of the arts the visualisation of this corporeal process takes a parallel course. Visual and sound artists who use bioacoustics (the process that combines biology and acoustics) evolve techniques of concentration on aspects of the physical and look at the different manifestations of breathing and the ways in which it becomes perceptible, through the use of diverse artistic media.

Beckett's *oeuvre* has infinite references to the corporeal function of breathing and concentrates on the notion of respiration in diverse ways. Steven Connor's statement that 'Beckett's texts are sustained upon an imagination of air'[6] portrays this process. The writer's output is juxtaposed with works by other artists and with art pieces that in some sense echo Beckett's world and aesthetics and offer an alternative to a particular history of modernism that is related to the idealisation of forms. Representative of a diverse assortment of historical moments and theoretical voices, these art practices continue to challenge the ideological effects of specific narratives of high modernism that focus on the separation and hierarchisation of artistic media, and map out an area beyond form and thematic content to interpret the visual arts. By challenging the viewer's expectations of the experience of coherent, bounded and unified form that can be *organised* as distinct media or in terms of a stylistic scheme, the selected artworks explore the act of the viewer on the art object.

Pneumatic Readymades: Duchamp, Beuys, Manzoni, Weseler, Fromanger, Navridis

The methodical act of formalisation in the medium, and the progressive aesthetic abstraction in Beckett's *Breath* are comparable to the selected artworks that highlight not the efficacy, but rather the limits of the medium, in the face of attempts to understand, represent or emulate the properties of breath.

'Form' has been identified as modernist and 'formless' as a process beyond the postmodern divide.[7] As Caroline Jones argues, 'few oppositions have organized post-1960s art as completely as form versus formless[8] (or, more pretentiously, informe)'. Both terms are accompanied by discourses that continue to influence the contemporary art world. The brief hegemony of the method called 'formalism' came in the 1950s and early 1960s, and its reign, according to Jones:

> is the crucial backdrop for contemporary antagonisms between form and formless [. . .] Form and informe have been particularly crucial discourses in Anglo-American art worlds, but the antinomy has its sources in Continental philosophies as old as modernism itself.[9]

Formalism was a compelling but always embattled component of aesthetic theory in a disjunctively modernising Europe, and theories attending to the 'formless' were, in several interesting respects, as Jones argues, 'less a rejection than an extension of formalism's earliest motivations, yet theorists of the informe have not moved beyond form as much as they have returned to a lost future rescued from formalism's complex past'.[10] The antinomy between form and formless defines the ways art treats 'appearance' and 'conception'. A shift occurs when emphasis is placed on the concept rather than the appearance ('shape', in Fried's terminology). The critique of modernist aesthetics fed an increased emphasis on concept over visual production.

Joseph Kosuth, who in recent times presented the work *For a Respirateur*, signals the emergence of conceptualism as minimalism's avant-garde successor, by arguing that all art (after Duchamp) is 'conceptual (in nature) because art only exists conceptually'.[11] Art movements, that are more or less indebted to the conceptual artist and inventor of the readymade, Marcel Duchamp, are considered as varieties of 'novelty' art[12] (minimalism), and Greenberg suggests that the 'aesthetic surprise' a viewer experiences on looking at 'true' works of art,[13] is long lasting and important, while the 'novelty' item provokes no more than a momentary effect that is 'superfluous'. The theorist attacks the tendency to produce art without the guidance of aesthetic judgement and argues that the readymades in their three-dimensionality are a spatial co-ordinate that art has to share with 'non-art'. Therefore, the minimalist artists' use of repeated and standardised units, like Duchamp's readymades, are elements of standardisation and repetition.[14]

Beckett's work is seen in the light of Duchampian practices by theorists such as Jonathan Kalb, who makes a comparison between Beckett and Duchamp by arguing that the former's relationship to language has always been quasi-Duchampian 'if one accepts the idea that Duchamp's greatness lies not so much in the fact that he stopped painting as in his managing to have that act recognized as significant. You have to be quite a writer before your refusal to write can be received as a statement in itself'.[15] Brater also notes that Duchamp's proclamation 'Reduce, reduce, reduce!' states a new credo for artistic composition. Beckett takes the manifesto at its word, for in his short prose pieces to 'construct' means quite literally to reduce. And Brater adds that

> definitively incomplete, Beckett's formal condensation undermines the elusive and sometimes suspicious relations between his minimalist prose and all other things: Objects give us everything. Duchamp continued but their representation no longer gives us anything. Disengaged from representational imagery and therefore not emblematic, Beckett's work makes us discover in residual prose the literary potential of compressed and frequently abstract patterns, their human overtones, their flesh colours, and, above all, their pervasive texture of mucous membrane.[16]

Duchamp notably stated that 'I just like – just breathing. I like breathing better than working. Each second, each breath is a work which is inscribed nowhere, which is neither visual nor cerebral, it's a sort of constant euphoria'[17] and this fascination with respiration was further developed in the artwork *Belle Haleine: Eau de Voilette or Beautiful Breath*, a readymade that was altered in several ways by Duchamp and his close friend and fellow artist Man Ray. The artist removed the original label 'Rigaud brand perfume bottle' and replaced it with a new one created by him and Man Ray. *Belle Haleine*[18] stands as one of the prominent readymades in Duchamp's *oeuvre*, and Man Ray's photograph of Duchamp, dressed as his female alter ego Rrose Selavy, stands at the top of the new label. This was the first visual appearance of Rrose Selavy. Duchamp's constant questioning of the 'nature' of the work of art and his emphasis on the work of art's 'completion' by the spectator highlights conceptual art's 'openness'.

Beckett's exceptional impact on conceptual and minimalist artists in relation to his fascination with respiration is comparable to conceptual pieces including Marcel Duchamp's *Paris Air* (1919), Piero Manzoni's *Artist's Breath* (1959), and Joseph Beuys' *The Breath* (*Der Atem*, 1966) among other works. Joseph Beuys is inspired by the Duchampian readymade in that he focuses less on the aesthetic (like Duchamp) and more on the social ramifications of the readymade.

Organic curves prevail in Beuys' work *Der Atem* (*The Breath*), and the artist uses liquid fat to create shapes that have been echoed in the curved lines of the pencil drawing. The materials Beuys employs are always selected for their particular significance to the artist. Christa-Maria Lerm Hayes draws attention to Gene Ray's interpretation of fat and felt in Beuys' work, 'as related to the Nazis' extermination camps' and stresses the fact that after the liberation, 'sacks of human hair and piles of other materials revealed the gruesome business with human remains that the Nazis had sustained there'.[19] According to

Lerm Hayes, Beuys' approach to Ireland and the Holocaust is indicative of the possibilities for art to deal with social trauma and situations where difference is not generating harmonious and prosperous relations.[20] Beuys shares an expanded conception of art as a form of 'social sculpture' that can contribute to political and ideological change.

The artist's 'Energy Plan'[21] is conceived as a vehicle of social change and his 'Weltanschauung' (world view) is perceived in relation to energies and alchemical polarities – cold and warm, soft and hard, life and death, past and present, east and west, north and south – and the ways in which energies are transferred through natural materials, plants and animals. Fat represents fuel and nurturing but is also associated with the production of warmth and energy, and copper is the conductor of electricity while heat transmits this energy. Respiration, and its rhythm, is one of the energies that has healing properties, a prominent element of Beuys' practice and philosophy.[22] The artist's multi-disciplinary interests in medicine, science, art, myth and history, and the ways he explores the qualities of natural materials are also influential on artist Günter Weseler[23] who created a work with Beuysian overtones in its unusual conjunction of materials: bread, fur, wood and electrical motors.

Duchampian readymades and especially his ampoule of *Paris Air* (1919), as well as his use of physical substances or residues, in conjunction with conceptual art's fascination with the visualisation of energy had an impact on Piero Manzoni's pneumatic sculptures. Manzoni fabricated forty-five *Corpi d'Aria* (*Pneumatic Sculptures*) of up to thirty-two inches in diameter that, when filled by the artist himself, were labelled *Artist's Breath* (*Fiato d'Artista*, 1959). The piece is Manzoni's first use of a body substance product, presented without alteration, certified as authentic, and traded by the volume. A series of red, white or blue balloons (medium-sized, that contained seventy-five imperial gallons of air) that were inflated and attached to a wooden base inscribed *Piero Manzoni – Artist's Breath,* would be sold by the artist if a person wished to order them.[24]

Manzoni offers his own body as an artwork, and the vestiges of the transfigured body become valuable relics. His practice parodies the traditional sculptural emphasis on permanence by using modern materials to suggest a modern aesthetic, whilst creating a poetic metaphor for the ephemerality of life itself. The artist uses his bodily resources as a 'material' within certain of his works, while the *Artist's Breath* works of the 1960s involve the artist blowing up balloons that allude to the notion of the philosophical 'pneuma', whereby the artist 'breathes life' into the work of art. The ephemerality of these balloons is subsequently memorialised with their remains being affixed to plaques.

Navridis' *Difficult Breaths* (2004)[25] is a pneumatic sculpture with lightweight elements such as latex, or ethereal like breath, while Gérard Fromanger's *Souffles* is an installation of large, colourful and translucent 'half-balloon' street sculptures that was presented one month after May 1968, in Place Blanche, Altuglas and Place d'Alésia in Paris, while Jean Luc Godard filmed the reactions of the people. The piece is conceived as a series of interventions in the public sphere; the police destroyed the installation the same night. Fromanger, one of the foremost proponents of the 'nouvelle figuration' movement in France, presented the same piece thirty-seven years later (2005), in the Jardin du Luxembourg.

RECORDING TEMPORALITY, BREATH RECORDERS: HILL, KANARINKA, DUPONT

Practitioners, writers and theorists arrive at the notion of respiration from different ends of both the formal and the thematic spectrum. Common to all, however, is the artwork's temporal extensiveness. Respiration, as a temporal and repetitive process, gives way to incalculable cycles of duration. As Levinas remarks, 'our time is already the breath of the human being in respect of another human being. Our time is the breath of the spirit'.[26]

The pneumatic sculptures by Duchamp, Beuys, Manzoni, Weseler, Navridis and Fromanger, like Beckett's *Breath*, appeal to the temporal sense of the viewer and experiment with notions of temporality, representational subtraction and visualisation of the process of respiration.

Artists attempt to represent the circular temporality of respiration with

Figures 7.1, 7.2 and 7.3: NIKOS NAVRIDIS. *Looking for a Place*: 2004. La Caixa Foundation's Exhibition Hall, Madrid

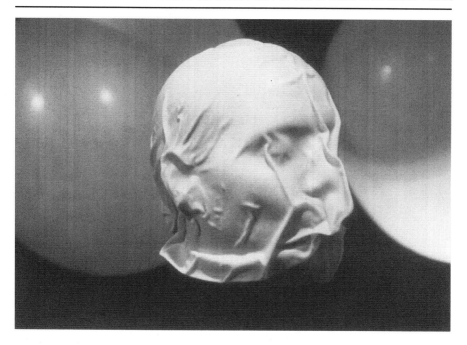

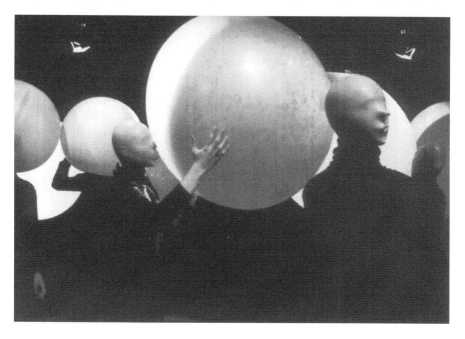

the persistent aspiration to visualise or record the phenomenon of breathing. Gary Hill's video installation *Circular Breathing* (1994) functions as a personal breath recorder. The viewer can record a breath pattern by breathing and blowing into the mouthpiece. The piece consists of projected large-scale (side-by-side) moving images of elderly hands playing the piano, the camera-eye view of someone walking up stairs, a man chopping wood, a freighter on the ocean, with the on-screen stereo sound of circular breathing. As the screens become activated, they are slowed to an almost photographic state of suspension. The cycle continues in the opposite direction and finishes when the screens become blank.

Jacques Derrida considers that Hill is one of the few (and maybe the only) video artists who is working with many different discourses in an attempt to depart from the rather conventional ways in which video artworks are usually presented. According to the philosopher, who examines the use of language in the medium of video, Hill is working with a new visual methodology and, as Derrida puts it,

> our first enigma – appears to be one of the most discursive, and not only with discourses but also with textual forms that are heterogeneous among themselves, whether literary or not that seem to be altogether at odds with such a working, with what one thought video art had to be, especially if, as seems to be the case, they are anything but the simple pretext assumed by the videogram.[27]

And yet, if this 'new art' arises, it is because within the vague terrain of the implicit, something is already enveloped – and developing.[28]

The representation of time is often brought to a condition that breaks down into 'abstract-objects', and the respiratory system as an abstract mechanism develops into an 'abstract-object' of meditation on the nature of time, the brevity of existence and the human condition. The individual is the seat of a constant process of decantation, as Beckett writes in his study of Proust, 'decantation from the vessel containing the fluid of future time, sluggish, pale and monochrome, to the vessel containing the fluid of past time, agitated and multi-coloured by the phenomena of its hours',[29] thus the human subject is but a sum of breaths, representing past and future time.

The multimedia artist Kanarinka investigates the notion that the human subject is a sum of breaths in a project that consists of a series of running performances in the public sphere (2007), a web podcast of breaths (2007), and a gallery installation of the archive of breaths (2008). The artist runs through the 'evacuation routes' that were formed in American cities after 9/11 so that civilians could escape the city in case of a terrorist attack.

Complex technological equipment is used to count, record and augment the artist's breaths through speakers (during her runs). The project is an attempt

Figure 7.4: Kanarinka AT ikatun DOT. *It takes 154,000 Breaths to Evacuate Boston*: 2007. Courtesy of the artist http://www.ikatun.com/

to measure the 'post-9/11 collective fear' in the individual breaths that it takes to traverse these new geographies of insecurity.[30]

Similarly, Sophie Dupont's *Marking Breath* (2011) is a day-long performance that consists of nothing more than a single, repetitive act of recording breathing. At each exhalation the artist carves a line into a small metal panel positioned in front of her. From sunrise to sunset, the artist sits silently at a table. Along the walls of the gallery stands a sequence of metal panels documenting some of the previous performances made in different parts of the world; from New York to Seoul, from Mexico City to Copenhagen.

The artist conceives of the work as an on-going performance to be created throughout her lifetime, using it as a moment to stop and silently mark her existence on a given day. Each time it is performed following a strict set of rules as described above; the panel is kept as a document of the action. A similarity can be drawn between *Marking Breath* and the date paintings created by Japanese conceptual artist On Kawara, where the latter makes a painting by recording onto canvas the date on which the painting was made. Over four decades, until his death in 2013, Kawara made over 3,000 date paintings, known collectively as *Today* (1966–2013). Similarly to Dupont, he observes a strict set of rules,

Figure 7.5: Kanarinka AT ikatun DOT. *It takes 154,000 Breaths to Evacuate Boston*: 2007. Courtesy of the artist http://www.ikatun.com/

always inscribing the date in white letters and numbers on a monochromatic ground, with each painting made during the course of a single day.

Medical discoveries and theories about corporeality in the twentieth century problematise the notion of representation and invite a reconsideration of the body both in 'real' and aesthetic forms. Respiration as a medium is commonly perceived as the physical basis of the organism and of the body's manifold sensory apparatus. Nevertheless, a fundamental reading of the term emphasises its formative value: breathing as a communicative agent between the individual, the outside world and time. The act of mediation is a process; in this sense the medium of breath always internalises a singular engagement with time. Any medium has the effect of reshaping the way in which we, collectively and individually, perceive and understand our environment. According to Stanley Cavell, 'medium' is not a given, it is not an a priori. He focuses on the communicative and therefore temporal contingency of the word 'medium': 'I characterized the task of the modern artist as one of creating not a new instance of his art but a new medium in it.'[31]

In our highly mediated world, technology becomes an important model for this process. Contemporary artists and writers explore the implications of the techno-human interface by investigating embodied technology and the technologised body. The impact of new technology rearranges the established hierarchy of the senses. Moreover, the modernist segmentation of the senses is now giving way to dramatic multi-sensory mixes or transpositions. The auditory, the olfactory and the tactile are similar to the visual crucial sites of embodied knowledge. The sensorium aims to encompass the ways humans co-ordinate all of the body's perpetual and proprioceptive signals, as well as the changing sensory envelope of the self and the ever-closer relationship between the sensuous and the technological. The sensorial intersects with the intermedial in the ways they construct sentient and experiential aspects of artistic creation and audience reception (Kanarinka and Lygia Clark).

Intermedial and sensorial artistic practices address the influence of technology on the senses and are involved in a mediated form of communication (where the viewer is imposed by the work of art), produced or transmitted not through a direct sensory contact but by means of a technological system for the processing of information. The effect of media on our senses (namely the sensorium) is a creation of the physical, biological, social and cultural environments of the individual organism and its relationships, while being in the world. Multiple sensory structures, as well as other modes of perception, the sum of their relations and the ratio of mixture and importance comprise a sensorium.

Philosophies of sensory embodiment and neuroscience reveal that the human sensorium has always been mediated, and that our sensing bodies are themselves mediating apparatuses without which there can be no knowledge of the world. Knowledge originates in experience and is mediated through the senses, while scientists argue that breathing is part of the body's sensorial spheres. Without the 'medium' of air or water, the anthropoid ear finds it impossible to hear. Yet over the past few decades that condition has greatly intensified and artists focus on the mediated sensorium, as Caroline Jones writes:

> Amplified, shielded, channelled, prosthetized, simulated, stimulated, irritated – our sensorium is more mediated today than ever before. Yet it bothers us less. The cyborg model of the 1980s and the virtual dreams of the 1990s have evolved into a twenty-first-century comfort zone: in which the prosthetic and supplemental are habitual. The micro speaker in the ear, the drug in the blood, the nanosurgical implant, the simulated taste in the mouth – these enhancements no longer provoke the apocalyptic excitement they did even a few years ago. The relative calm this situation provides gives us time for reflection: a propitious moment for artists and other culture workers to interpret, think and reckon with the sense of our mediated sensorium.[32]

Some scholars treat the respiratory system as an autonomous discipline and focus on its impact on the nervous and visceral systems of the body; whereas neuroarthistorians like Heinrich Wölfflin argue about the involvement of the respiratory system in the interaction of our visual and motor systems, and suggest that lines relate to the tempo of respiration and that the idea that our response to lines is determined by our eye movement carries little weight. In his view, the observation of the varying height of the waves in a line suggests that variations of speed of respiration can be widely applied not just to individual people, but to whole cultures, in relation to the significance of tempos of breathing for the expression of moods. This point is significant for historical characterisation and the theorist analyses architecture as a paradigm for human behaviour. According to Wölfflin, the older a person is, 'the faster s/he begins to breathe in its architecture, the more excited it becomes'. He observes:

> How quiet and restfully run the lines of an early Doric temple [. . .] Then in the Ionic there is a quicker mobility [. . .] and as ancient culture comes to its end, the more it pursues a febrile, hasty movement. Peoples that from the very beginning are quick of blood go the furthest. One thinks of the suffocating pace of the lines in Arabic decorations. Unfortunately, I must here content myself with hints, a historical psychology, much more a psychological history, would have to be able to follow the growing speed of lines in all exactitude and would certainly find that the development comes always first in decoration.[33]

Scientific research principally focuses on the nature of the respiratory system, from the standpoint of anatomical studies, kinaesthetic consciousness, somatic learning, voice study, practical exercises, bodywork, physical and spiritual awareness, medical prognosis and physiological psychology, and control of posture and movement. The influence of respiration in the work of artists and theorists and its manifestations in art and culture have not been extensively theorised. Inquiry into the complexities of respiration, as an area of intense cross-disciplinary focus, can offer an insight into a possible new interdisciplinary reading of breathing.

BREATHING MACHINES: LYGIA CLARK, ANN HAMILTON AND JOHN LATHAM

Lygia Clark's *Respire Comigo* (*Breathe with Me*) is an interactive sensorial art piece where the two ends of a rubber tube (of the kind used for sub-aqua fishing) are placed together to form a circle that the artist stretches and contracts rhythmically beside the viewer's ear; and Ann Hamilton's *Flour Breath – Body Object Series* is a piece that explores the relationship between 'humanness' and 'object-ness', animate body and inanimate object, so as to 'materialize voice [. . .] the form of language (verbal, written and visual) [which], when spoken, leaves no material trace'.[34]

Clark and Hélio Oiticica (1937–80) also centre their work on the body, and on the experiential aspects of the viewer's participation, by exploring haptic space through tactile, auditory, olfactory and kinetic propositions. Their emphasis on meaning encompasses both a sensory experience and an aesthetic potential. Clark's artworks are not limited to the aesthetic field, but rather attempt to integrate art and life, by displacing art's boundaries and by going against institutionalised art processes. A later and new stage of her work is based on bodily sensory experience, with therapeutic objectives, while the artist deals with the viewer's 'memory files', fears and weaknesses. Her methods are articulated in *Objetos Sensoriais* (*Sensorial Objects*, 1966–8), simple everyday objects including water, shells, rubber and seeds, and *Objetos Relacionais* (*Relational Objects*), that draw from the duality of objects (light/heavy, soft/hard, full/empty).

The artistic preoccupation with the visualisation of the process of breathing is generally associated with techniques of 'abstraction' that can capture this visually restricted organic function. Respiration as an 'immaterial' and invisible medium exceeds the sphere of representation and textual signification, and thus reinforces the role of the concept within the art object and the de-emphasis of material aspects.[35] The conceptual artist John Latham (1921–2006) considers that verbal language is inadequate to describe the dimensionality of the universe, given that it is constituted by the common-sense view of the relation of objects in space. Latham's *The Big Breather Project* (1973) is a machine that extracts energy from the sea. This device, that consists of a thirty-two foot high 'lung', is filled and emptied by the six-hour cycle of tide levels in river estuaries, and was erected in estuary waters where it would use the six-hour

Figure 7.6: JOHN LATHAM. *Big Breather*: 1973. Second version, installed Imperial College, London. Photo courtesy of the John Latham Foundation

cycles to make energy available for a number of purposes such as fog lamps and sound-warnings.

In the interface of art and science, the source and inspiration for this artwork are the artist's visionary theories and the notion of 'flat-time' that expresses the theoretical physics of 'event-structure'. According to this theory, everything that exists can be explained not as atomic particles and waves, but as recurring time-based 'events' of finite duration. Thus, a 'least event' – the shortest departure from a state of nothingness – is, according to the theory, the fundamental unit of existence. The recurrence of such events establishes a 'habit' that forms the basis for structures in reality. Recurring events of longer duration result in more complex phenomena such as objects, mental images and, ultimately, the cosmos.

Latham's machine certifies that the experience of the 'forces of nature' is in so many instances today a graphic one, mediated through seismographs, remote sensors, bubble-chamber photographs, encephalograms and so forth. Artists have in the past sometimes responded, as Brett suggests:

> by offering up their canvas as a straightforward blank surface to receive the imprint of natural energies, such as Yves Klein *Cosmogonies*, one of which was an attempt to capture wind patterns by strapping a still wet canvas to the roof of his car on a journey from Paris to Nice (a somewhat quixotic gesture), or his fire paintings. The relationship between a literal trace and a sign – a configuration with pre-thought and more complex meanings – therefore becomes multivalent and ambivalent, with traces acting as signs and signs acting as traces. In the transcription of energies drawing often approaches script, or writing.[36]

The relationship between a literal trace and a sign can operate as an analogy to the abstract and the representational in art; these two compositional systems activate other areas of the visual brain. Abstract compositions activate a less extensive part than representational or figurative compositions, that is, abstract works activate more restricted parts of the visual brain than narrative or representational art.[37]

Contemporary art practices encompass multi-layered strategies to understand or traverse the threshold between the chiasmus of the 'visible' (elements of representation, in the classic sense of the word) from the 'invisible' (elements of abstraction). The interface between the visible and invisible is associated to temporality and to the chiasmus between presence and absence. In 'The Visible and the Invisible' and the chapter on 'The Intertwining – The Chiasm',[38] Maurice Merleau-Ponty traces a constitutive 'invisibility' at the heart of the visible, something that cannot be seen, that is beyond 'appearance', and considers that our bodies are part of both the tangible world, as well as the world through which we perceive the tangible things that lie beyond our bodies.

Figure 7.7: GABRIEL OROZCO. *Breath on Piano*: 1993. Chromogenic color print 40.6 x 50.8 cm. Courtesy of the artist and Marian Goodman Gallery

IN/VISIBLE TRACES: GABRIEL OROZCO, GIUSEPPE PENONE AND ANA MENDIETA

Gabriel Orozco's *Breath on Piano* investigates the interplay between the visible and the invisible, and the ways breath can leave a trace on materials as well as the nexus between materiality and immateriality. The piece records a trace of the artist's breath in the brief seconds before it evaporates, a captured moment of the pattern of a hot breath created on a shiny piano. The ephemerality and fleeting nature of the physical world is marked in this 'formless structure', suggesting an unseen presence of a body that produces this breath. Merleau-Ponty's conception of the body as a chiasm[39] or crossing-over juxtaposes subjective experience and objective existence. The artistic exploration of the idea of a body as a system rather than mere biological organism implies – as in Merleau-Ponty's chiasmus – a questioning of the body as a subject.

The chiasmus implies the interweaving of scientific and aesthetic aspects, as well as of the individual with the world, and alludes to the phenomenological body that seems to exist as a metaphor, a disembodied fragment or a trace. Breath is in essence beyond appearance; in close contact with and 'inside' of the body; it is distanced by sight and consequently the organic process becomes crucial in working out the relationship between abstraction, visuality and cor-

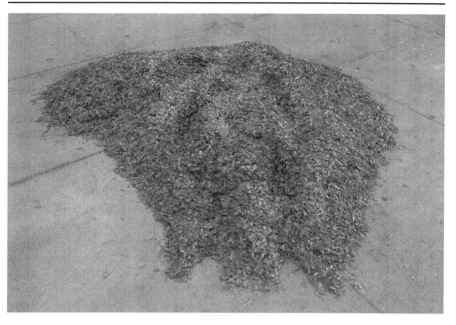

Figure 7.8: GIUSEPPE PENONE. *Soffio di Foglie (Breath of Leaves)*: 1979-2015.
Dimensions variable. Courtesy of the artist and Marian Goodman Gallery.
Photo Cathy Carver

poreality in the realm of the arts. If the theory of the body, as Merleau-Ponty states in the *Phenomenology of Perception*, is already a theory of perception, then audio-visual perception is located not just in the brain, in the purely cognitive realm of nerve endings, cortical regions and neurotransmitters, but also in the body and its embedment in its surroundings.[40]

Giuseppe Penone's installation *To Breathe the Shadow* (*Respirare I' Ombra*, 1979–91)[41] and Ana Mendieta's *Untitled (Grass Breathing)* (Mexico, 1975) leave the trace of the artists' absent bodies on a space lined by laurel leaves (Penone) and grass-covered ground (Mendieta). The earth-body sculptures consist of the outline of the artists' bodies and draw from the ephemerality of breath and the passage of time. According to Penone, the clarity of the well-marked path is sterile: 'to find the path, to follow it, to examine it, and to clear away the tangled undergrowth: that is sculpture'.[42]

The visible and the invisible aspects of the body often mark a lack of correspondence. As Michel Foucault articulates in his essay, 'The Utopian Body,'[43] the body can be visible in one sense, and yet this same body, that is so visible, is also withdrawn, captured by a kind of invisibility from which he can never really detach it. Accordingly, the skull and the back of the skull can be experienced and felt with the finger, but cannot be seen. As he questions:

But see it? Never. This back, which I can feel leaning, against the pressures of the matters, against the couch when I am lying down, and which I might catch but only by the ruse of the mirror. And what is this shoulder, whose movements and positions I know nothing with precision, but that I will never be able to see without dreadfully contorting myself? The body-phantom that only appears in the mirage of the mirror, and then only in fragmentary fashion – do I really need genies and fairies, and death and the soul, in order to be, at the same time both visible and invisible?[44]

Respiration and spectatorial engagement are ultimately interrelated. Our breathing is affected by being aware of someone else's breathing and scientists argue about the involvement of breathing in the interaction of our visual and motor systems. Mondrian was pleased when a viewer compared his painting with the rhythm of breathing. Looking at a picture this person had said simply, 'Je respire,' and as Mondrian writes, 'that's exactly what it should be in my view, namely, that one breathes, feels free through seeing the canvas'.[45] The spectator becomes a participant in these expanded works that not only demand her/his active perceptual engagement, but often also generate explicit awareness of this activity. The selected artists, through the use of visual, auditory, olfactory and tactile artistic media, explore and expand the ways of making breath perceptible, often through the viewer's participation.

NOTES

1. Stéphane Mallarmé. 'Brise Marine' [1887]. In Anthony Hartley (ed.), *Mallarmé*. Baltimore: Penguin Books, 1965: 29.
2. Irigaray, Luce. *The Forgetting of Air in Martin Heidegger*. London: Athlone Press, 1999: 12.
3. Mondzain, Marie-José. *Homo Spectator*. Paris: Bayard, 2007. In http://dominique-vivant.blogspot.gr/2012/01/homo-spectator.html [accessed 1/11/2016].
4. See Lippard, Lucy (ed.). *Six Years: The Dematerialization of the Art Object from 1966 to 1972*. London: Studio Vista, 1973: 5.
5. See Brett, Guy. *Force Fields: Phases of the Kinetic*. Barcelona: Museu d'Art Contemporani de Barcelona (MACBA), Actar, 2000.
6. Connor, Steven. 'Beckett's Atmospheres' In S. E. Gontarski and Anthony Uhlmann (eds), *Beckett after Beckett*, Gainesville: University of Florida Press, 2006: 52. In http://stevenconnor.com/atmospheres-2.html [accessed 18/7/2017].
7. Jones, Caroline A. 'Form and Formless'. In Amelia Jones (ed.), *A Companion to Contemporary Art since 1945*, Malden, MA: Blackwell Publishing, 2006: 127.
8. According to Jones: 'If the revival of "formless" in the 1990s was accompanied by a method, it was deconstructive in nature, committed to process and naturalized in contemporary art discourse at least since the postmodern turn against art writer Clement Greenberg in the 1980s.' Ibid.
9. Ibid.
10. Ibid.
11. Kosuth, Joseph. 'Art after Philosophy, part 1', *Studio International* (October), 1969: 845. In http://www.lot.at/sfu_sabine_bitter/Art_After_Philosophy.pdf

12. Greenberg, Clement. 'Recentness of Sculpture'. In Maurice Tuchman, *American Sculpture of the Sixties*. Los Angeles: Los Angeles County Museum, 1967: 24.
13. For example paintings by Raphael or Jackson Pollock.
14. Marcel Duchamp's concept of the readymade was invented in 1917 with the creation of the renowned porcelain urinal entitled *Fountain, 1917* that was remade in 1964.
15. See Kalb, Jonathan. *Beckett in Performance*. Cambridge: Cambridge University Press, 1989: 160.
16. Brater, Enoch. 'Why Beckett's "Enough" Is More or Less Enough', *Contemporary Literature*, 21.2 (Spring 1980): 266.
17. See Pierre Cabanne. *Dialogues with Marcel Duchamp*. London: Thames and Hudson, 1971: 23.
18. Perfume bottle with collage label inside oval violet cardboard box, assisted readymade bottle.
19. In Lerm Hayes, Maria-Christa. 'Unity in Diversity through Art? Joseph Beuys' Models of Cultural Dialogue'. KTHC – Knowledge, Technology, Human Capital, Eurodiv Paper, 2006: 3. In http://www.feem.it/userfiles/attach/Publication/ NDL2006/NDL2006-060.pdf [accessed 1/11/16].
20. Ibid.
21. See: http://sydney.edu.au/museums/pdfs/Art_Gallery/666%20Beuys_catalogue_ finalextra.pdf [accessed 1/11/16].
22. See Beuys' lecture tour to the United States in 1974, entitled 'Energy Plan for the Western Man', organised by the Ronald Feldman Gallery. He included in his lectures an explanation of the ways in which his work was influenced by Rudolf Steiner's writings and theories.
23. In the 1960s and 1970s Günter Weseler was one of the most prominent German artists together with Blinky Palermo, Gerhard Richter, Joseph Beuys and Sigmar Polke. The work mentioned is *New Species (14 Breathing Objects)* (1972–2012). See http://www.artnet.com/artists/günter-weseler/past-auction-results/2
24. During the same period Manzoni planned a group of spherical bodies of air of approximate 2.5 metres diameter to go in a park. By means of an air compressor these were to pulsate with a slow unsynchronised rhythm of breathing (experimental example with a membrane of small dimensions, 1959). On the same principle he constructed an architectural proposal of a pneumatically pulsating ceiling and wall. As he remarked in 1959, 'as another scheme for a park I had thought of a cluster of pneumatic cylinders, elongated in shape, like steel, which would vibrate in the blowing of the wind [. . .] which would have produced sounds in the wind'. In Manzoni, Piero. *Paintings, Reliefs and Objects*. Exhibition catalogue. London: The Tate Gallery (20 March–15 May) 1974. In 1961, Manzoni composed two *Aphonies*, the *Aphonia Herning* (for orchestra and public), and the *'Milan' Aphonia* (for heart and breath) (1962).
25. The exhibition in which this work appeared was curated by Rosa Martínez and was organised and produced by la Caixa Foundation, in la Caixa Foundation's Exhibition Hall in Madrid, from 30 January to 14 March 2004.
26. Ettinger, Bracha. *Time is the Breath of Spirit: Emmanuel Levinas in Conversation with Bracha Lichtenberg Ettinger*. Trans. Joseph Simas and Carolyn Ducker. Oxford: MOMA, 1993: 93.
27. Derrida suggests that we should take into consideration what 'happens to language' 'partitioned or distributed, cut strung or tucked together, delinearized, palindromanagrammatized in more than one language and passing like a serpent across seven monitors at the same time with regard to the "video event"'. As he writes,

anything but a mutism, a certain being silent of this writing – new but very impure and all the newer for that – which stages discourses or texts that are thought to be of the most 'interior' sort. Is it just by chance that Gary Hill solicits, among others, gnostic texts or the writings of Blanchot? One never sees a new art, one thinks one sees it; but a 'new art', as people say a little loosely, may be recognized by the fact that it is not recognized, one would say that it cannot be seen because one lacks not only a ready discourse, with which to talk about it, but also that implicit discourse which organizes the experience of this art itself and is working even on our optical apparatus, our most elementary vision.

Derrida, Jacques. 'Videor. Passage de l' Images'. Group show catalogue. Paris: Musée National d'Art Moderne, Centre Georges Pompidou, 1990.
28. Ibid.
29. Beckett, Samuel. *Proust*. New York: Grove Press, 1957: 4–5.
30. The project involves the study of 'experimental geography', a term invented by geographer Trevor Paglen (2002). The term denotes an amalgam of science and art in a manner that deploys aesthetics, ambiguity, poetry and empiricism. This alternative practice explores the distinctions between geographical study and artistic experience of the earth, as well as the juncture where the two realms collide, and possibly make a new field altogether. It employs a wide range of mediums including sound and video installations, photography, sculpture and experimental cartography. Source: www.kanarinka.com [accessed 1/11/2016].
31. Cavell, Stanley. 'Knowing and Acknowledging'. In *Must We Mean What We Say?* Cambridge: Cambridge University Press, 1976: 238.
32. Jones, Caroline and Arning, Bill (eds). *Sensorium: Embodied Experience, Technology and Contemporary Art*. Cambridge, MA: MIT Press, the MIT List Visual Arts Center, 2006: 5.
33. In Onians, John. *Neuroarthistory: From Aristotle and Pliny to Baxandall and Zeki*. New Haven and London: Yale University Press, 2007: 117.
34. 'The Body and the Object: Ann Hamilton 1984–1996', *Dialogue Arts in the Midwest* (May/June 1996): 35. Also see, 'Ann Hamilton, 1984–1996: The Body and the Object', *Forum* (1997): 29; Abrams, Janet, 'The Body and the Object: Ann Hamilton 1984–1996', *I.D. Magazine*, 44.1 (January/February 1997): 102. Staniszewski, Mary Anne. 'The Body and the Object: Ann Hamilton 1984–1996', *Artforum*, 36.5 (January 1998): 36.
35. In 1968 Lucy Lippard and John Chandler's influential essay, 'The Dematerialization of Art' marked the outset of conceptual art. This essay was followed by the essential anthology Lippard, Lucy R. *Six Years: The Dematerialization of the Art Object from 1966 to 1972*. New York: Praeger, 1973. In http://cast.b-ap.net/wp-content/uploads/sites/8/2011/09/lippard-theDematerializationofArt.pdf
36. Brett, Guy. *Force Fields: Phases of the Kinetic*. Barcelona: Museu d'Art Contemporani de Barcelona (MACBA), Actar, 2000: 40.
37. See Zeki, Semir. *Inner Vision: An Exploration of Art, Vision and the Brain*. Oxford: Oxford University Press, 1999: 207.
38. Maurice Merleau-Ponty's 'The Intertwining – The Chiasm' is the last and incomplete chapter from *The Visible and the Invisible* written before his death. Merleau-Ponty's thoughts on perception eventually culminated in his concept of 'chiasm' or flesh, which is the crossing over between subjective experience and objective existence. Merleau-Ponty, Maurice. *The Visible and the Invisible*. Evanston: Northwestern University Press, 1969.
39. The term comes from the Greek letter X: Chi.

40. Merleau-Ponty, Maurice. *Phenomenology of Perception*. Trans. Colin Smith. New York: Humanities Press, 1962.
41. The Installation at the Centre Pompidou (1999) consists of bronze, metal cages and laurel leaves.
42. See http://fauxberliner.blogspot.com/2010/01/hamburger-bahnhof-and-other-deli-cacies.html [accessed 1/11/2016].
43. 'Le Corps Utopique', translated by Lucia Allais in consultation with Caroline A. Jones and Arnold Davidson, from Foucault, Michel. *Utopies et Heterotopies*, a CD release of two 1966 radio broadcasts published in 2004 by the Institut National de l' Audiovisuel, Paris.
44. Ibid.
45. Piet Mondrian quoted in Matthes, Hendrik. 'Aphorisms and Reflections by Piet Mondrian', *Kunst & Museumjournaal*, 6.1 (1995): 57.

CONCLUSION: THE AFTERLIVES OF
BREATH – BREATHE, BREATHE AGAIN . . .
BREATHE BETTER

It will never have been given to me to finish anything, except
perhaps breathing[1]

You write in order to be able to breathe.[2]

Grace to breathe that void.[3]

You are living in your breathing. Stop. Think. You are dying in your
breathing. Stop. Think. You are living in your breathing. You are dying
in your breathing. You are living in your dying, dying in your living.
(Take time, breathing.) Stop. Show. The doing without the showing
is merely experience. The showing is critical, what makes it theatre.
What makes it show (by nothing but breathing) is the radiance of
inner conviction.[4]

This book has explored the dynamic interface between the theatrical and the
visual in Beckett's *Breath*, and appraised the writer's exceptional impact on
conceptual and minimalist artists in relation to his fascination with respiration,
that is comparable to conceptual pieces including Marcel Duchamp`s *Paris Air*
(1919), Piero Manzoni`s *Artist's Breath* (1959), Joseph Beuys' *The Breath* (*Der
Atem*, 1966) and Art & Language *There were Sighs Trapped by Liars* (1997)

among others. The abeyance of the mimetic, the exposition of the components of a medium in skeletal form, the disengagement from representational imagery and the ambiguity of meaning are pivotal for understanding aspects of Beckett's impact on conceptual art. However, his pervasiveness in contemporary art is also the result of his experimentation with media and technology. The late stage plays foreground the notion of changing media environments so as to draw attention to the artifice of the dramatic form, and Beckett explores certain cardinal aspects of technology so as to challenge the limitations of the artistic medium.

The perspective on a wide range of artworks about respiration engaged with alternative contributions to the question and provocative intervention in contemporary and modernist debates on the relationship between the visual arts and the theatre, both within the context of respiration and of Beckett. The majority of the artworks involve intermediality, whilst they belong to a transitional space between the plastic arts, the theatre and other media. The endeavour to represent silence, absence and emptiness (notions not associated with representational art), the methodical act of formalisation in the medium and the progressive aesthetic abstraction in Beckett's *Breath* are juxtaposed to these artworks which highlight not the efficacy, but rather the limits of the medium, in the face of attempts to understand, represent or emulate the properties of breath.

The book has attempted to demonstrate the broad challenge of intermedial approaches to received disciplinary categories and forms of practice, capturing their nascent reworking of art and criticism by focusing on the formation of the inter-medium as a space in-between art and science, the verbal and visual, the audible and scenic, visibility and invisibility, presence and absence, appearance and emptiness, embodiment and dis-embodiment, life and death, inhalation and exhalation, silence and sound, the three dimensional and the static image. Beckett's reductionist strategies, the quasi-generic and inter-generic features of his late style in the theatre, the decentred field of subjectivity and its polysemous modes of absence and presence highpoint these intermedial exchanges.

INTERMEDIAL PRACTICE: A TOTAL WORK OF ART OR A SYSTEM OF RELAYS?

The transient and limitless formal possibilities of the artwork and the methods associated with movements that originated in the 1960s and 1970s subsequently determined art practice and theory. Whereas the artistic focus on notions of intermediality shares a lot of common elements with the synaesthetic unity of the Wagnerian 'total work of art' (Gesamtkunstwerk)[5] that engages in interrelating or even unifying theatre,[6] Wagner's notion of the 'total work of art' expresses his attempt to reconceptualise the theatre as a hyper-medium that integrates a variety of technical media into its performance. Theatre thus becomes a large medial framework that incorporates different media without negotiating the assumed live quality of the theatrical body.[7]

Intermediality challenges specific notions of the total work of art, while the term characterises the roles the disciplines play in an integrative and interactive process. This encounter between two or three disciplines doesn't take place when one begins to reflect on the other, but when one discipline realises that it has to resolve, for itself and by its own means, a problem similar to one confronted by the other. Analogous problems confront the sciences, painting, music, philosophy, literature and cinema, on different occasions, and under different circumstances. As Gilles Deleuze argues:

> the same tremors occur on totally different terrains. The only true criticism is comparative [. . .] because any work in a field is itself imbricated within other fields [. . .] There is no work that doesn't have its beginnings or end in other art forms [. . .] All work is inserted in a system of relays.[8]

The system of relays was analysed by means of this specialised paradigm of intersection of critical discourses on aesthetics, in the theatre and the visual arts, in the expanded field of respiration. The physical act of respiration becomes the starting point for a new understanding of the body's intermedial relationship to the world. The medium of breath and the body's intermedial relationship to the world is treated as a conceptual guide, so as to investigate points of intersection (connections, linkages, overlaps) of the theatre and the visual arts, in the expanded field of art practice and the mobility of practices like minimalism and conceptual art in these different contexts. The expanded field is generated by problematising a set of concepts concerning issues of genre, medium and discipline in relation to different artworks in the field of respiration. These artistic fields are based on an expanded notion of art and theatre that involves other disciplines, such as architecture and sound art, thus contemporary art practice presupposes an expanded theoretical approach.

The contextual analysis of genre, discipline and the interrelationship between performance and literary studies, namely, the relationship between the textual and the visual, challenges the misconception that dramatic performance is a reiteration of texts, a citation that imports literary or textual authority into performance. The relation of staging and performance to the written text is multifaceted, given that a text is a connection and an interweaving of signifying elements. The written and/or verbal text is transferred onto theatre and becomes the 'text' of the staging. The linguistic text, the text of the staging (*mise en scène*) and the 'performance text', shape three different kinds of text,[9] yet the intermedial text can include all these elements and involves mediation.

The mode of relationship of the performance to the spectators, the temporal and spatial situation, and the place and function of the theatrical process become decisive for the creation of meaning and signification. As Malgorzata Sugiera argues, nowadays the basic structural principle of texts written for the theatre increasingly often turns out to be their immanent theatricality. She considers that theatricality can no longer be understood as a reflection upon theatre that is the domain of artistic activity or as an extensive metaphor of human life, but rather as a 'means of inducing the audience to watch themselves as subjects which perceive, acquire knowledge and partly create the objects of their cognition'.[10]

Theatricality is the philosophical discourse of performance, and is considered the conceptual machinery of representation. In theatre theory and historiography the term is applied in diverse ways, yet studies in philosophy, anthropology, ethnology and sociology, political, historical and communication sciences, cultural semiotics, history of art and literature have identified and applied the concept of theatricality as a cultural model beyond a purely metaphorical use of the term, and they have also employed the concept of the theatre as a heuristic model to a wide extent. According to Timothy Murray, Foucault conceived the notion of 'theatrum Philosophicum'; Lyotard analyses the 'political stage'; Baudrillard studies the 'stage of the body'; Clifford Geertz explores the 'theatre state of Bali'; Paul Zumthor proclaims the performance of narrators in oral cultures to be 'theatre'; Ferdinard Mount investigates the 'theatre of politics'; Hayden White explains 'historical realism as tragedy'; and Richard van Dulmen analyses the history of tribunal practice and penal ritual as a 'theatre of terror culture'.[11]

The existence of philosophical anti-theatricalism is a symptom of the conflictual entanglement that binds the theatre and theory together. Theatre and theory are engaged, as Puchner remarks:

> in a struggle over visibility, material mimesis, and the presence and liveness of the theatre, notions that theory wants to wrest from the theatre in order to revise and integrate them into its own apparatus. Theory thus creates its own concepts of theatricality, which are prone to be at odds with the real theatre. The struggle between theory and the theatre is fought through a variety of genres and art forms, including the closet drama and the manifestos of the avant-garde's conceptual theatre.[12]

Puchner stresses that it is important to recognise that critique of the theatre and its modes of representation is not limited to theory, but can occur within the domain of the theatre itself, and he gives as examples Wagner's programmatic designs and Artaud's utopian hallucinations. As he writes:

> as soon as the critique of the theatre is launched from within the domain of the theatre, theory is free to use theatrical concepts and models that are no longer firmly tied to actual bodies on a stage. This turn on the part of theory to the theatre, the theatrical turn, is thus made possible by the fundamental self-critique of avant-garde theatre.[13]

Consequently, what Jonas Barish calls the 'anti-theatrical prejudice' is common both to theatrical theory and practice as it is for other disciplines, and a historical grounding of any approach to anti-theatricalism is essential, so as to understand how different art forms create their own versions of anti-theatricalism. Contemporary art and theatre reciprocally pose interesting challenges to the legacy of theatricality through interdisciplinary artistic activity, working with diverse artistic disciplines, connecting and integrating the aural and visual media by way of developing new media forms (combinations of film, video, computers, etc.), application of various technologies, spatial installations, and finding new ways of presenting art.

Beckett tests the autonomy of artistic genres and media by questioning the tenability of the various antitheses that seem to govern the medium, and by his technical experiments on extra linguistic media, such as mime, gesture, posture, lighting, sound, rhythm and stage set. The writer's work is indicative of the necessity of working across the media in an interdisciplinary way; he concentrated on what Adorno, disapprovingly, called 'pseudomorphoses', that is, attempts by one medium to imitate the technical procedures of an alien medium. For Beckett, as Albright remarks, 'any morph is a pseudomorph and his work, whether for the stage, radio, television or film, goes against the grain of the medium it exploits'. Beckett being Beckett, as Albright puts it, was less interested in what a medium could do than in what it couldn't do.[14]

ANTI-THEATRICAL PREJUDICE

The view of a duality between concepts (theatricality/anti-theatricality) is based on the premise that there is an unbridgeable division between them and it therefore necessarily excludes the perspective that reconciles in practice what seems paradoxical in theory. The anti-theatrical prejudice is shared both in Beckett's works and Fried's theory, and a particular critique of the actor is motivating both Fried's and Beckett's anti-theatrical stance. Modernist discourse criticises literalist works for being fundamentally naturalistic and claims that a kind of latent or hidden naturalism, indeed anthropomorphism, lies at the core of literalist theory and practice. In Fried's often metaphorical formulations, as Puchner notes, 'theatrical' paintings or sculptures are described as if they were actors; these sculptures are 'aware' of the audience and thus lose their self-sufficient unity and integrity, in the process of which they start to resemble vain human actors pandering to the audience. Indeed, Fried ascribes to such theatrical works an anthropomorphic quality that leads to a form of personalised 'naturalism'. The suspicion of the live actor that speaks through Fried's figurative language becomes apparent, when he reveals that:

> the one art form safe from such deplorable anthropomorphic effects is film. In contrast to the endlessly personalizing theatre, film not only

removes the actors from the presence of the audience but also cuts them into pieces through close-ups and montage.[15]

Barish draws from the Beckettian world in order to illuminate what he considers to be drama's anti-theatrical prejudice. In the later plays, the scraping away process continues unrelentingly, attacking the characters in their vitals, leaving them not only without memory, or with only the merest shred of memory, but – according to the case – without locomotion, without speech or even without visibility. As Barish notes:

> they come imprisoned in urns or ashcans or pyramids of earth, reduced to trunkless heads or legless torsos, or else deprived of language so that they can only gesticulate frantically in pantomime, or reduced to a single disembodied mouth hysterically jabbering away in shrill monologue, or – extremest of all – reduced to total absence except for two faint cries and an intake of breath heard on a bare stage with nothing on it but a pile of rubbish.[16]

According to Barish, it is hard to imagine a theatre more negative, more calculatedly eviscerated of everything the world has always thought of as theatre. Adding to that, it is hard to imagine human substance coming so close to absolute nullity and yet retaining, in some strange and stunted fashion, a meaningful semblance of humanity. As he argues, 'in all these cases the playwright assaults the theatre, undermines it with high explosives, in order to delve to bedrock of consciousness'.[17]

The theorist formulates a correlation between anti-theatricality and anti-humanism when he discusses Beckett's wish to blast the theatre loose from its specious theatricality, as well as from its complacent reliance on mimicry, spectacle and its facile trust in the rational, the social and the objective. Yet:

> in so doing he topples one by one the stones that held the edifice together. With personality challenged as a value and even as a reality with impersonation less and less honored as an art, the actor undergoes a transformation into a ritual vessel, an impersonal symbol of existence, a depersonalized building-block with which the architect of the theater tinkers his constructions together. Antitheatricalism links itself with antihumanism as it does when with Artaud it aims to offend rather than please.[18]

Various forms of anti-theatricalism seem to be symptoms of this prejudice that, as discussed, can play a productive role in the theatre. Anti-theatrical associations between the theoretical systems of both Fried and Beckett illustrate that both the theatre and the visual arts share similar prejudices against theatricality, while they appropriate similar conceptual systems and share a common theoretical ground about issues of representation. The critical overview of Fried's problematic approach concerning the relation of the theatre with the visual arts considered the limitations of his approach, in the context of an inventive reconsideration of the conceptual and aesthetic fields with which the art and theatre are inextricably linked. The intention is to explore these different treatments of theatricality and to examine their implications for rethinking visual and theatrical representation.

Rereadings and reconsiderations of these art discourses, in critical relation to broadly contemporaneous writings on art demonstrated their relevance to art criticism, art historical questions and interdisciplinary concerns. The 'Three Dialogues' and the ways that Beckettian aesthetics translates into practice were discussed in relation to *Breath*, given that the playlet is the culmination of Beckett's experimental vision and artistic self-reflection as an artwork that ventures to go beyond 'the field of the possible', even if that attempt results in an 'art of failure'.[19]

Beckett confesses in the 'Three Dialogues' that he knows that 'all that is required, in order to bring even this "horrible" matter to an acceptable conclusion is to make [. . . of . . .] this fidelity to failure, a new occasion a new term of relation'.[20] Art is often considered by the artist as something to be overthrown, for it denies the artist the realisation, the transcendence s/he desires. Susan Sontag describes the process in which art itself becomes the enemy of the artist. Therefore a new element enters the individual artwork and becomes constitutive of it. As she argues: 'the appeal (tacit or overt) for its own abolition – and, ultimately for the abolition of art itself [. . .] Committed to the idea that the power of art is located in its power to negate, the ultimate weapon in the artist's inconsistent war with the audience is to verge closer and closer to silence'.[21]

There is no escapefor the artist from this cyclical process of composition, as there is no diversionfor the human, from the cycle of respiration. Beckett's concentrated 'drama', in *Breath*, articulates and distils this process of the human condition in an existential crossing that is determined by representation in the rise and fall of the curtain. As an integral part of the 'performance', the classic raising and lowering of the curtain establishes the temporal boundaries of the drama. Beckett telescopes an entire life within a period of time roughly equivalent to that of one respiration.

When the curtain rises, we see that a large rubbish heap occupies the stage and that there is no cast. Yet every one of the thirty seconds of the play is filled with dramatic tension, since one virtually holds one's breath from the moment the curtain rises until it mercifully falls once more, for what Beckett dramatises so incisively in these brief moments is the ceaseless perpetuation of mankind's futile existence, as Herbert Blau suggests:

four poignant utterances span the seconds, taking man from the silence of nonexistence to the shock of birth, through maturity, and finally to a slow and agonized death; but at this moment (which might seem to signal a conclusion) a second natal cry reveals that the process is a cycle from which there is no escape. Here, then, is the distilled essence of the human condition captured in the essence of theatre itself. For what is theatre but the experience framed by the rise and fall of the curtain?[22]

The writer's decision to fill the stage with rubbish is not just an allegorical statement about the human condition, as it is often stated, it is an ideological[23] statement that encapsulates Beckett's ultimate aspiration to go beyond representation (and beyond the representation of 'reality'). *Breath* is unfolding in the dialectic of birth and death, and its ideological context turns out to be central. To fail for Beckett, means to fail to represent and his fidelity to the 'art of failure', namely, the inevitability of the artist's failure, becomes an expressive recourse, intimately related to the representation of the human condition.

The absence of the human reveals what has been human and, as Derrida proclaims, 'the trace I leave signifies to me at once my death, either to come or already come upon me, and the hope that this trace survives me'.[24] In our respiratory system lies the essence of human experience, nonetheless, in Beckett's late theatre the fragmentation of the human body discloses a subjectivity that is beyond embodiment. For Beckett, as Boulter argues, 'the total elimination of the human is a total impossibility',[25] but in *Breath* the body is missing despite the fact that it is protagonistic in several stagings (Coogan, Guimaraes, Tynan).

A wide acceptance of anthropomorphism is monitored that could be interpreted as a manifestation of the increasing intention for art to have agency. The use and omnipresence of the mannequin[26] in contemporary installation practice and the revival of a minimalist vocabulary that embraces anthropomorphism are signs of tendencies to reconcile minimalism with the presence of the human figure.[27] This new artistic convention becomes rather questionable when discussed in the light of theorists like Fried who intended to eliminate anthropomorphism. Didi-Huberman acknowledges minimalism's anthropomorphism, but in contrast to Fried, instead of the presence of objects, he supports their subject-like power and the notion that artworks have agency, that objects are quasi-subjects.

According to Isabelle Graw, linking art to subjecthood is not exactly a new move. There is an aesthetic tradition – from Hegel to Adorno – that treats artworks like 'rhetorical figures of the subject'. Hegel considers painting to be the art form that the 'principle of subjectivity' had broken into. Moreover, Adorno considers the artwork to be a stand-in for the universal subject ('Statthalter des Gesamtsubjekts'). An anthropomorphisation of minimal art was set in motion by artists like Janine Antoni, John Miller and Mike Kelley in the late 1980s, while, as Graw argues, 'the insistence on the dark or repressed side of Minimalism was motivated by the insights of identity politics and cultural studies and amounted to a necessary strategic provocation, the animation of Minimalist forms has since turned into what can be described as an aesthetic convention'.[28]

SUBLIME EMPTINESS

For Beckett, we are always already post-human insofar as we are controlled by discourses (history-ideology-language). Human always remains human, as Boulter argues, but only as phantom, as trace, as spectre. As he writes:

> the figure of the posthuman is always a figure of the boundary or limit: she exists just at the threshold of the recognizable at the limit of what we expect to be the human (the figure of the ghost, the specter – the literal post-human). Beckett, for all his interest in the limits of the human, in what Boulter has been calling the posthuman, thus really does remain fundamentally a humanist. Indeed, the trajectory of his career demonstrates that posthumanism, defined in a limited sense as the elimination of the human – its body; it claims to a transparent consciousness – is a patent impossibility: traces of the human, of the (spectral) body, of (spectral) desires, insistently reanimate what seems to have vanished.[29]

Posthumanism is defined as the theory that radically critiques the idea that the individual subject is the centre of all things, the beginning and end of all knowledge and experience. Thus, this is a radical critique of humanist philosophy which would posit, as Boulter argues, 'the human's reason and rationality as being transparently available to the thinking subject. Posthumanism begins by countering humanism's belief that the human is self-producing, self-coincidental, that it is somehow responsible for the production of its world and its experience of the world'.[30]

Beckett's concern with the limits of the human discloses his preoccupation with history and humanity, yet in an inverted manner (via negativa); in negative representation. Herbert Blau associates the ideological context of *Breath* with topics encountered in critical theory, most specifically with Walter Benjamin's *Theses on the Philosophy of History*. A Klee painting named *Angelus Novus* shows an angel looking as though he is about to move away from something he is fixedly contemplating. As Benjamin writes:

> his eyes are staring, his mouth is open, his wings are spread. This is how one pictures the angel of history. His face is turned toward the past. Where we perceive a chain of events, he sees one single catastrophe which keeps piling wreckage upon wreckage and hurls it in front of his feet. The

angel would like to stay, awaken the dead, and make whole what has been smashed. But a storm is blowing from Paradise; it has got caught in his wings with such violence that the angel can no longer close them. The storm irresistibly propels him into the future to which his back is turned, while the pile of debris before him grows skyward. This storm is what we call progress.[31]

According to Blau, the phrase 'Know minimum', that Beckett includes in *Worstward Ho* and the 'meremost minimum of pitiful rubbish' in *Breath* is proleptic and reminiscent of Benjamin's view of history, for it suggests the wreckage of time accumulating before the 'Angelus Novus'. Described by Benjamin in the painting by Paul Klee as wings outspread, caught up in a violent storm from Paradise, the angel is being blown backward into the future:

> facing the catastrophe of the past, the debris growing skyward before him, from which Beckett might have gathered the litter, as a kind of bricolage, scraps and tatters from those ruins of time, 'no verticals, all scattered and lying', not flat out, but at minima, if not Benjamin's 'chips of Messianic time', an ideographic suggestion of the Beckettian view of history.[32]

The theorist suggests that the waste onstage might also be a corrective to what Theodor Adorno writes, in his essay on *Endgame*, with 'profounds of mind'[33] about the play not meaning anything becoming the only meaning, and with that certain certitudes about the writer's indifference to history.

Nevertheless, as analysed in the Introduction, what seems to be, at first reading, Beckett's indifference to history might be a manifestation of Beckett's sensibility between the desire to respond to the ethical problems entailed by the representation of historical facts, as the imperative to remember, and his pluralistic approach to an art that evades representation. The writer is ideologically committed to the sufferings of post-war devastated humanity, and through the negative representation and criticism of any philosophical certainty he points beyond the scope of representation, to a view of history and humanity that is yet to be uncovered. Beckett manages to provoke a critical historical reflexivity by composing an open dialectics (inhalation-exhalation) that attempts to depict the singularity and incomprehensibility of the past, while it remains receptive to the pluralism of modes of understanding.

Emptiness on stage is further illuminated with the presence of the pile of miscellaneous scattered and lying rubbish. This still image that resembles a temporalised[34] installation (tableau) depicts a moribund humanity on the verge of death. The writer is interrogating the dialectics of presence (liveness) and absence, the presence of miscellaneous rubbish in juxtaposition with the absence of the human figure. The 'terror' of the decay of humanity and death is juxtaposed with the presence of the rubbish heap (waste) that co-exists with the 'sublime', the life-giving force of respiration. *Breath* oscillates between the sublime expression of life that is respiration's basic characteristic and the 'negative representation'[35] of waste.

Michael Fried would probably endorse Beckett's 'negative representation' and anti-theatrical strategies, but he wouldn't support its intermedial ramifications. Beckett's opposition to the 'traditional unity' of the work and to medium specificity is counter to Fried's fixation with art's autonomy and medium specificity. The specificity of both the visual arts and the theatre has become difficult to define in Beckett's intermedia aesthetics.

The notion of 'failure'[36] is central to the account of human subjectivity within the existential/phenomenological philosophical tradition, and as Cormac Power argues, 'there are analogies to be drawn between the notion of performance as failure and the phenomenological account of human consciousness as perpetually attempting/failing to realise itself and its own possibilities'.[37] Performance fails to exist in perpetuity like an object. Unlike a visual art piece, a theatrical performance is disappearing as it is being experienced. Peggy Phelan emphasises the contingent aspects of performance by considering that its most irretrievable failure of all is its 'total disappearance and non-existence'. Phelan also celebrates the staging of disappearance in performance as 'representation without reproduction'.[38] Embedded in this notion is the singularity of live performance, its immediacy and its non-repeatability.

Beckett's 'aesthetics of failure' has anti-theatrical overtones, but is also a conscious strategy against triumphalism and often in favour of a form of indeterminacy characteristic of an 'art of impoverishment'. Representation seems no longer possible for the writer, because of the absence of relation between subject and object, while Fried is also anxious about how the subject perceives the object and about the collapsing distinction between subject and object, although from a different standpoint. The performance of objecthood, the new relation to objecthood and the engagement of the subject obscures artworks' autonomy and medium specificity. The emergence of time-based art, the endurance of a piece and the encounter with objecthood produces discomfort to modernist discourse. In this context the two writers are seen in contradistinction to each other.

Fried is an exponent of medium purity and against artworks that reduce their medium to its most basic form of objecthood, and Beckett is an exponent of the exhaustion of media. Thus, the two writers provide different accounts of modernity. Fried is fascinated by high-modernity and medium specificity, in contrast to Beckett's late works, that stem from a desire to 'exhaust' the art object, pointing to the exhausted project of modernity and to the exhausted artistic endeavour. Beckett's final piece of discursive writing considers the exhaustion of possibilities as a fundamental artistic strategy,[39] as well as the tension between abstraction and expression, the dilemma of artistic expression and the impossibility of expression in painting.

Ultimately, Beckett's impact on contemporary artistic practice lies in the dilemma between expression and abstraction as well as in the desire to 'exhaust the possible'. The urgency to substitute the human figure with an amplified sound and the focus on the spatial, gestural and durational extensions of artistic innovation demonstrates the writer's struggle with the exhaustion of representation. Nonetheless, this exhaustion becomes as vital and generating for Beckett's art, as breathing is for life.

NOTES

1. Samuel Beckett. *Malone Dies*. New York: Grove, 1951. (http://www.themodern-word.com/beckett/beckett_quotes.html).
2. Charles, Juliet. *Conversations with Samuel Beckett and Bram van Velde*. French Literature Series. Champaign: Dalkey Archive Press, 2009: 157.
3. Samuel, Beckett. *Ill Seen Ill Said*. In *Nohow On: Company, Ill Seen Ill Said, Worstward Ho*. Grove Press, 1981: 59.
4. Blau, Herbert. *Take Up the Bodies, Theatre at the Vanishing Point*. Urbana: University of Illinois Press, 1982: 86.
5. The modernist (principally Michael Fried's) understanding of the theatre as a compound art form, a type of Gesamtkunstwerk in the romantic Wagnerian tradition, is significant to Fried's negative view of the theatre and theatricality, since the theatre 'lies between art forms', as Fried argued.
6. Theatre is interdisciplinary par excellence, since different disciplines are integrated in the theatrical process. As Yury Annenkov argues, 'the theatre is not an independent, self-sufficient, pure form of art, but merely a treaty drawn up by a bunch of different arts, a treaty according to which they promise to reproduce, supplement, explain, and reveal by visual and acoustic media – the fortuitous, miraculous elements of the theatre [. . .]'. Annenkov, Yury. *Teatr Chistogo Metoda* (*The Theatre of Pure Method*). Moscow: Russian State Archive of Literature and Art, c. 1920: 48. In https://archive.org/stream/amazonsofavantga00exte/amazonsofavant-ga00exte_djvu.txt
7. See Barton, Bruce. 'Paradox as Process: Intermedial Anxiety and the Betrayals of Intimacy', *Theatre Journal*, 61.4 (December 2009): 575–601.
8. Deleuze, Gilles. 'The Brain is the Screen: An Interview with Gilles Deleuze', trans. Marie Therese Guirgis. In Gregory Flaxman (ed.), *The Brain in the Screen: Deleuze and the Philosophy of Cinema*. Minneapolis: University of Minnesota Press, 2000: 367. See https://monoskop.org/images/4/4d/0816634467BrainB.pdf
9. In the 'German Letter' (1937), which is part of the correspondence between Beckett and his friend publisher Axel Kaun, whom he met in Germany, written three months after Beckett's return to Dublin from his trip to Germany, Beckett asked Axel Kaun, 'Is there something paralyzingly holy in the vicious nature of the word that is not found in the elements of the other arts?' Oppenheim, Lois. *The Painted Word: Beckett's Dialogue with Art*. Ann Arbor: University of Michigan Press, 2000: 7.
10. Sugiera, Malgorzata. 'Theatricality and Cognitive Science: The Audience's Perception and Reception', *SubStance*, 31.2/3, special issue 98/99 (2002): 225.
11. Murray, Timothy (ed.). *Mimesis, Masochism, and Mime: The Politics of Theatricality in Contemporary French Thought*. Ann Arbor: University of Michigan Press, 1997: 218–20.

12. Puchner, Martin, *Against Theatre: Creative Destructions on the Modernist Stage* (edited collection with Alann Ackerman), New York: Palgrave Macmillan, 2006. In http://www.people.fas.harvard.edu/~puchner/theaterinmodernistthought.pdf

13. Puchner, Martin. 'The Theatre in Modernist Thought', *New Literary History*, 33.3. The Book as Character, Composition, Criticism, and Creation (Summer 2002): 522.

14. See Albright, Daniel. *Beckett and Aesthetics*. Cambridge: Cambridge University Press, 2003: 1 and 2.

15. Puchner, Martin, *Stage Fright: Modernism, Anti-Theatricality and Drama*, Baltimore and London: Johns Hopkins University Press, 2002: 3.

16. Barish, Jonas. *The Anti-Theatrical Prejudice*. London: California University Press, 1981: 458.

17. Ibid.

18. Ibid.

19. The 'field of the possible', and the 'art of failure' are extensively discussed in Beckett, Samuel. 'Three Dialogues'. In Ruby Cohn (ed.), *Disjecta: Miscellaneous Writings and a Dramatic Fragment*. New York: Grove Press, 1984: 138.

20. Ibid.

21. Sontag, Susan. 'The Aesthetics of Silence'. In *Styles of Radical Will*, London: Vintage, 1994. See p. 2 in http://www.kim-cohen.com/Assets/CourseAssets/Texts/Sontag_The%20Aesthetics%20of%20Silence.pdf

22. Blau, Herbert. 'Apnea and True Illusion: Breath(less) in Beckett'. In Linda Ben-Zvi and Angela Moorjani (eds), *Beckett at 100: Revolving It All*. Oxford: Oxford University Press, 2008: 53.

23. Beckett was one of the few modernist artists to become a militant of the left rather than the right. See Terry Eagleton. 'Political Beckett?', *New Left Review*, 40 (July/August) 2006: 67–75.

24. Naas, Michael. *Derrida From Now On*. New York: Fordham University Press, 2008: 5.

25. Boulter, Jonathan. *Beckett: A Guide for the Perplexed*. London: Continuum, 2008: 14.

26. Artists like John Miller, Thomas Hirschhorn, Heimo Zobernig, David Lieske, Isa Genzken and Rachel Harrison have focused their work on replicas of the human subject. See Daniel Birnbaum, Isabelle Graw and Nikolaus Hirsch (eds). *Art and Subjecthood: The Return of the Human Figure in Semiocapitalism*. New York: Sternberg Press, 2012.

27. Ibid. The book is based on the conference proceedings *Art and Subjecthood: The Return of the Human Figure in Semiocapitalism*, part of the project 'Art and Life', made possible by Kulturfonds Frankfurt Rhein Main and organised by the Institut für Kunstkritik (Isabelle Graw, Daniel Birnbaum, Nikolaus Hirsch).

28. Ibid.: 15.

29. Boulter, Jonathan. *Beckett*: 12.

30. Ibid.

31. Benjamin, Walter. 'Theses on the Philosophy of History'. In *Illuminations*. New York: Schoken Books, 1969: 257 and 258.

32. Blau, Herbert. 'Apnea and True Illusion': 458.

33. The two writers disagreed on the philosophical context of Adorno's text.

34. According to Stimson,

> instead of the usual modernist alternatives of instrumental beauty or universal sublimity, here the beholder would submit him/herself to the flux of a polytemporal aesthetic experience neither outside of time nor subject to its singular iron

rule. In so doing, the great companion myths of time and timelessness, history and transcendence, would be sundered and the many component parts, the many and sundry bits of local time generated by that break-up would be disseminated to various (often-conflicting) narratives of temporal ebbs and flows.

Stimson quotes Smithson who succinctly says in *Entropy* that 'time breaks into many times'. Stimson, Blake. 'Conceptual Work and Conceptual Waste', *Discourse*, 24.2 (Spring 2001): 137; and 'Rhizome ... Conceptual Work and Conceptual Waste', *Discourse* (Spring 2002). In http://arthistory.ucdavis.edu/people/faculty/publications/stimson.html [accessed 1/11/16].

35. On the history of negative presentation in the visual arts after 1945, see Ray, Gene. 'Mourning and Cosmopolitics: With and Beyond Beuys'. In Christa-Maria Lerm-Hayes and Victoria Walters (eds), *Beuysian Legacies in Ireland and Beyond: Art, Culture and Politics*. Berlin and Muenster: LIT Verlag, 2011: 118–46; Ray, Gene. *Terror and the Sublime in Art and Critical Theory*. New York: Palgrave Macmillan, 2005; and Ray, Gene. 'History, the Sublime, Terror: Notes on the Politics of Fear'. *Static*, 7 (July 2007): 1–15.

36. The notion of 'failure' in performance is an area of growing concern within the field. See www.institute-of-failure.com [accessed 1/11/2016].

37. See Power, Cormac. 'Performing to Fail: Perspectives on Failure in Performance and Philosophy'. In Daniel Meyer-Dinkgraffe and Daniel Watt (eds), *Ethical Encounters: Boundaries of Theatre, Performance and Philosophy*. Newcastle: CSP, 2010: 127.

38. Phelan, Peggy. *Unmarked: The Politics of Performance*. London: Routledge, 1993: 148.

39. See Deleuze, Gilles. 'The Exhausted', *SubStance*, 24.3 (1995): 24.

BIBLIOGRAPHY

PRIMARY SOURCES

Beckett, Samuel. *Proust*. New York: Grove Press, 1957.
——. *Bram van Velde*. New York: Grove Press, 1960.
——. *Proust and Three Dialogues with Georges Duthuit*. London: John Calder, 1965.
——. *Ends and Odds*. New York: Grove Press, 1976.
——. *Ill Seen Ill Said*. In *Nohow On: Company, Ill Seen Ill Said, Worstward Ho*. New York: Grove Press, 1981.
——. *Worstward Ho*. London: John Calder, 1983.
——. *Breath and the Complete Dramatic Works* [1984]. London: Faber and Faber, 1986.
Fried, Michael. *Art and Objecthood Essays and Reviews*. Chicago and London: The University of Chicago Press, 1998.

SECONDARY SOURCES

Abbott, H. Porter. 'Tyranny and Theatricality: The Example of Samuel Beckett', *Theatre Journal*, 40.1 (March 1988): 77–87.
——. *Beckett Writing Beckett: The Author in the Autograph*. Ithaca: Cornell University Press, 1996.
Abramović, Marina and Ratti, Antonio (eds). *Body Art*. Milan: Charta, 2002.
Acheson, James. *Samuel Beckett's Artistic Theory and Practice: Criticism, Drama and Early Fiction*. New York: St Martin's Press, 1997.
Adorno, Theodor W. *Minima Moralia: Reflections from Damaged Life* [1951]. Trans. E. F. N. Jephcott. London: Verso, 1974.
——. *Negative Dialectics*. Trans. E. B. Ashton [1966]. New York: Continuum, 1995.
——. *Aesthetic Theory*. Trans. Robert Hullot-Kentor. Minneapolis: University of Minnesota Press, 1997.
——. *Can One Live After Auschwitz? A Philosophical Reader*. Ed. Rolf Tiedemann. Trans. Rodney Livingstone and Others. Stanford: Stanford University Press, 2003.

Agamben, Giorgio. *Remnants of Auschwitz: The Witness and the Archive*. New York: Zone Books, 1999.

Albright, Daniel. *Beckett and Aesthetics*. Cambridge: Cambridge University Press, 2003.

Alvarez, Alfred. *Beckett*. London: Collins, 1973.

Annenkov, Yury. *Teatr Chistogo Metoda (The Theatre of Pure Method)*. Moscow: Russian State Archive of Literature and Art, c. 1920.

Apple, Jacki. 'Introduction'. In *Alternatives in Retrospect: An Historical Overview, 1969–1975*, exhibition catalogue. New York: New Museum, 1981: 5–7.

Aristotle, *Poetics*, ed. and trans. Stephen Halliwell. Cambridge, MA: Harvard University Press, 1999.

Artaud, Antonin. *The Theatre and its Double*. New York: Grove Press, 1958.

Auslander, Philip. 'Presence and Theatricality in the Discourse of Performance and the Visual Arts'. In *From Acting to Performance: Essays in Modernism and Postmodernism*, London and New York: Routledge, 1997: 49–57.

——. *Liveness, Performance in a Mediatized Culture*. London and New York: Routledge, 1999.

Bachelard, Gaston. *Air and Dreams: An Essay on the Imagination of Movements*. Dallas: Dallas Institute Publications, 1988.

——. *The Poetics of Space*. Boston, MA: Beacon Press, 1994.

Bacon, Francis. *The History of Winds in the Works of Frances Bacon, Baron Verulam, Viscount St Alban and Lord High Chancellor of England*, vol. 12. London, 1815.

Bailes, Sarah Jane. *Performance Theatre and the Poetics of Failure: Forced Entertainment, Goat Island, Elevator Repair Service*. New Brunswick, NJ: Routledge, 2010.

Bair, Deidre. *Samuel Beckett: A Biography*. London: Cape, 1978.

Bal, Mieke. *Double Exposures: The Subject of Cultural Analysis*. New York: Routledge, 1996.

Bal, Mieke and Marx-Macdonald, Sherry (eds). *Travelling Concepts in the Humanities: A Rough Guide*. Toronto: University of Toronto Press, 2002.

Banes, Sally. *Democracy's Body: Judson Dance Theatre, 1962–1964*. Durham, NC: Duke University Press, 1993.

Barish, Jonas. *The Anti-Theatrical Prejudice*. London: California University Press, 1981.

Barthes, Roland. *Critical Essays*. Evanston: Northwestern University Press, 1972.

——. *Image Music Text*. New York: Noonday Press/Farrar, Stauss and Giroux, 1977.

——. *The Responsibility of Forms: Critical Essays on Music, Art, and Representation*. New York: Hill and Wang, 1985.

Barton, Bruce. 'Paradox as Process: Intermedial Anxiety and the Betrayals of Intimacy', *Theatre Journal*, 61.4 (December 2009): 575–601.

Batchelor, David. *Minimalism*. Cambridge: Cambridge University Press, 1997.

Battcock, Gregory (ed.). *Minimal Art: A Critical Anthology*. New York, 1968.

——. *Minimal Art: A Critical Anthology*, Berkeley and London: University of California Press, 1995.

Bauman, Zygmunt. *Legislators and Interpreters: On Modernity, Post-Modernity and Intellectuals*. Ithaca: Cornell University Press.

Bay-Cheng, Sara, Kattenbelt, Chiel, Lavender, Andy and Nelson, Robin. *Mapping Intermediality in Performance*. Amsterdam: Amsterdam University Press, 2010.

Beckett, Samuel. 'Peintres de l'empêchement'. In Ruby Cohn (ed.). *Disjecta: Miscellaneous Writings and a Dramatic Fragment*. New York: Grove Press, 1984: 133–7.

——. 'German Letter of 1937'. In Ruby Cohn (ed.), *Disjecta: Miscellaneous Writings and a Dramatic Fragment*. New York: Grove Press, 1984: 51–4.

Beckett, Samuel et al. *Our Examination Round his Factification for Incamination of Work in Progress*. London: Faber and Faber, 1929.

Beer, Gillian. *Open Fields: Science in Cultural Encounter*. Oxford: Oxford University Press, 1999.

Benjamin, Walter. 'Theses on the Philosophy of History'. In *Illuminations*. New York: Schocken Books, 1969: 253–64.

——. 'Paralipomena to "On the Concept of History"'. In Howard Eiland and Michael W. Jennings (eds), *Selected Writings* [vol. 4, 1938–40]. Cambridge, MA: Belknap/Harvard University Press, 2003: 402.

Ben-Zvi, Linda. 'Samuel Beckett, Fritz Mauthner and the Limits of Language', *PMLA*, 95 (1980): 183–200.

——. 'Samuel Beckett's Media Plays', *Modern Drama*, 28 (1985): 22–37.

——. 'Beckett and Television: In a Different Context', *Modern Drama*, 49.4 (Winter 2006): 469–90.

Bertram, Theo. *Samuel Beckett and the Little Things of Life*. Bristol: University of Bristol, 2000.

Bersani, Leo and Dutoit, Ulysse. *Arts of Impoverishment: Beckett, Rothko, Resnais*. Cambridge, MA: Harvard University Press, 1993.

Best, Steven and Douglas Kellner. *The Postmodern Turn*. New York: Guilford Press, 1997.

Birnbaum, Daniel, Graw, Isabelle and Hirsch, Nikolaus (eds). *Art and Subjecthood: The Return of the Human Figure in Semiocapitalism*. New York: Sternberg Press, 2012.

Blackman, Maurice. 'Acting without Words: Artaud and Beckett's Theatrical Language', *Journal of Australian Universities*, 55, Modern Language Association (1981): 68–76.

Blau, Herbert. *Take Up the Bodies, Theatre at the Vanishing Point*. Urbana: University of Illinois Press, 1982.

——. *Blooded Thought: Occasions of Theatre*. New York: Performing Arts Journal Publications, 1982.

——. *The Audience*. Baltimore: Johns Hopkins University Press, 1990.

——. *Sails of the Herring Fleet: Essays on Beckett*. Ann Arbor: University of Michigan Press, 2000.

——. *The Dubious Spectacle, Extremities of Theatre 1976–2000*. Minneapolis: University of Minnesota Press, 2002.

——. 'Apnea and True Illusion: Breath(less) in Beckett', *Modern Drama*, 49.4 (Winter 2006): 452–68.

Bleeker, Maaike. *Visuality in the Theatre: The Locus of Looking*. London: Palgrave Macmillan, 2008.

——. (ed.). *Anatomy Live: Performance and the Operating Theatre*. Amsterdam: Amsterdam University Press, 2008.

——. 'Passages in Post-Modern Theory: Mapping the Apparatus', Parallax, 14.1 (2008): 55–67.

——. 'Corporeal Literacy: New Modes of Embodied Interaction in Digital Culture'. In Sara Bay-Cheng, Chiel Kattenbelt, Andy Lavender and Robin Nelson (eds), *Mapping Intermediality*. Amsterdam: Amsterdam University Press, 2010: 39–44.

Boenisch, Peter. 'Aesthetic Art to Aisthetic Act: Theatre, Media, Intermedial Performance'. In Frieda Chapple and Chiel Kattenbelt, *Intermediality in Theatre and Performance*. Amsterdam: Amsterdam University Press, 2006: 103–16.

Bois, Yves-Alain. *Painting as Model*. Cambridge, MA: The MIT Press, 1990.

Bois, Yves-Alain and Krauss, Rosalind E. *Formless. A User's Guide*. Cambridge, MA: MIT Press, 1997.

Bolter, Jay David and Grusin, Richard. *Remediation: Understanding New Media*. Cambridge, MA: MIT Press, 2000.

Boulter, Jonathan. *Beckett: A Guide for the Perplexed*. London: Continuum, 2008.

Bouriaud, Nicholas. *Relational Aesthetics*. Paris: Les Presses du Réel, 1998.

Bousso, Vitória Daniela. 'Interstice Zone in Adriano and Fernando Guimarães'. 'Todos Os Que Caem / All That Fall' catalogue. Rio de Janeiro: Centro Cultural Banco do Brasil, 2004: 97–9.

Boyland, Patrick J. 'British Art in the 1980s and 1990s: The Social and Political Background'. In Bernice Murphy (ed. and cur.), *Pictura Brittanica: Art from Britain*. Sydney: Museum of Contemporary Art, 1997.

Bradby, David. *Beckett: Waiting for Godot.* 'Plays in Production'. Cambridge: Cambridge University Press, 2001.

Branden, Joseph. *Anthony McCall: The Solid Light Films and Related Works. Artist Interview by Jonathan Walley,* ed. Christopher Eamon. Evanston: New Art Trust, Northwestern University Press.

Brater, Enoch. 'Fragment and Beckett's Form in *That Time* and *Footfalls*', *Journal of Beckett Studies,* 2 (Summer 1977): 70–81. http://www.english. fsu.edu/jobs/num02/Num2EnochBrater.htm

——. 'Why Beckett's "Enough" Is More or Less Enough', *Contemporary Literature,* 21.2 (Spring 1980): 252–66.

——. *Beyond Minimalism: Beckett's Late Style in the Theatre.* Oxford: Oxford University Press, 1987.

——. *The Drama in the Text, Beckett's Late Fiction.* Oxford: Oxford University Press, 1994.

Breder, Hans and Busse, Klaus-Peter. *Intermedia: Enacting the Liminal.* Dortmund: Dortmunder Schriften zur Kunst, 2005.

Brett, Guy. *Force Fields: Phases of the Kinetic.* Barcelona: Museu d'Art Contemporani de Barcelona (MACBA), Actar, 2000.

Brook, Peter. *The Empty Space.* New York: Atheneum, 1984.

Brown, Kathryn. 'Undoing Urban Modernity: Contemporary Art's Confrontation with Waste', *European Journal of Cultural Studies,* 65.1 (July 2013): 131–43.

Buchloh, Benjamin H. D. *Neo-Avantgarde and Culture Industry: Essays on European and American Art from 1955 to 1975.* Cambridge, MA: MIT Press, 2000.

——. 'Detritus and Decrepitude: The Sculpture of Thomas Hirschhorn', *Oxford Art Journal,* 24.2 (2001): 41–56.

Buning, Marius (ed.). *Historicising Beckett: Issues of Performance.* Amsterdam: Rodopi, 2005.

Bürger, Peter. *The Decline of Modernism.* Cambridge, MA: Polity Press, 1992.

Burns, Elizabeth. *Theatricality: A Study of Convention in the Theatre and in Social Life.* London: Longman, 1972.

Buskirk, Martha. *The Contingent Object of Contemporary Art.* Cambridge, MA: MIT Press, 2003.

Busse, Klaus-Peter. 'Intermedia: The Aesthetic Experience of Cultural Interspaces'. In Hans Breder and Klaus-Peter Busse (eds), *Intermedia: Enacting the Liminal.* Dortmund: Dortmunder Schriften zur Kunst, 2005: 262–70.

Butler, Lance St John. *Samuel Beckett and the Meaning of Being.* London: MacMillan, 1984.

Butt, Gavin (ed.). *After Criticism: New Responses to Art and Performance.* Malden: Blackwell, 2005.

Cabanne, Pierre. *Dialogues with Marcel Duchamp*. London: Thames and Hudson, 1971.

Carlson, Marvin. 'The Resistance to Theatricality', *SubStance*, 31.2/3, special issue 98/99 (2002): 238–50.

Casanova, Pascale. *Samuel Beckett: Anatomy of a Literary Revolution*. London: Verso, 2006.

Cavell, Stanley. *Must We Mean What We Say?* Cambridge: Cambridge University Press, 1976.

Chabert, Pierre. 'The Body In Beckett's Theatre', *Journal of Beckett Studies*, 8 (Autumn 1982): 23–8.

Chaikin, Joseph. *The Presence of the Actor*. New York: Atheneum, 1972.

Chapple, Frieda and Kattenbelt, Chiel. 'Key Issues in Intermediality in Theatre and Performance'. In Frieda Chapple and Chiel Kattenbelt (eds), *Intermediality in Theatre and Performance*. Amsterdam and New York: Rodopi, 2006: 13–29.

Charles, Juliet. *Conversations with Samuel Beckett and Bram van Velde*. French Literature Series. Champaign: Dalkey Archive Press, 2009.

Chawla, Nishi. *Samuel Beckett: Reading the Body in his Writing*. New Delhi: Prestige, 1999.

Cixous, Hélène. 'The Laugh of the Medusa', *Signs*, 1.4 (Summer 1976): 875–93.

Clüver, Claus. 'Intermediality and Interarts Studies'. In Jens Arvidson, Mikael Askander, Jørgen Bruhn, Heidrun Führer, *Changing Borders: Contemporary Positions in Intermediality*. Lund: Intermedia Studies Press, 2007: 19–37.

Cohn, Ruby. *Just Play Beckett's Theatre*. Princeton: Princeton University Press, 1980.

——. (ed.). *Disjecta: Miscellaneous Writings and a Dramatic Fragment*. London: John Calder, 1983 and New York: Grove Press, 1984.

——. *A Beckett Canon*. Ann Arbor: University of Michigan Press, 2001.

Collings, Matthew. *Blimey: From Bohemia to Britpop: The London Art World from Francis Bacon to Damien Hirst*. Cambridge: 21 Publishing, 1997.

——. *This is Modern Art*. London: Seven Dials, 2000.

Connor, Steven. *Samuel Beckett: Repetition, Theory and Text*. New York: Blackwell, 1988.

——. 'Oxygen Debt: Little Dorrit's Pneumatics'. Lecture given at Birkbeck College, London, 28 September 2002.

——. 'Beckett's Atmospheres'. In S. E. Gontarski and Anthony Uhlmann (eds), *Beckett after Beckett*, Gainesville: University of Florida Press, 2006: 52–65. In http://stevenconnor.com/atmospheres-2.html

Cope, Richard. *Re-reading Samuel Beckett's Three Dialogues with George Duthuit within the Context of the Continuum it Nourished*, PhD thesis. London South Bank University, 2006.

Costello, Diarmuid. 'Greenberg's Kant and the Fate of Aesthetics in Contemporary Art Theory', *The Journal of Aesthetics and Art Criticism* (2007): 217–28.

——. 'On the Very Idea of a Specific Medium: Michael Fried and Stanley Cavell on Painting and Photography as Arts', *Critical Inquiry*, 34 (Winter 2008): 274–312.

Costello, Diarmuid and Vickery, Jonathan. *Art: Key Contemporary Thinkers*. Oxford: Oxford University Press, 2007.

Crimp, Douglas. *Art after Modernism: Rethinking Representation*. New York: New Museum of Contemporary Art, 1984.

Critchley, Simon. *Very Little . . . Almost Nothing, Death, Philosophy, Literature*. London: Routledge, 1997.

——. 'To Be or Not to Be is Not the Question: On Beckett's Film', *Film-Philosophy*, 11.2 (August 2007): 108–21.

——. *On Humour*. London: Routledge, 2010.

Crowther, Paul. 'Greenberg's Kant and the Problem of Modernist Painting', *British Journal of Aesthetics*, 25.4 (1985): 317–25.

Cunningham, David and Cunningham, Conor. *Genealogy of Nihilism*. London: Routledge, 2002.

——. 'Ex Minimis: Greenberg, Modernism and Beckett's Three Dialogues', *Samuel Beckett Today / Aujourd'hui*, 13 (2003): 29–41.

——. 'Asceticism against Colour, or, Modernism, Abstraction and the Lateness of Beckett', *New Formations*, 55 (Spring 2005): 104–19.

Davis, Tracy and Postlewait, Thomas (eds). *Theatricality*. Cambridge: Cambridge University Press, 2004.

Deleuze, Gilles. *L'Épuise*. London: Faber, 1973.

——. 'The Exhausted', *SubStance*, 24.3 (1995): 3–28.

——. 'The Brain is the Screen: An Interview with Gilles Deleuze', trans. Marie Therese Guirgis. In Gregory Flaxman (ed.), *The Brain in the Screen: Deleuze and the Philosophy of Cinema*. Minneapolis: University of Minnesota Press, 2000. See https://monoskop.org/images/4/4d/0816634467BrainB.pdf

Derrida, Jacques. 'The Theatre of Cruelty and the Closure of Representation'. In *Writing and Difference*. Chicago: University of Chicago Press, 1978: 232–50.

——. 'La Parole Soufflée'. In *Writing and Difference*. Chicago: University of Chicago Press, 1978: 169–95.

——. *Writing and Difference*. Trans. Alan Bass. Oxford: Routledge, 2008.

Derrida, Jacques and Birnbaum, Jean (eds). *Learning to Live Finally: The Last*

Interview. Hoboken, NJ: Melville, 2007. In http://www.rhizomes.net/issue20/burt/index.html [accessed 1/11/16].

Devlin, Devis. 'Intercessions' (15 poems), *Transition*, 27 (May–April 1938).

Didi-Huberman, Georges. *Confronting Images: Questioning the Ends of a Certain History of Art*. University Park: Pennsylvania State University Press, 2005.

——. *Ce Que nous voyons, ce qui nous regarde*. Paris: Les Éditions de Minuit, 1992: 33. Translated in Juliane Rebentisch. *Aesthetics of Installation Art*. Berlin: Sternberg Press, 2012.

Doherty, Francis. *Samuel Beckett*. London: Hutchinson, 1971.

Dowd, Garin. *Abstract Machines: Samuel Beckett and Philosophy after Deleuze and Guattari*. Amsterdam/New York: Rodopi, 2007.

Driver, T. F. 'Beckett by the Madeleine', *Columbia University Forum*, iv (Summer 1961): 22–3.

Duve, Thierry de. 'Performance Here and Now: Minimal Art, a Plea for a New Genre of Theatre'. *Open Letter*, 5–6 (Summer/Fall 1983): 234–60.

Eagleton, Terry. 'Political Beckett?', *New Left Review*, 40 (July/August) 2006: 67–75.

Eco, Umberto. *The Open Work*. Cambridge, MA: Harvard University Press, 1989.

Elam, Keir. *The Semiotics of Theatre and Drama*. New York: Methuen, 1980.

Elkins, James. 'What Do we Want Photography to Be? A Response to Michael Fried,' *Critical Inquiry*, 31 (Summer 2005): 176–7.

Elleström, Lars. *Media Borders, Multimodality and Intermediality*. Basingstoke: Palgrave Macmillan, 2010.Erickson, Jon. *The Fate of the Object: From Modern Object to Postmodern Sign in Performance, Art, and Poetry*. Ann Arbor: University of Michigan Press, 1995.

Essif, Les. 'Introducing the Hyper Theatrical Subject: The Mise en Abyme of Empty Space', *Journal of Dramatic Theory and Criticism*, 9.1 (1994): 67–87.

——. *Empty Figure on an Empty Stage: The Theatre of Samuel Beckett and his Generation*. Bloomington: Indiana University Press, 2001.

Esslin, Martin. (ed.), *Samuel Beckett: A Collection of Critical Essays*. New York: Prentice-Hall, 1965.

——. 'A Poetry of Moving Images'. In Alan-Warren Friedman, Charles Rossman and Dina Sherzer (eds), *Beckett Translating/ Translating Beckett*. University Park: Pennsylvania State University Press, 1987: 65–76.

Ettinger, Bracha. *Time is the Breath of Spirit: Emmanuel Levinas in Conversation with Bracha Lichtenberg Ettinger*. Trans. Joseph Simas and Carolyn Ducker. Oxford: MOMA, 1993.

Fehsenfield, Martha. 'Beckett's Late Works: An Appraisal', *Modern Drama*, 35 (1982): 355–62.

Feldman, Mark B. 'Inside the Sanitation System: Mierle Ukeles, Urban Ecology, and the Social Circulation of Garbage', *Iowa Journal of Cultural Studies*, 10/11 (Spring/Fall 2009). In http://ir.uiowa.edu/cgi/viewcontent. cgi?article=1082&context=ijcs [accessed 15/7/17].

Fer, Brian. 'The Somnambulist's Story: Installation and the Tableau', *Oxford Art Journal*, 2 (2001): 75–92.

Feral, Josette. 'Theatricality: The Specificity of Theatrical Language', *SubStance*, 31.2/3, special issue 98/99 (2002): 94–108.

Fifield, Peter. *Late Modernist Style in Samuel Beckett and Emmanuel Levinas, New Interpretations of Beckett in the 21st Century*. London: Palgrave Macmillan, 2013.

Fischer-Lichte, Erika. 'Theatricality: A Key Concept in Theatre and Cultural Studies', *Theatre Research International*, 20.2 (Summer 1995): 85–9.

——. *Theatre, Sacrifice, Ritual*. London and New York: Routledge, 2005.

Foster, Hal. 'The Crux of Minimalism'. In *Individuals: A Selected History of Contemporary Art*. Los Angeles: Museum of Contemporary Art, 1986: 162–83.

——. *The Return of the Real: The Avant-Garde at the End of the Century*. Cambridge, MA: MIT Press, 1996.

——. *The Art-Architecture Complex*, London: Verso, 2011.

——. 'After the White Cube', *London Review of Books*, 37.6 (2015): 25–6. In https://www.lrb.co.uk/v37/n06/hal-foster/after-the-white-cube

Foster, Hal, Krauss, Rosalind, Bois, Yve-Alain and Buchloh, Benjamin. *Art since 1900: Modernism, Antimodernism, Postmodernism*. New York: Thames and Hudson, 2011.

Francis, Frascina. *Art, Politics and Dissent: Aspects of the Art Left in Sixties America*. Manchester and New York: Manchester University Press, 1999.

Fried, Michael. 'Art and Objecthood'. In *Minimal Art: A Critical Anthology*, New York: E. P. Dutton, 1968: 139–41.

——. *Absorption and Theatricality: Painter and Beholder in the Age of Diderot*. Chicago: University of Chicago Press, 1988.

——. 'Shape as Form: Frank Stella's Irregular Polygons' [1966]. In *Art and Objecthood: Essays and Reviews*. Chicago: University of Chicago Press, 1998: 77–99.

——. 'An Introduction to my Art Criticism'. In *Art and Objecthood Essays and Reviews*. Chicago and London: University of Chicago Press, 1998: 1–74.

——. 'Critical Response to Caroline A. Jones', *Critical Inquiry*, 27.4 (Summer 2001): 703–5.

——. *Why Photography Matters as Art as Never Before*. New Haven, CT and London: Yale University Press, 2008.

Fuchs, Elinor. *The Death of Character: Perspectives on Theater after Modernism*. Bloomington: Indiana University Press, 1996.

Fuery, Patrick. *Theory of Absence: Subjectivity, Signification, and Desire*. Westport, CT: Greenwood Press, 1996.

Gade, Rune and Jerslev, Anne (eds). *Performative Realism*. Copenhagen: Museum Tusculanum Press, University of Copenhagen, 2005.

Garner, Stanton. 'Visual Field in Beckett's Late Plays', *Comparative Drama*, XXI, 4 (1987–8): 349–73.

——. *Bodied Spaces: Phenomenology and Performance in Contemporary Drama*. Ithaca: Cornell University Press, 1994.

Gasset, José Ortega y. *The Dehumanization of Art, and Other Writings on Art and Culture*. Ann Arbor: Doubleday Anchor Books, 1956.

Gelikman, Oleg. 'Intermediality and Aesthetic Theory in Shklovsky's and Adorno's Thought', *Comparative Literature and Culture*, 13.3 (2011): 2–10.

Gene, Ray. *Terror and the Sublime in Art and Critical Theory: From Auschwitz to Hiroschima to September 11*. New York, and Basingstoke: Palgrave Macmillan, 2005.

——. 'Mourning and Cosmopolitics: With and Beyond Beuys'. In Christa-Maria Lerm Hayes and Victoria Walters (eds), *Beuysian Legacies in Ireland and Beyond: Art, Culture and Politics*. Berlin and Muenster: LIT Verlag, 2011: 118–46.

Gidal, Peter. *Understanding Beckett*. London: Macmillan, 1986.

Gilbert-Rolfe, Jeremy. *Beauty and the Contemporary Sublime*. London: Allworth Press, 1999.

Gilbert-Rolfe, Jeremy and Melville, Stephen W. *Seams: Art as a Philosophical Context*. London: Taylor and Francis, 1996.

Goldberg, RoseLee. *Performance Art: From Futurism to the Present*. New York: Harry Abrams, 1988.

——. *Performance: Live Art since 1960*. New York: Harry Abrams, 1998.

Goldstein, Ann. *A Minimal Future? Art As Object 1958–1968*. Cambridge, MA: The MIT Press, 2004.

Goldstein, Ann and Rorimer, Anne (eds). *Reconsidering the Object of Art: 1965–1975*. Cambridge, MA: The MIT Press, 1995.

Gontarski, Stanley. *The Intent of Undoing in Samuel Beckett's Dramatic Texts*. Bloomington: Indiana University Press, 1985.

——. 'Revising Himself: Performance as Text in Samuel Beckett's Theatre', *Journal of Modern Literature*, XXII.1 (Fall 1998): 131–55.

——. 'Reinventing Beckett', *Modern Drama*, 49.4 (Winter 2006): 428–51.

——. 'Redirecting Beckett'. In Daniela Guardamagna and Rosanna M. Sebellin (eds), *The Tragic Comedy of Samuel Beckett, Beckett in Rome*. Rome: Università degli Studi di Roma. 'Tor Vergata' o Editori Laterza, 2009: 327–41.

Gontarski, S. E. and Uhlmann, Anthony. *Beckett after Beckett*. Gainsville: University Press of Florida, 2006.

Graham, Amanda Jane. 'Assisted Breathing: Developing Embodied Exposure in Oscar Muñoz's *Aliento*', *Latin American Perspectives* (15 December 2011). In http://0-lap.sagepub.com.opac.sfsu.edu/content/early/2011/12/15/0094582X11431807.abstract?rss=1

Greenberg, Clement. *Art and Culture: Critical Essays*. Boston, MA: Beacon Press, 1961.

——. 'Recentness of Sculpture'. In Maurice Tuchman, *American Sculpture of the Sixties*. Los Angeles: Los Angeles County Museum, 1967: 24–6.

——. *Clement Greenberg: The Collected Essays and Criticism*, ed. John O'Brian. Chicago: University of Chicago Press, 1986–93.

——. 'Modernist Painting.' In John O'Brian (ed.), *Clement Greenberg: The Collected Essays and Criticism*. Chicago: University of Chicago Press, 1986–93, vol. 4: 85–93.

——. 'After Abstract Expressionism.' In John O'Brian (ed.), *Clement Greenberg: The Collected Essays and Criticism*. Chicago: University of Chicago Press, 1986–93, vol. 4: 121–34.

——. *Homemade Esthetics*. Oxford: Oxford University Press, 1999.

——. *Clement Greenberg: Late Writings*. Ed. Robert C. Morgan. Minneapolis: University of Minnesota Press, 2003.

——. 'Intermedia'. In Robert C. Morgan (ed.), *Clement Greenberg: Late Writings*. Minneapolis: University of Minnesota Press, 2003: 93–8.

Gronberg, Tag. 'Performing Modernism'. In Christopher Wilk (ed.), *Modernism: Designing a New World*. London: V and A Publications, 2006: 125–6.

Gropius, Walter (ed.), *Oscar Schlemmer, László Moholy-Nagy, Farkas Molnar, The Theatre of the Bauhaus*. Baltimore: Johns Hopkins University Press, 1996.

Gruber, William. *Missing Persons: Character and Characterization in Modern Drama*. Athens: University of Georgia Press, 1994.

Guimarães, Adriano and Guimarães, Fernando. *Happily Ever After / Felizes para Sempre*. Catalogue. Rio de Janeiro: Centro Cultural Banco do Brasil, 2001.

Harmon, Maurice (ed.). *No Author Better Served: The Correspondence of Samuel Beckett and Alan Schneider*. Cambridge, MA and London: Harvard University Press, 1998.

Harrison, Charles and Wood, Paul (eds). *Art in Theory 1900–1990: An Anthology of Changing Ideas*. Blackwell, Oxford and Cambridge: 1992.

Hartoonian, Gevork. *Crisis of the Object:The Architecture of Theatricality.* London: Routledge, 2006.

Harvie, Jen. 'Being Her: Presence, Absence, and Performance in the Art of Janet Cardiff and Tracey Emin'. In Maggie B. Gale and Viv Gardner (eds), *Auto/Biography and Identity: Women, Theatre and Performance.* Manchester: Manchester University Press, 2004: 194–215.

Hauck, Gerhard. *Reductionism in Drama and the Theatre: The Case of Samuel Beckett.* Potomac, MD: Scripta Humanistica, 1992.

Hawker, Rosemary. 'The Idiom in Photography as the Truth in Painting', *The South Atlantic Quarterly*, 101.3 (Summer 2002): 541–54.

——. 'Painting over Photography: Questions of Medium in Richter's Overpaintings', *Australian and New Zealand Journal of Art*, 8.1, Post-Medium (2007): 42–59.

——. 'Callum Morton's Architecture of Disguised Difference'. In A. L. Macarthur and J. Macarthur (eds), *Architecture, Disciplinarity, and the Arts.* Brussels: A&S Books, 2009: 151–65.

——. 'Idiom Post-medium: Richter Painting Photography', *Oxford Art Journal*, 32.2 (June 2009): 263–80.

Hayman, Ronald. *Theatre and Anti-Theatre: New Movements since Beckett.* New York: Oxford University Press, 1979.

Hesla, David H. *The Shape of Chaos: An Interpretation of the Art of Samuel Beckett.* Minneapolis: University of Minnesota Press, 1971.

Heuvel, Michael Vanden. *Performing Drama/Dramatizing Performance: Alternative Theatre and the Dramatic Text.* Ann Arbor: University of Michigan Press, 1991.

——. 'Good Vibrations: Avant-Garde Theatre and Ethereal Aesthetics, Kandinsky to Futurism'. In Anthony Enns and Shelley Trower (eds), *Vibratory Modernism.* Basingstoke: Palgrave Macmillan, 2013: 198–214.

Hutchings, William. 'Abated Drama: Samuel Beckett's Unabated Breath', *ARIEL: A Review of International English Literature*, 17.1 (1986): 85–94.

Hoffman, Frederic. *Samuel Beckett: The Language of Self.* New York: Dutton and Co., 1964.

Ibarra, Paola. 'Beautiful Trash: Art and Transformation', *Revista Harvard Review of Latin America*, 14.2 (Winter 2015): 41–3.

Irigaray, Luce. *The Forgetting of Air in Martin Heidegger.* London: Athlone Press, 1999. See also *L'Oubli de l'air chez Martin Heidegger.* Paris: Éditions de Minuit, 1983.

Issacharoff, Michael. 'Space and Reference in Drama', *Poetics Today*, 2.3 (1981): 211–24.

Jeffers, Jennifer M. 'The Image of Thought: Achromatics in O'Keefe and Beckett', *Mosaic*, 29.4 (December 1996): 59–78.

Jones, Amelia and Stephenson, Andrew (eds). *Performing the Body/Performing the Text*. London: Routledge, 1999.

Jones, Caroline A. 'The Modernist Paradigm: The Artworld and Thomas Kuhn', *Critical Inquiry*, 26 (Spring 2000): 488–528.

——. 'Form and Formless'. In Amelia Jones (ed.), *A Companion to Contemporary Art since 1945*, Malden, MA: Blackwell Publishing, 2006: 127–44.

Jones, Caroline and Arning, Bill (eds). *Sensorium: Embodied Experience, Technology and Contemporary Art*. Cambridge, MA: MIT Press, the MIT List Visual Arts Center, 2006.

Kalb, Jonathan. *Beckett in Performance*. Cambridge: Cambridge University Press, 1989.

Kant, Immanuel. *Critique of Pure Reason*. Trans. Paul Guyer and Allen Wood. New York: Cambridge University Press, 1997.

——. *Critique of the Power of Judgment*. Trans. Paul Guyer and Eric Matthews. New York: Cambridge University Press, 2000.

Kenner, Hugh. *A Reader's Guide to Samuel Beckett*. New York: Farrar, 1973.

Knezevic, Barbara. 'Review of Amanda Coogan: The Fall, Kevin Kavanagh Gallery, Dublin, 25 June 2009', *Circa: Contemporary Art in Ireland*. In http://circaartmagazine.website/reviews/amanda-coogan-the-fall-kevin-kavanagh-gallery-dublin-25-june-2009/ [accessed 28/11/10].

Knowlson, James. *Light and Darkness in the Theatre of Samuel Beckett*. London: Turret, 1972.

——. *Damned to Fame: The Life of Samuel Beckett*. New York: Grove Press, 1996.

Knowlson, James and Knowlson, Elizabeth (eds). *Beckett Remembering Beckett: A Centenary Celebration*. New York: Arcade, 2006.

Koch, Gertrude. 'The Richter Scale of Blur', *October*, 62 (Fall 1992): 133–42.

Kosuth, Joseph. 'Art after Philosophy, part 1', *Studio International* (October), 1969. In http://www.lot.at/sfu_sabine_bitter/Art_After_Philosophy.pdf

Krauss, Rosalind. *Passages in Modern Sculpture*. New York: Viking Press, 1977.

——. *The Originality of the Avant-Garde and Other Modernist Myths*. Cambridge, MA: MIT Press, 1986.

——. *A Voyage on the North Sea: Art in the Age of the Post-Medium Condition*. London: Thames and Hudson, 2000.

Kubiak, Anthony. 'Post Apocalypse with Out Figures: The Trauma of Theatre in Samuel Beckett'. In Joseph H. Smith (ed.), *The World of Samuel Beckett*. Baltimore: Johns Hopkins University Press, 1991: 107–24.

Lambert, Carrie. 'More or Less Minimalism: Performance and Visual Art in the 1960s'. In *A Minimal Future? Art as Object 1958–1968*. Cambridge, MA: The MIT Press, 2004: 103–10.

Lane, Richard (ed.). *Beckett and Philosophy*. New York: Palgrave, 2002.

Langbaum, Robert. *The Mysteries of Identity: A Theme in Modern Literature*. London and Chicago: University of Chicago Press, 1982.

Latham, John. *Event Structure: Approach to a Basic Contradiction* Calgary: Syntax, 1981.

Leder, Drew. *The Absent Body*. Chicago: University of Chicago Press, 1990.

Lee, Pamela. *Chronophobia: On Time in the Art of the 1960s*. Cambridge, MA: The MIT Press, 2004.

Lehmann, Hans-Thies. *Postdramatic Theatre*. London and New York: Routledge, 2006.

Lerm Hayes, Christa-Maria. 'Nauman . . . Beckett . . . Beckett . . . Nauman: The Necessity of Working in an Interdisciplinary Way', *CIRCA*, 104 (Summer 2003): 47–50.

——. *Joyce in Art: Visual Art Inspired by James Joyce*. Dublin: Lilliput Press, Dufour Editions, 2004.

——. 'Unity in Diversity through Art? Joseph Beuys' Models of Cultural Dialogue'.' KTHC – Knowledge, Technology, Human Capital, Eurodiv Paper, 2006. In http://www.feem.it/userfiles/attach/Publication/NDL2006/NDL2006-060.pdf [accessed 20/11/12].

——. 'In the Wake (of) – as a Theory of Participatory Practice', *The Recorder: The Journal of the American Irish Historical Society*, 21.2/22, no. 1 (2009): 41–8.

Lerm Hayes, Christa-Maria and Walters, Victoria (eds), *Beuysian Legacies in Ireland and Beyond: Art, Culture and Politics*. Berlin and Muenster: LIT Verlag, 2011.

Lessing, Gotthold-Ephraim. *Laocoön: An Essay on the Limits of Painting and Poetry*. Indianapolis: Bobbs-Merrill, 1962.

Levy, Shimon. *Samuel Beckett's Self-Referential Drama: The Sensitive Chaos*. Brighton: Sussex Academic Press, 2002.

LeWitt, Sol. 'Sentences on Conceptual Art'. In Alexander Alberro and Blake Simpson (eds), *Conceptual Art: A Critical Anthology*. Cambridge, MA: MIT Press, 2000: 105–8.

Lippard, Lucy (ed.). *Six Years: The Dematerialization of the Art Object from 1966 to 1972*. New York: Praeger, 1973. In http://cast.b-ap.net/wp-content/uploads/sites/8/2011/09/lippard-theDematerializationofArt.pdf

Locatelli, Carla. *Unwording the World: Samuel's Beckett's Fiction after the Nobel Prize*. Philadelphia: University of Pennsylvania Press, 1990.

Lozier, Claire. 'Breath as Vanitas: Beckett's Debt to a Baroque Genre'. In Erik Tonning, Matthew Feldman, Matthijs Engelberts and Dirk Van Hulle (eds), *Samuel Beckett: Debts and Legacies*. Amsterdam and New York: Rodopi, 2010; 241–51.

Lyons, Charles. *Samuel Beckett*. New York: Grove Press, 1984.

——. 'Character and Theatrical Space'. In James Redmond (ed.), *The Theatrical Space*. Cambridge: Cambridge University Press, 1987: 27–44.

Lyotard, Jean-Francois. *The Inhuman: Reflections on Time*. Trans. Geoffrey Bennington and Rachel Bowlby. Cambridge: Polity Press, 1991.

McCarthy, Gerry. 'Emptying the Theatre: On Directing the Plays of Samuel Beckett'. In Lois Oppenheim (ed.), *Directing Beckett*. Ann Arbor: University of Michigan Press, 1997: 250–67.

McCarthy, Sean. 'Giving Sam a Second Life: Beckett's Plays in the Age of Convergent Media', *Texas Studies in Literature and Language*, 51.1 (Spring 2009): 102–17.

McMullan, Anna. *Theatre on Trial: Samuel Beckett's Later Drama*. New York: Routledge, 1993.

Manzoni, Piero. *Paintings, Reliefs and Objects*. Exhibition catalogue. London: The Tate Gallery (20 March–15 May) 1974.

Massumi, Brian. *Parables for the Virtual. Movement, Affect, Sensation*. Durham, NC: Duke University Press, 2002.

Matthes, Hendrik. 'Aphorisms and Reflections by Piet Mondrian', *Kunst & Museumjournaal*, 6.1 (1995): 57–62.

Maude, Ulrika. 'Beckett and Aesthetics and Images of Beckett' (review), *Modernism/Modernity*, 11.4 (November 2004): 845–8.

Mazzio, Carla. 'The History of Air: Hamlet and the Trouble with Instruments', *South Central Review*, 26.1/2 (Winter and Spring) (2009): 153–96.

Merleau-Ponty, Maurice. *Phenomenology of Perception*. Trans. Colin Smith. New York: Humanities Press, 1962.

——. *The Visible and the Invisible*. Evanston: Northwestern University Press, 1969.

Meyer, James. *Minimalism: Art and Polemics in the Sixties*. New Haven and London: Yale University Press, 2001.

Middeke, Martin. 'Minimal Art: On the Intermedial Aesthetic Context of Samuel Beckett's Late Theatre and Drama', *Anglia*, 123.3 (2005): 359–80.

Moloney, Ciara. 'Review of Barbara Knezevic: *Breath* and Other Shorts, The Joinery, 2–11 June, 2010', *Paper Visual Art Journal* (26 July 2010). In http://papervisualart.com/2010/07/26/barbara-knezevic-breath-and-other-shorts-the-joinery-2-11-june-2010/ [accessed 20/11/2012].

Mondzain, Marie-José. *Homo Spectator*. Paris: Bayard, 2007. In http://dominiquevivant.blogspot.gr/2012/01/homo-spectator.html [accessed 1/11/2016].

Moorjani, A., Ben-Zvi, Linda (eds). *Beckett, McLuhan and Television: The Medium, the Message and the Mess in Beckett at 100 Revolving It All*. Oxford: Oxford University Press, 2008.

Morgan, Stuart. *Damien Hirst: No Sense of Absolute Corruption.* Ed. Raymond Foye. New York: Gagosian Gallery, 1996.

Mowitt, John. *Text: The Genealogy of an Antidisciplinary Object.* Durham, NC: Duke University Press: 1992.

Murray, Timothy (ed.). *Mimesis, Masochism, and Mime: The Politics of Theatricality in Contemporary French Thought.* Ann Arbor: University of Michigan Press, 1997.

Naas, Michael. *Derrida From Now On.* New York: Fordham University Press, 2008.

Oliveira, Nicholas. 'The Space of Memory: Installation Plays by the Brothers Guimares'. In *Happily Ever After.* Catalogue. Rio de Janeiro: Centro Cultural Banco do Brasil, 2001: 11–17.

Oliveira, Nicolas de, Oxley, Nicola, and Petry, Michael. *Installation Art in the New Millennium. The Empire of the Senses* [1994]. London: Thames and Hudson, 2003.

Olson, Charles. *Projective Verse, Human Universe and Other Essays.* New York: Grove Press, 1967.

Onians, John. *Neuroarthistory: From Aristotle and Pliny to Baxandall and Zeki.* New Haven and London: Yale University Press, 2007.

Oppenheim, Lois. *The Painted Word: Beckett's Dialogue with Art.* Ann Arbor: University of Michigan Press, 2000.

——. (ed.). *Palgrave Advances in Samuel Beckett Studies.* London: Palgrave Macmillan, 2004.

Oppenheim, Lois and Buning, Marius (eds). *Beckett On and On . . . .* Madison and London: Associated University Presses, 1996.

Osborne, Peter. 'Conceptual Art and/as Philosophy'. In Michael Newman and Jon Bird (eds), *Rewriting Conceptual Art.* London: Reaktion Books, 1999: 47–65.

——. (ed.). *Conceptual Art.* London and New York: Phaidon, 2002.

Panofsky, Erwin. 'The Concept of Artistic Volition', trans. Kenneth J. Northcott and Joel Snyder, *Critical Inquiry,* VIII.1 (Autumn 1981): 17–33.

Pattie, David. 'Space, Time, and the Self in Beckett's Late Theatre'. *Modern Drama,* 43.3 (Fall 2000): 393–403.

——. *The Complete Critical Guide to Samuel Beckett.* London: Routledge, 2004: 246.

Pavis, Patrice. *Analyzing Performance. Theatre, Dance, and Film.* Ann Arbor: The University of Michigan Press, 2003.

Perloff, Marjorie, 'The Silence That is Not Silence: Acoustic Art in Beckett's Embers'. In Lois Oppenheim (ed.), *Samuel Beckett and the Arts: Music, Visual Arts and Non-Print Media.* New York: Garland, 1999: 247–68.

Petersen, Anne Ring. 'Between Image and Stage: The Theatricality and Performativity of Installation Art'. In Rude Gade and Anne Jerslev (eds), *Performative Realism: Interdisciplinary Studies in Art and Media* Copenhagen: Museum Tusculanum Press, University of Copenhagen, 2005: 209–34.

Phelan, Peggy. *Unmarked: The Politics of Performance*. London: Routledge, 1993.

Potts, Alex. *The Sculptural Imagination: Figurative, Modernist, Minimalist*. New Haven, CT: Yale University Press, 2000.

——. 'Installation and Sculpture', *Oxford Art Journal*, 24.2 (2001): 6–24.

Pountney, Rosemary. *Theatre of Shadows: Samuel Beckett's Drama: 1956–76*. Gerrard's Cross: Colin Smythe Ltd, 1988.

Power, Cormac. *Presence in Play: A Critique of Theories of Presence in the Theatre*. Amsterdam and New York: Rodopi, 2008.

——. 'Performing to Fail: Perspectives on Failure in Performance and Philosophy'. In Daniel Meyer-Dinkgraffe and Daniel Watt (eds), *Ethical Encounters: Boundaries of Theatre, Performance and Philosophy*. Newcastle: CSP, 2010: 125–34.

Puchner, Martin. *Stage Fright: Modernism, Anti-Theatricality and Drama*. Baltimore and London: Johns Hopkins University Press, 2002.

——. 'The Theatre in Modernist Thought', *New Literary History*, 33.3. The Book as Character, Composition, Criticism, and Creation (Summer 2002): 521–32.

——. *Against Theatre: Creative Destructions on the Modernist Stage* (edited collection with Alann Ackerman). New York: Palgrave Macmillan, 2006.

Quinn, Michael. 'Concepts of Theatricality in Contemporary Art History', *Theater Research International*, 20.2 (Summer 1995): 106–13.

Ratcliff, Carter. *Out of the Box: The Reinvention of Art, 1965–1975*. New York: Allworth Press, 2000.

Ray, Gene. 'The Use and Abuse of the Sublime: Joseph Beuys and Art after Auschwitz', PhD Coral Gables: University of Miami Press, 1997.

——. 'Joseph Beuys and the After-Auschwitz Sublime' In *Joseph Beuys: Mapping the Legacy*. New York and Sarasota, FL: Distributed Art Publishers and the John and Mabel Ringling Museum of Art, 2001: 5–18.

——. 'Little Glass House of Horrors: High Art Lite, the Culture Industry and Damien Hirst', *Third Text*, 18.2 (2004): 119–33.

——. *Terror and the Sublime in Art and Critical Theory: From Auschwitz to Hiroshima to September 11*. New York: Palgrave, 2005.

——. 'History, The Sublime, Terror: Notes on the Politics of Fear', *Static*, 7 (2007): 1–15.

Read, Alan. *Theatre and Everyday Life*. London: Routledge, 1993.

Rebentisch, Juliane. *Aesthetics of Installation Art*. Berlin: Sternberg Press, 2012.

Reinhardt, Ad. *Art-As-Art: The Selected Writings of Ad Reinhardt*. Berkeley and London: University of California Press, 1991.

Robbe-Grillet, Alain. 'Samuel Beckett, or Presence in the Theatre'. In Martin Esslin (ed.), *Samuel Beckett: A Collection of Critical Essays*. New York: Prentice-Hall, 1965: 113.

Roesler-Friedenthal, Antoinette and Nathan, Johannes (eds). 'The Enduring Instant: Time and the Spectator in the Visual Arts'. A section of the XXXth International Congress for the History of Art. London, 2000.

Salter, Chris. *Entangled: Technology and the Transformation of Performance*. Cambridge, MA and London: MIT Press.

Saltz, David. 'Live Media: Interactive Technology and Theatre', *Theatre Topics*, 11.2 (September 2001): 107–30.

Sarrazac, Jean-Pierre. 'The Invention of Theatricality: Rereading Bernard Dort and Roland Barthes', *SubStance*, 98/99, 31.2 and 31.3 (2002): 57–72.

Sayre, Henry. *The Object of Performance: The American Avant Garde since 1970*. Chicago and London: University of Chicago Press, 1989.

Serreau, Geneviève. *Histoire du Nouveau Théâtre*. Paris: Galimard, 1966.

Siraganian, Lisa. *Modernism's Other Work: The Art Object's Political Life*. New York: Oxford University Press, 2012.

Sloterdijk, Peter. *Terror from the Air*, trans. Amy Patton and Steve Corcoran. Los Angeles: Semiotext(e), 2009.

Smith, Henry. *Breath and the Actor*. CD-ROM, Exeter Digital Archives, 1997.

Smith, Joseph (ed.). *The World of Samuel Beckett, Psychiatry and the Humanities*. Baltimore and London: Johns Hopkins University Press, 1991.

Smith, Terry. *Impossible Presence: Surface and Screen in the Photogenic Era*. Chicago and London: University of Chicago Press, 2001.

Smith, Tony. 'Interview with Samuel Wagstaff Jr', *Artforum*, 5.4 (December 1966): 14–19.

Sontag, Susan. 'The Aesthetics of Silence'. In *Styles of Radical Will*, London: Vintage, 1994: 3–34.

Sparrow, Felicity (ed.). *Bill Viola, The Messenger*. Durham: The Chaplaincy to the Arts and Recreation in North East England, 1996.

Spielmann, Yvonne. 'Synesthesia and Intersenses, Intermedia in Electronic Images'. *Leonardo*, 34.1 (2001): 55–61.

Stafford, Barbara-Maria. *Echo Objects: The Cognitive Work of Images*. Chicago: University of Chicago Press, 2007.

Stallabrass, Julian. *High Art Lite: British Art in the 1990s*. London: Verso, 1996.

States, Bert O. *Great Reckonings in Little Rooms: On the Phenomenology of Theatre*. Los Angeles: University of California Press: 1985.

Stewart, Paul. *Zone of Evaporation: Samuel Beckett's Disjunctions*. Amsterdam and New York: Rodopi, 2006.

Stimson, Blake. 'Conceptual Work and Conceptual Waste', *Discourse*, 24.2 (Spring 2001): 137.

——. 'Rhizome ... Conceptual Work and Conceptual Waste', *Discourse* (Spring 2002). http://arthistory.ucdavis.edu/people/faculty/publications/stimson.html

Strickland, Edward. *Minimalism: Origins*. Bloomington and Indianapolis: Indiana University Press, 1993.

Sugiera, Malgorzata. 'Theatricality and Cognitive Science: The Audience's Perception and Reception', *SubStance*, 31.2/3, special issue 98/99, 31.2 & 31.3 (2002): 225–35.

Therese, Tierney. 'Formulating Abstraction: Conceptual Art and the Architectural Object', *Leonardo*, 40.1 (February 2007): 51–7.

Tonning, Erik. *Abstraction in Samuel Beckett's Drama for Stage and Screen 1962–1985*. Oxford: Peter Lang, 2007.

Trod, Tamara Jane. *Mediums and Technologies of Art beyond Modernism*. London: University of London, 2005.

Tronstad, Ragnhild. 'Could the World become a Stage? Theatricality and Metaphorical Structures'. *SubStance*, 31.2/3, special issue 98/99: Theatricality (2002): 216–20.

Turbity, Derval. 'Beckett's Spectral Silence: *Breath* and the Sublime', *Limit(e) Beckett*, 1 (2010): 102–22.

Uhlmann, Anthony. *Samuel Beckett and the Philosophical Image*. Cambridge: Cambridge University Press, 2006.

Unsal, Merve. 'Minimalist Art vs Modernist Sensibility: A Close Reading of Michael Fried's Art and Objecthood', in http://www.artandeducation.net/paper/minimalist-art-vs-modernist-sensibility-a-close-reading-of-michael-frieds-art-and-objecthood/

Vickery, Jonathan. 'Art and the Ethical: Modernism and the Problem of Minimalism'. In Dana Arnold and Margaret Iversen (eds), *Art and Thought*. Oxford: Blackwell, 2002: 111–28.

Walley, Jonathan. 'An Interview with Anthony McCall', *The Velvet Light Trap*, 54 (Fall 2004): 65–75. In http://muse.jhu.edu/login?auth=0&type=summary&url=/journals/the_velvet_light_trap/v054/54.1walley.html

Walker, Julia A. 'Why Performance? Why Now? Textuality and the Rearticulation of Human Presence', *The Yale Journal of Criticism*, 16.1 (Spring 2003): 149–75.

Weber, Samuel, *Demarcating the Disciplines: Philosophy, Literature, Art*. Minneapolis: University of Minnesota Press, 1986.

——. *Theatricality as Medium*. Ashland, NY: Fordham University Press, 2004.

Weller, Shane. *A Taste for the Negative: Beckett and Nihilism*. Oxford: Legenda, 2005.

Wiles, Timothy. *The Theatre Event: Modern Theories of Performance*. Chicago: University of Chicago Press, 1980.

Wilshire, Bruce. *Role Playing and Identity: The Limits of Theatre as Metaphor*. Bloomington: Bloomington University Press, 1982.

Wölfflin, Heinrich. *Principles of Art History: The Problem of the Development of Style in Later Art*. Trans. M. D. Hottinger. New York: Dover, 1950.

Vostell, Wolf (ed.). *Dé-Coll/age (décollage)*. New York: Something Else Press, 1967.

Zarrilli, Philip (ed.). '. . . On the Edge of Breath, Looking'. In *Acting (Re) Considered: A Theoretical and Practical Guide*. London: Routledge, 1995: 181–99.

——. 'Acting at the Nerves Ends: Beckett, Blau and the Necessary', *Theatre Topics*, 7.2 (1997): 103–16.

Zeki, Semir. *Inner Vision: An Exploration of Art, Vision and the Brain*. Oxford: Oxford University Press, 1999.

INDEX